William Harrison Ainsworth

Myddleton Pomfret

A Novel

William Harrison Ainsworth

Myddleton Pomfret
A Novel

ISBN/EAN: 9783337028558

Printed in Europe, USA, Canada, Australia, Japan

Cover: Foto ©Thomas Meinert / pixelio.de

More available books at **www.hansebooks.com**

MYDDLETON POMFRET.

A Novel.

.

BY

WILLIAM HARRISON AINSWORTH,

AUTHOR OF

"THE TOWER OF LONDON,"

"LEAGUER OF LATHOM,"

"WINDSOR CASTLE,"

"CARDINAL POLE,"

ETC.

LONDON:

CHAPMAN AND HALL, 193 PICCADILLY.

1878.

BY THE SAME AUTHOR,

PRICE 2s., PICTURE BOARDS.

The Spanish Match	*Old Court*
Cardinal Pole	*The Leaguer of Lathom*
Chetwynd Calverley	*Myddleton Pomfret*
The Constable of the Tower	*Hilary St. Ives*
The Lord Mayor of London	*John Law*

The Constable de Bourbon

LONDON: CHAPMAN AND HALL.

MYDDLETON POMFRET.

PROLOGUE.

A SAD HONEYMOON.

CHAPTER I.

JULIAN CURZON.

SOME of my readers must recollect Julian Curzon. A few years ago Julian was accounted one of the handsomest men about town, and was very popular, owing to his agreeable manners. His brilliant career in the world of fashion was cut short by an imprudent marriage. Beyond doubt he might have won a rich heiress or a wealthy widow, but he threw himself away on a penniless girl. The only excuse that can be offered for his folly is, that he was madly in love, and certainly a more charming creature than Sophy Leycester, whom he married, cannot be imagined.

Sophy was the daughter of a Yorkshire gentleman of very moderate means, who could give her no portion. When Julian first beheld her, she was just nineteen, and a marvel of beauty. She had a ravishingly fair complexion, a graceful slender figure, a swan-like throat, features cast in the loveliest mould, large soft blue eyes shaded by long silken lashes and overarched by pencilled brows, a forehead smooth and white as Parian marble, and a cloud of light

fleecy locks.   Despite her want of fortune, Sophy Leycester
might have married well.   She had many admirers, some of
whom were rich.   But she preferred Julian Curzon to any
of them.

His daughter's choice was far from agreeable to Mr.
Leycester.   He had made sure of marrying her to Lord
Cranley or General Sir John Hawkesbury, both of whom
were captivated by her charms, but finding her deaf to his
representations, he gave way, though not without considerable reluctance.   No settlements were made on the marriage,
for Julian had nothing to settle, and Mr. Leycester, in giving
his consent to his daughter's marriage, gave nothing more.

In order that their bliss might be wholly undisturbed, the
young couple determined to spend their honeymoon at the
English lakes, and immediately after the performance of
the ceremony proceeded by rail to Bowness.   For a few
weeks they seemed to be in Paradise.   The weather was
enchanting.   Windermere displayed all its beauties—mirror-
like expanse, lovely islands, woody promontories, mountain
and fell.   The happy pair passed almost all their time upon
the lake, admiring the surrounding scenery, or moored in
some sequestered bay, where they seemed shut out from the
rest of the world.

During all this time, Julian scarcely took up a newspaper.
The world might go on as it pleased for aught he cared
about it.   He wrote no letters, and received none, and this
is not surprising, since, in order to ensure perfect privacy,
he had given out that he had gone with his bride upon the
Continent.

Mrs. Curzon was almost as indifferent about news as her
husband.   She had brought a lady's-maid with her on the
wedding trip, but Julian had dispensed with the attendance
of his valet.   Nevertheless, though they occupied private
apartments in a wing of the hotel overlooking the garden,
and secluded themselves as much as possible, their movements were curiously watched by the other guests, and
whenever Julian went out with his lovely bride to embark
in the little skiff which was kept constantly in readiness for
them, many an eye followed them, and many a glass tracked
their passage across the lake.

One morning they were proceeding, as usual, to the place

of embarkation, followed by a boatman carrying a hamper containing materials for an excellent luncheon. The beautiful Mrs. Curzon looked perfectly bewitching in her straw hat and batiste dress, and Julian showed to advantage in a cool Nankin summer costume and Panama hat. They were hastening towards the strand, not expecting interruption, when a person, who had been evidently on the look-out, stepped forward. He was a middle-aged man, in a short Oxford grey coat, and with nothing particular in his appearance, except that he had sharp features and keen grey eyes.

"Good-morning, Mr. Curzon," he said, raising his hat as he approached. "I am surprised to see you here. I fancied you were in Switzerland."

"I have changed my plans," replied Julian, who was perceptibly embarrassed. "I did think of going to Switzerland, but my wife is so charmed with this place that we have stayed here. My love, give me leave to present to you my old friend, Mr. Stonehouse," he added to Sophy.

The newly married lady rather superciliously acknowledged the obsequious bow addressed to her by the gentleman in the short Oxford grey coat.

"What brings you to this part of the world, may I ask, Stonehouse?" said Julian.

"Business. I had business at Kendal, and I thought I would come on here," replied the other. "I should like to have a word with you, if you will spare me a few minutes."

"Not now, Stonehouse," replied Julian. "You're not going away to-day, I'm sure. Dine with me quietly at seven, and then we can have a chat over our wine."

"I didn't intend to stay so long," rejoined the other, "but I really have something important to say to you, so I accept the invitation."

"Delighted to hear it," returned Julian. "You'll have no difficulty in amusing yourself. Plenty to see here. We shall expect you at seven."

So saying, he moved off with his wife. Mr. Stonehouse looked after them for a few moments with a very peculiar expression of countenance, and then entered the hotel.

"Why did you ask that horrid man to dinner, Julian?" remarked Sophy, as they walked along.

"I couldn't help it, my dear," he replied. "He's an awful bore; but I must be civil to him, and so must you, darling. I didn't expect to see him here."

They then embarked in the boat, and were rowed slowly towards one of the islands. Julian was so full of thought that he found it impossible to keep up a lively conversation.

"Apparently Mr. Stonehouse has cast a gloom over you," remarked his wife. "Who is he? I never heard you speak of him."

"He's a money-lender, my love, and really not a bad fellow. He has helped me out of many a scrape. I wish he hadn't come here though, for I fear I shall find it hard to get rid of him. After all, I wish we had gone to Switzer-land, or to the Italian lakes."

"It's not too late to do so yet," she rejoined, "though I am certain we shan't find anything so charming as Winder-mere. Oh! how happy we have been here."

"I never knew what real happiness was till now. But we will go to Switzerland—that is, if I can shake off this troublesome fellow."

"Shake him off!" exclaimed Sophy, in surprise. "You can easily get rid of him, I suppose."

"Not so easily as you imagine, my love. There's only one way of getting rid of him—paying what I owe him."

"Well, pay him then."

"It would be rather inconvenient to me to do so now, my dear. But say no more on the subject. It bores me to talk about him."

Sophy, however, was not to be put off in this way. Pre-sently she inquired,—

"Do you owe Mr. Stonehouse much, Julian?"

"I forget the exact amount," he replied, evasively; "but it's more than I can manage just now."

"I was not aware you were in debt," she remarked.

"I haven't troubled you much with my private affairs, darling, and I don't care to discuss them now. I've no doubt I shall be able to settle matters with Stonehouse. But to enable me to do so you must be civil to him. You'll find him tolerably agreeable when you know him better."

Sophy looked grave—graver than Julian had ever seen her look before. Finding all his efforts to enliven her futile, he became moody and silent in his turn. This was the first day since their union that had not passed off delightfully. They came back earlier than they intended, and Mrs. Curzon immediately retired to her own room.

At the hour appointed Mr. Stonehouse made his appearance. Sophy received him very coldly, but he did not seem put out by her manner. A very nice little dinner was served—including char from the lake. Exhilarated by the champagne, Mr. Stonehouse talked pleasantly and well, but Mrs. Curzon could not overcome her dislike to him, and did not care to conceal it. Almost immediately after dinner she disappeared.

"Evidently your wife does not like me," remarked Mr. Stonehouse, helping himself to a glass of claret. "She is a very charming creature, I must own. But circumstanced as you are, you ought not to have married her. I always counselled you to marry a fortune."

"So you did, Stonehouse—so you did, but you see I have married to please myself."

"Well, I'm afraid you'll repent it. I can't help feeling sorry for the poor young lady."

"Spare your pity, Stonehouse," rejoined Julian, rather sharply. "You are the only person likely to cause her anxiety. If you don't trouble me she'll be all right."

"That's just it. I don't want to trouble you. It will distress me greatly to interfere with the last few days of your honeymoon, and I shall be grieved beyond measure to cause your wife distress, but what am I to do?"

"Wait patiently, my good fellow, till it suits me to pay you," replied Julian, indifferently.

"I shall have to wait long enough if I wait till then," replied Stonehouse. "No, no, Mr. Curzon, I must speak out plainly. You've not behaved honourably. You've tried to swindle me."

"Swindle you! Come, come, Stonehouse, that's a little too strong."

"Swindle's the word, and no other. You've not met your engagements. I won't be trifled with any longer. If you don't settle with me I'll clap you in Kendal jail. That's flat. Any appeal to my feelings in regard to your wife will be useless. You ought not to have placed the young lady in such a position. Why didn't you marry Miss Lake, or the other heiress, Miss Glenlyon? or, better still, the wealthy Mrs. Dundas? You might then have set yourself straight. But you have been fool enough to throw away your last chance."

" Never mind what I've done, Stonehouse. It is nothing to you."

" It is everything to me, Sir. By your folly you have deprived yourself of the sole power left you of paying me. And for what? You can't live with your charming wife now you've got her, for I suppose you won't take her to jail with you."

" Harsh language, Stonehouse—harsh language. But I know you don't mean to put your threats into execution."

" Don't I? You'll see. There's no use wasting time in idle talk. I'll leave you in peace to-night, but I shall come back in the morning, and, unless you are prepared to settle, I'll lock you up. I will, by Jupiter!"

Having delivered this menace, he was about to depart, when Mrs. Curzon entered the room.

"What has happened?" she exclaimed, startled by her husband's looks.

" I'll tell you, Madam," replied Stonehouse. " It's proper you should know the truth."

"For Heaven's sake if you are a man, spare her feelings!" implored Julian.

" Whatever it may be, let me hear it," said Sophy, closing the door.

"Well, then, the case is simply this," rejoined Stonehouse, totally disregarding the imploring looks thrown at him by Julian. "Your husband has given me a bond for a large sum of money. The bond has been dishonoured. For your sake, I assure you, I shall extremely regret if I am forced to adopt unpleasant measures."

"What is the amount of my husband's debt, Sir?" asked Sophy, quietly. "I have some jewels and ornaments which cost more than two hundred pounds. You shall have them."

"Your husband owes me upwards of two thousand pounds, so that your offer of jewels to the amount of two hundred won't go very far towards paying me; but I thank you, nevertheless."

"You must not—shall not—give up your jewels, Sophy," said Julian. "Leave me to bear the consequences of my folly."

"Don't mind what he says, Sir," she cried to the money-lender. "I don't care about my jewels. I'll fetch them for you at once, if you'll promise to be lenient to him."

"I can give no promise just now," rejoined Stonehouse, coldly. "Much will depend upon what he offers to-morrow."

"You see you can produce no effect upon the flinty-hearted rascal," said Julian.

"Give him time, Sir; he will pay you—I am sure he will," implored Sophy.

"I have just said, Madam, that I cannot be content with mere promises," rejoined Stonehouse. "Your husband has disappointed me so often that I can no longer trust him. I give him till to-morrow at noon for reflection. If he is then prepared to satisfy me, well and good. If not, he knows what will ensue. I wish you a good-evening, Madam."

So saying, he bowed to her and left the room.

For some minutes not a word was uttered. During this interval, Sophy continued to regard her husband, who remained at the table with his head buried in his hands. At last she broke the painful silence.

"And so it has come to this already! Our brief dream of happiness is over."

Julian looked up as she spoke, and gazed vacantly at her. The blow appeared to have partially stunned him.

"Have you any means of paying this man?" she continued. "Tell me frankly."

"None whatever," he replied. "I am hopelessly ruined."

She became very pale, but did not lose her composure. Fixing her fine eyes steadily and compassionately upon him, she said:—

"I won't reproach you, Julian; but if you really loved me as devotedly as you professed, I cannot understand how you could conceal your difficulties from me."

"Love for you, Sophy, was the motive for concealment. Had I confessed the truth, I should have lost you. I therefore practised the deception."

"You have acted cruelly—very cruelly, Julian, and have placed me in a most painful position. Should Mr. Stonehouse put his threat into execution, and imprison you, what is to become of me?"

"Go back to your father. It will be your best plan."

"And you coolly recommend me to do this, Julian?" she rejoined, somewhat contemptuously. "You appear to care little for the humiliation and annoyance I must necessarily experience in taking such a step. But I am rightly served. I would not listen to papa's counsel. I would have my own way, because I believed you. I now know what your love is worth. I now thoroughly understand you. I pity you, but at the same time I despise you."

"Despise me! oh, recal that word, Sophy!"

"Julian, you must not expect that I can ever more love and respect you. Had unforeseen calamities overtaken you, I would have stood faithfully by your side, and have helped you to the best of my power. But you have acted dishonourably. You carefully concealed your embarrassed circumstances from me and from papa. Conduct like this cannot be pardoned. Henceforward it is impossible that we can live together. To-morrow I shall return home."

"I didn't mean what I said, darling. I won't consent to your return. You shall not leave me."

"You cannot help yourself. Mr. Stonehouse will prevent all interference on your part. Good-night. I shall occupy Charlotte's room."

So saying, she went out, leaving him in a state bordering upon frenzy.

CHAPTER II.

A DESPERATE ACT.

TURN which way he would, there seemed no escape for the luckless Julian. He was in the clutches of an inexorable creditor. Pay him he must, either in purse or person. His lovely young wife, to whom he was passionately attached, had announced her determination to leave him, and he entertained no doubt that she would execute her threat. Dark thoughts swept through his brain, and he almost yielded to the promptings of despair.

Julian Curzon was by no means devoid of good qualities. Though reckless and extravagant, he was warm-hearted and generous. To such an extent had he practised self-deception as really to persuade himself that in marrying Sophy Leycester, a girl without money, he had acted a very disinterested part. Blind to the consequences of his imprudence, he succeeded for a time in stifling all self-reproach. But he was now rudely and unexpectedly awakened from his dream, and compelled to look his frightful position fully in the face.

Pacing to and fro within the room, he tried to reflect. But his brain was on fire, and he could not assemble his thoughts. At last he became more composed, and the changed expression of his countenance denoted that he had formed some resolution. Whatever his design might be, he set about it at once. Opening the door gently, he proceeded with noiseless footsteps to his dressing-room. The apartments which he occupied, as we have already stated, were in a private part of the hotel, so he encountered no one on the stairs. After remaining in his dressing-room for nearly half-an-hour, he descended in the same quiet manner, with a small bundle in his hand, wrapped in a silk handkerchief,

He had also changed his attire, and had put on a morning dress. Re-entering the room, he opened the window softly, and stepped out upon the lawn in front of the hotel, taking the little bundle with him.

Noiselessly as he did this, his movements were overheard by his wife, who was in a room above, the window of which commanded the garden and the lake. The night was cloudy, but there was light enough to enable her to distinguish her husband as he crossed the lawn. She saw him pass through the garden gate, and proceed towards a wood skirting the lake. Then he was lost to view.

Long before this, Sophy's anger had subsided. She was filled with terrible misgivings. Had he left her? Had she driven him away by her reproaches? She had worked herself up to a fearful state of anxiety when Julian suddenly reappeared. He had now got rid of the bundle. On beholding him a fresh revulsion took place in her feelings, and she blamed herself for the weakness she had exhibited. Listening intently, she heard him enter the room and close the window softly, and then, believing her fears groundless, retired to rest—no, not to rest.

With Julian, however, the business of the night was not ended. On re-entering the room he sat down and wrote a long letter to his wife. The composition was extremely painful to him, and he several times abandoned his task. After many ineffectual efforts, he finished the letter, but on reading it over he was so dissatisfied, that he tore it up, and burnt the fragments.

At this juncture a sleepy-looking waiter entered the room to inquire whether Mr. Curzon had any further commands for the night, and being answered sternly in the negative, departed.

Julian then flung himself upon a sofa, and fell into a troubled sleep, which lasted till daybreak. The first beams of the sun shining in through the window aroused him, and he started up. All the painful thoughts which had been suspended during slumber rushed upon him at once with added poignancy.

Again he rushed up-stairs to his dressing-room. He was an admirable swimmer, and accustomed each morning to bathe in the lake. Snatching up the towels laid out for him, he went down-stairs, and once more threw open the window, but just as he was about to issue forth his wife appeared. She had risen an hour ago from a sleepless couch.

"Stay a moment, Julian," she said. "I want to speak to you."

"Not now—not now," he rejoined. "I am about to cool my fevered brow in the lake. On my return I will talk to you."

"You will kill yourself, if you bathe now. I am sorry for what I said last night. I have come to tell you so."

He looked hard at her. His breast was torn by conflicting emotions.

"You were quite right in what you said," he cried. "My conduct has been infamous—unpardonable. I know I have forfeited your respect—perhaps your love."

"No, no, I love you still—I shall ever love you, Julian."

He looked as if he would have strained her to his heart, but he controlled the impulse.

"Sophy," he said, in broken accents, "you must forget me. I do not deserve your love. I am a worthless fellow, who ought never to have aspired to the hand of an angelic being like you. I see my folly too late, and can find no excuse for it—none! I fully comprehend the baseness of which I have been guilty. I would make reparation if I could. But since that is impossible, I won't be a further encumbrance to you."

"Your looks and words seem to point to something dreadful, Julian. I was wrong to reproach you so sharply. Don't let misfortune overwhelm you. Think not of the sombre present, but of a bright future. Whatever may be your lot I am prepared to share it with you."

"It must not, cannot be, Sophy. We must part this day for ever. You have nothing to regret in the separation. I could not make you happy."

"Oh yes, you could, Julian," she cried, bursting into tears.

"I once thought so," he rejoined. "But I must not make another mistake."

"You will make a second mistake—worse, far worse than the first, if you act as I fear you intend, Julian. Do not yield to the promptings of despair. Struggle manfully against your difficulties, and you will overcome them."

"Had you spoken thus last night, Sophy, I might have listened to you, but all hope is now crushed within me. I can only see one way out of the frightful labyrinth in which I am involved, and that way I shall take. Forgive me the wrong I have done you. Think of me charitably, and may Heaven bless you!"

And he turned to depart.

"Stay, Julian, I conjure you. You must not—shall not go!" she cried.

But he dashed through the window, and hurried across the lawn in the direction of the lake. She called to him again and again, but he paid no heed, and never once looked back.

A fearful sickness of heart deprived her for a minute or two of strength, but as soon as she recovered she ran out. She saw him enter the boat, and again called out, but he heeded her not, and before she reached the strand he was rowing swiftly towards a woody and secluded bay about half a mile off.

In vain she renewed her cries—in vain she waved her handkerchief, hoping to attract his attention. He continued his course unmoved.

The morning was exquisite, and the glassy surface of the lake reflected the objects on its banks, and even the mountains around it. Nothing was heard but the dip of oars as the boat speeded away, or the plash of some large fish as it rose. The lovely islands studding the lake seemed invested with magical beauty. But at that early hour no boat except Julian's could be descried on the water.

But what was the splendour of the morning, what was the beauty of the lake to Sophy? She was insensible to everything save her anguish. She had long ceased to call to her husband, for he was now too distant for her cries to reach him, even if he would have attended to them.

By this time he had gained the further side of the bay, and approached so close to the shore that she fancied he was about to land. But no!—when within about thirty yards from the wood-fringed bank he ceased to row, and the boat became motionless,

For some minutes, during which she watched him with intense anxiety, he did not appear to stir. Then hastily divesting himself of his apparel, he sprang over the side of the boat and dived into the lake. She looked anxiously for his reappearance on the surface of the water, but he did not rise again.

Several minutes elapsed—minutes of frightful agony!— and still she could see nothing of him.

But he might be hidden from her view by the boat. Ten minutes had now flown, and yet he had not reappeared. Her fears had almost become certainties. Still she clung to hope.

But time went on—five minutes more—and the placid surface of the lake was still undisturbed.

Yielding now to despair, she made the place echo with her shrieks. The attention of two men who had just put off in a boat from Bowness, being attracted by her outcries, they rowed towards her. As soon as they drew near, she made them understand what had happened. At her solicitation they took her on board, and rowed swiftly towards the scene of the accident.

Ere long they neared the boat, which by this time had drifted further from shore. In it could be seen the unfortunate man's clothes. The boatmen scanned the smooth surface of the water, thinking he might have swum to a distance. But he could not be distinguished. They shouted loudly, but no answer was returned.

Poor Sophy, who looked as pale as death, perceived that they had lost all hope; but she scarcely dared to question them, and they did not proffer a remark, but muttered a few words to each other.

"You think I have lost him?" she gasped, at length, in accents that pierced their hearts. "You think he is drowned?"

"I daren't give you any hope, Ma'am," replied the elder boatman, in a tone of deep commiseration. "I'm awmost afeared your husband has been seized by cramp. The lake is very deep hereabouts, and the water icy cowld owing to the springs."

"Ay, there were a gen'l'man drownded in this very bay about six years ago—you mind it, Isaac?"

"Ay, ay. But don't talk about it now, Mat. Don't you see how you frighten the poor lady? Do let us take you to the hotel, Ma'am. We'll then go and get the drags and search for the body."

"No, put me on board the other boat, and then lose no time in fetching the drags."

"Take my advice, Ma'am," remonstrated Isaac. "Go ashore. You can do no good here."

But she refused to quit the spot, and the boatmen, finding her resolute, assisted her into the other boat, and then pulled vigorously towards Bowness, where they knew they could obtain drags.

Left to herself in the little bark lately occupied by her husband, the miserable lady gave vent to an outburst of grief, which she had restrained while the boatmen were present. Mingled with her heart-bursting sobs were self-reproaches of indescribable bitterness, for she felt assured that Julian had destroyed himself, and that she was the cause of the dreadful act. What would she have given to recall her words? Julian's difficulties now appeared as nothing. Willingly would she have shared his adverse fortune, if he could only have been restored to her. But he was gone—gone for ever! The deep blue waters of the lake hid him from her. And if she ever beheld him more, she shuddered to think it would be in death.

How ill did the lovely scene assort with her distress. The smiling lake seemed to mock her with its beauty. How often had she admired this enchanting picture with Julian. How often had she listened to his rapturous admiration of the scene. All these recollections crowding upon her increased her anguish tenfold. But even the faintest sound —the cry of a bird—the plash of a fish—roused her, and she started up as if expecting to behold him. Alas! alas! she was ever disappointed.

After a frightful long interval, as it seemed to her, shouts were heard, and a number of boats were seen approaching. Several of the boats were crowded—tidings of the disastrous occurrence having spread like wildfire through Bowness. Foremost amongst the throng of little barks were the boatmen with the drags. On arriving at the spot, the men at once commenced operations, and dragged the lake some fifty yards nearer the shore where they supposed the unfortunate man had `sunk. The search was made with great care, and long persevered in, but the body could not be found.

Owing to the presence of the unhappy lady, the scene was of the most painful kind. Looks of deep commiseration were directed towards her as she sat in the boat anxiously watching the operations. All wondered how she could sustain so severe a trial. Among the spectators was the iron-hearted Stonehouse, and even he was touched.

After continuing the search for several hours, the men desisted from their fruitless toil. Poor Sophy entreated them to go on, but they shook their heads, saying it was useless, and finding that nothing more could be done, she consented to go ashore. The boat in which she sat was then taken in tow, and as soon as it reached the landing-place, she was carefully and considerately lifted out, and carried in a state of half insensibility to the hotel, where every attention was shown her.

Later on in the day, the portion of the lake in which the ill-fated man had sunk was again dragged, and every expedient resorted to to recover the body, but without success.

Next day the efforts were renewed, but with a like unsatisfactory result. The lake never yielded up its prey, and the notion propounded by the boatmen was confirmed —namely, that the body had got lodged in a deep hole, from which it was impossible to extricate it. Subsequently a skilful diver was employed in the search, but he made no discovery.

End of the Prologue.

BOOK I.

AN ILL-OMENED MARRIAGE.

———◆———

CHAPTER I.

HOW JULIAN'S DEBTS WERE PAID, AND HOW SOPHY
OBTAINED A THOUSAND A YEAR.

LONG did Sophy mourn her unfortunate husband. Though she never confided the dread secret to any one, she felt convinced that his death was not accidental; and she ceased not to reproach herself with being the cause of his untimely end.

She returned to her father's residence in Yorkshire, where she lived in complete retirement for nearly four years. At the end of that time an event occurred which produced an important change in her circumstances.

One day a letter, bearing her address, arrived from Madras. Sophy had no correspondent in India, and the handwriting, which was bold and business-like, was perfectly strange to her. So she examined the letter carefully, wondering whom it came from. At last she opened it, and read as follows :—

"Madras, May 10, 186—.

"MADAM,—You will be surprised to receive a letter from an entire stranger, with whose very name you are probably unacquainted. I must premise, therefore, by explaining who I am, as well as my motive for venturing to address you.

"I am a Madras merchant, junior partner of the house of Bracebridge, Clegg, and Pomfret, and I may as well state that I have been very successful in business. Your late husband, Julian Curzon, was my intimate friend, and rendered me a most important service, which I have never forgotten, and which at length I trust I may be able partially to requite.

"It is no secret from me that poor Julian, at the time of his death, was greatly in debt, and I can easily conceive how much he must have suffered from inability to set himself straight. I do not think I can show greater respect for his memory than by acting as he would have desired to act. I mean to pay the whole of his debts, with interest up to the present time. With this design I have placed to your credit at Drummonds' the sum. of six thousand pounds, which I beg you will apply in the liquidation of your husband's debts. If the sum should prove insufficient, I trust you will unhesitatingly apply to me for more."

"I feel sure it will be an agreeable task to you to free your husband's name from reproach, and I therefore make no apology for requesting you to act for me in the matter. I will only beg you to kindly let me know that my wishes have been complied with.

"I remain, Madam,
"Your obedient servant,
"MYDDLETON POMFRET."

This letter, which filled Sophy with the greatest astonishment, was quickly followed by another from Drummonds', informing her that six thousand pounds had been deposited with them in her name by Messrs. Bracebridge and Co., of Madras ; thus removing any lingering doubts from her mind as to the genuineness of Mr. Pomfret's communication.

Sophy did not hesitate. Her desire to clear Julian's name from reproach was paramount to every other consideration. It was not necessary to make any inquiries as to his debts, for she had a complete list of them, all his creditors having applied to her. None had been paid, and of course they had long since abandoned expectation of repayment. The total amounted to somewhat more than four thousand pounds. To this four years' interest had to be added, raising the amount to nearly another thousand pounds. Mrs. Curzon confided the arrangement of the affair to her father's man of business, Mr. Blair, of Throg-morton Street, and in less than a week every account was paid. When forwarding her the receipts, Mr. Blair informed her that nothing could exceed the gratitude of the creditors. Mr. Stonehouse declined the interest, but Mr. Blair forced it upon him.

All having been settled, Sophy wrote a letter overflowing with gratitude to Mr. Myddelton Pomfret, informing him that his instructions had been fully carried out, and at the same time mentioning that he had sent her a larger sum than required. A thousand pounds belonging to him was left at Drummonds' to be returned, or applied as he might direct. In conclusion, she assured him she should .never forget his kindness—never cease to pray for his welfare.

Nearly three months elapsed before Sophy again heard from her generous correspondent. She then received another letter, which we proceed to lay before the · reader :—

"MADAM,—I am at Ootacumand, on the Neilgherry hills, where I have come to recruit myself after a sharp attack of illness which brought me almost to death's door. Though much better, I am still not very strong. Nothing but inability to write would have prevented me from thanking you for your kind attention to my wishes. You have given me inexpressible relief, for poor Julian's debts weighed upon me as heavily as if they had been my own. But I do not yet feel quite easy, and I trust you will accede to the request I am now about to make as readily as you did to my former proposition.

"The circumstances in which you have been placed by Julian's untimely death have caused me great distress. You ought to have an income sufficient to enable you to maintain your proper position. This income it is my wish to provide ; and I trust you will not thwart my intentions.

"Julian's debts have turned out less than I expected. A thousand pounds, you tell me, is still left at Drummonds'. This sum, then, will constitute the first year's allowance, and I pledge myself that a like amount shall be regularly continued to you, and secured after my death.

"In confirmation of what I state, let me mention that

when seized with the dangerous illness to which I have adverted, I made my will, and bequeathed you a sum sufficient
to provide you with an ample income. I consider myself
justified in doing this, since I have no near relatives.

"My conduct may appear singular, and you will deem
perhaps, that I am influenced by over-strained feelings. It
is not every man, I admit, who would act in this way. But
I claim no merit, because I am simply performing what I
hold to be a sacred duty.

"After this explanation, you will not, I am sure, oppose
my wishes.

"Yours very sincerely,
"MYDDLETON POMFRET."

"What unheard-of generosity!" exclaimed Sophy, as she
read this letter. "Would you believe it, Celia?" she added
to her sister, who was with her at the time. "This kind-
hearted Mr. Myddleton Pomfret means to allow me a
thousand a year. He has fully explained his motives for
his extraordinarily liberal conduct, and I can perfectly
understand and appreciate them."

"Well, you are lucky, indeed!" cried Celia. "I congratulate you upon your good fortune. Why, Mr. Pomfret
must be a prince."

"No, he is only a Madras merchant," replied Sophy;
"but he certainly has a princely disposition. Really the
circumstances are so extraordinary that I can scarcely credit
them. Through the instrumentality of this noble-hearted
man, whom I have never seen, I have been enabled to pay
off poor Julian's debts, and now he provides me with a
large income. But I don't think I ought to accept it."

"Is the offer clogged by any disagreeable conditions?"
inquired Celia.

"On the contrary, it is made in the handsomest manner
possible. Mr. Pomfret considers himself under deep obligations to my poor dear husband, which can only be
discharged by the course he proposes to pursue."

"Since it is put in that way, I do not see why you should
decline the offer," observed Celia. "I wonder what Mr.
Pomfret is like? He can't be very old, since he was
Julian's friend."

2—2

"I know nothing whatever about him, beyond what his letters communicate," said Sophy; "but Mr. Blair informed me that the house to which he belongs is one of the first in Madras."

"Is he a bachelor?"

"How can I possibly tell, you silly creature? I fancy he is unmarried, because he expressly states in his letter that he has no near relations."

"Indeed! what a nice man he must be—very rich, since he can afford to give away a thousand a year to a friend's widow—and no relations. Perhaps he will follow up his present proposition by an offer of his hand."

"Don't tease in this way, I beg of you, Celia," said Mrs. Curzon, the tears starting in her eyes. "I shall never— never be faithless to my dear Julian's memory. You shake my design of accepting Mr. Pomfret's offer. I would never lay myself under such great obligations to him if I thought he would presume upon his liberality."

"Nay, I was but joking," said Celia. "Don't be such a goose as to refuse this wonderful offer. I hope your magnificent friend will soon come back from Madras. Be sure to tell him how charmed we shall all be to see him, and put in a word for me if you can manage it," she added, laughing.

"I shall not come to a hasty decision in the matter," said Sophy. "The proposal is so singular that it requires consideration."

"I don't think it requires a moment's consideration," cried Celia. "What! you who haven't got fifty pounds a year —who have scarcely enough for your milliner's bill—who are completely dependent upon papa—you refuse a thousand a year—a fortune! Think what such a sum implies. A thousand a year will give you a nice little establishment in town, in a fashionable quarter. A thousand a year will give you a pretty little brougham or a pretty phaeton, servants, charming dresses, every luxury. A thousand a year will enable you to live well, dress well, and keep up society. A thousand a year will do wonders. You'll soon be thought a charming young widow, for you are still young, Sophy, and haven't lost your good looks. Oh, I wish I had a thousand a year! Shouldn't I be happy? Shouldn't I know how to spend it?"

And she clapped her hands and laughed joyously.

"I shall lead a very quiet life," remarked Sophy.

"No you won't," cried Celia. "You've lived in retirement quite long enough. You'll live in town, I say, and let me live with you."

Mrs. Curzon shook her head.

"I have not spirits enough for society," she said.

"Then I'll find spirits for you," cried the gay Celia. "Live in town you must, and shall. Write by the first Indian mail to Mr. Myddleton Pomfret, and accept his proposition."

"Only if papa approves," said Sophy.

Papa, on being consulted, *did* approve, and thus enunciated his opinion.

"This is an extraordinary circumstance," he said, "and quite passes my comprehension. Such an instance of friendship is of very rare occurrence in these degenerate times, and proves Mr. Pomfret to be no common man. The delicacy and good feeling manifested by him in making the offer to you will enable you to accept it; and I must sincerely congratulate you upon your good fortune in finding such a friend. You ought to look upon the income you will receive as a legacy from poor Julian. In reality you owe it to him."

"I shall look upon it in that light, dear papa," she replied. "You have removed all the scruples I felt in accepting the offer."

"You need have no scruples, my dear," he returned. "You richly deserve your good fortune, and I again congratulate you upon it."

Satisfied that she could, with propriety, accept his offer, Sophy thus wrote to her benefactor :—

"MY DEAR MR. MYDDLETON POMFRET,—I accept your noble offer, and fully appreciate the motives that have induced you to make it. But really the large income you are generous enough to allow me is more than adequate to my wants. Ever since the irreparable loss I have sustained, I have lived a life of perfect seclusion, and scarcely desire to emerge from it. Hence society can have few attractions for me, and were it not for my sister, I should prefer remaining as I am. Celia, however, is eager to mix with the world, and ever since she has heard of your generous intentions towards me, has not ceased to urge me to live in town. Perhaps I may yield to her entreaties, but as yet I am undecided. I should like to have your opinion. Pray give it me frankly, and be sure I will be guided by it.

"I feel utterly incapable of thanking you as I ought for your great generosity, and if I fail in doing so, you will not impute it, I am sure, to want of gratitude.

"That you should have thought of me during the dangerous illness with which I grieve to hear you have been afflicted, affords another proof of the depth of your friendship for Julian. Need I say how deeply I am touched by the manifestation? Only the noblest natures are capable of such exalted feelings. To ordinary minds your conduct would be unintelligible, but believe me *I* comprehend it. Long before this reaches you, I trust you will have entirely recovered.

"Again thanking you from my heart,
"I remain,
"Your very grateful,
"SOPHIA CURZON."

Before changing her abode, though strongly urged to do so both by her father and sister, Sophy awaited Mr. Pomfret's reply. After the lapse of a couple of months the ensuing letter came :—

"MY DEAR MRS. CURZON,—As you are good enough to express some anxiety about my health, I will relieve you at once by stating that I am now much better. All I suffer from is debility, but that I owe to the climate. Were it possible, I would return to my native country without delay ; but I must, perforce, remain here for a couple of years longer, when, if I am spared, I shall leave India altogether, and then I trust I shall have the pleasure of making your personal acquaintance. By that time you will have come, I hope, to consider me in the light of an old friend.

"I am rejoiced to find that you have allowed no scruples to interfere with the acceptance of my offer. You would

have hurt me greatly if you had. Never consider yourself
under any obligation to me, but regard the gift as coming
from Julian. The estimation in which you hold his memory
gratifies me inexpressibly.

" You flatter me very much by asking my advice as to
your future plans. I should not have presumed to say a
word on the subject; but since you request my opinion, I
declare at once that I agree with your sister. Society, I
hope, will not be much longer deprived of one of its
brightest ornaments. Take a suitable house in town, and
live as your tastes and inclinations dictate. Julian, I am
sure, would not have wished you to seclude yourself.

"I have heard your sister Celia, who, I believe, is unmarried, described as lively and light-hearted, and I shall be
glad to hear she is living with you. You could not have a
more agreeable companion.

" One word more. Though I have limited your allowance
to a thousand a year, if your expenses should, at any time,
from unforeseen circumstances, exceed that amount, do not
hesitate to apply to me.

" Naturally I shall feel a lively interest in your proceedings, ·
and I trust I am not asking you too much in begging you to
write to me frequently.

" Write confidentially and without reserve. Make me
the depository of your secrets, if you have any to communicate. Ask my advice on any subject, and I will give
it you sincerely.

" In your next letter I hope to hear that you have taken a
nice little house somewhere in the neighbourhood of Hyde
Park. Pray make my compliments to Mr. Leycester and
your sister,

" And believe me, dear Madam,
" Sincerely yours,
" MYDDLETON POMFRET."

Mrs. Curzon communicated the contents of this letter to
her father and sister, both of whom agreed that the writer
must be the most amiable of men. Celia was enchanted
with the allusion to herself, and declared it was quite
wonderful how thoroughly Mr. Pomfret understood her
character.

"Julian must have described me to him," she said. "Oh,
how I wish he would come back from India! What a pity
he is obliged to remain there for two years longer, and he
seems to suffer so much from the climate."

In less than a month afterwards Mrs. Curzon was able to
inform her generous correspondent that she was installed
with her sister at a charming little house in Hertford Street,
May Fair. She only wished Mr. Pomfret could see how
elegantly it was furnished. Nothing was wanting. Her
little establishment was complete, and she had a well-
appointed brougham. In pursuance of his recommendation,
though contrary to her own inclinations, she had made up
her mind to enter into society once more, and had, consequently, called upon several old friends. Invitations were
showering upon her on all sides.

CHAPTER II.

NE morning in June two tall and handsome young men, both of very distinguished appearance, were walking slowly along Pall Mall in the direction of Saint James's Street, engaged in earnest converse. One of them was Captain St. Quintin, of the Grenadiers; the other Captain Scrope Musgrave, of the Bengal Rifles, lately returned from India. Very handsome they both were, as we have just intimated, though in different styles. St. Quintin had a slight, elegant figure, features of almost feminine delicacy, relieved by a pale mustache, and loosely flowing whiskers of the same hue. His companion, on the contrary, who though equally well-proportioned, possessed a more muscular frame, was so exceedingly swarthy, that he was nicknamed by his intimates "Black Musgrave." Skin, beard, hair, eyes were dark as those of a Hindoo. Captain Musgrave's physiognomy was very marked and striking—more striking, perhaps, than pleasing. His features were regular, his eyes large and brilliant, and his dazzling white teeth contrasted with a jetty beard. His expression, however, was haughty and disdainful, and marred the effect which must have been otherwise produced by his good looks. He was a few years older than his companion, but still under thirty. The two young men were going to make a call at the house of a lady in May Fair, and were talking about her as they sauntered along.

"And so you are struck by the lovely widow, Scrope?" remarked St. Quintin.

"Struck all of a heap," replied Musgrave. "She's a charming creature—precisely the sort of a woman I have been looking for all my life, but have never seen till last night, when I met this enchantress at Lady Northbroke's. I

lost my heart to her the very moment I beheld her, and
yet, as you well know, St. Quintin, I'm not exactly the man
to fall in love at first sight."

" I should never have suspected you of the weakness if
you hadn't owned to it," remarked the other, laughing.

" To my mind, I have never seen so charming a face as
Mrs. Curzon's," continued Musgrave. " I studied it for
more than an hour, as if contemplating a beautiful picture,
and the longer I looked the more enamoured I became.   I
was just considering how I could manage to get presented
to her, when you kindly performed the office for me."

" Only too happy to oblige a friend," returned St.
Quintin. " And let me tell you that no one could have
served you better than myself.   I paved the way for your
introduction by saying the right thing to Mrs. Curzon, for
she is monstrously particular, and won't know everybody.   I
think you must have contrived to please her, for she appeared
more than usually gracious to you.   In a general way, she is
exceedingly cold and reserved."

" I certainly did not find her cold," said Musgrave,
displaying his white teeth.   " On the contrary, she appeared
to me remarkably amiable, in proof of which she did not
object when I ventured to ask permission to call upon her
this morning.   And now, my good fellow, tell me something
more about her.   How long has she been a widow? And how
about her jointure?   I hope she is well endowed.   She
deserves to be."

" You mustn't raise your expectations too high in regard
to her jointure," returned St. Quintin.   " Put it down at a
thousand or twelve hundred a year, and you won't be far
wide of the mark."

" Twelve hundred a year is not so bad.   It will do very
well with such a charming person," said Musgrave.   " I
would rather have her with twelve hundred than another
with twelve thousand."

" But I'm not quite clear that it won't go away in the
event of her marriage," rejoined St. Quintin.   " So you must
look well before you leap.   In reply to your first inquiry, I
may tell you that she has been a widow nearly four years.
Her matrimonial fetters did not hold her long, and were
severed before the honeymoon was over."

"The deuce! what happened to her husband?" cried Musgrave.

"Drowned one fine morning while bathing in Windermere," replied St. Quintin.

"Ah, I now recollect the circumstance. It occurred just before I went to India. So she was the wife of Julian Curzon. There was something strange about his death, if I'm not mistaken."

"Some people fancied he made away with himself because he was desperately in debt at the time," replied St. Quintin; "but there was nothing to justify the supposition, I believe. The strangest part of the story is that the body was never found, though every search was made for it."

"That's strange indeed," said Musgrave, reflectively. "If Curzon died in debt, how happens it that his widow has so good a jointure?"

"She doesn't derive her income from him," returned St. Quintin. "Julian made no settlement upon her, for the best of all reasons, that he had nothing to settle. For a long time after his death she had nothing and was obliged to live in absolute retirement. Then a turn came for the better. A Madras merchant, Mr. Myddleton Pomfret, who had been under considerable obligations to Julian—though what they were I can't say—took upon himself to pay the poor fellow's debts, and insisted upon making a handsome allowance to the widow."

"Oh, that's how she gets her income, is it?" cried Musgrave. "I know Myddleton Pomfret. He's a partner in Bracebridge's house at Madras. Is he Julian's relative?"

"No, he seems merely actuated by friendship."

"Hum!" exclaimed Musgrave. "If this is really the case, and I suppose there's no mistake ——"

"No mistake whatever. I had it all from Mrs. Curzon's sister, Celia."

"In that case," pursued Musgrave, "it is quite clear that the fair widow's income will cease if she marries again. Rather a bad look out, eh?"

"Draw your own conclusions, Musgrave. I can't help you further."

This conversation brought them to the pretty little house in Hertford Street, in which Mrs. Curzon was established with her sister. They found Celia alone in the charmingly furnished drawing-room. Exquisite flowers were in the balcony, and their odour came through the open windows, which were screened by flowing white curtains.

Celia received the visitors with smiles, and at once entered into a lively conversation with them. She was two years younger than Mrs. Curzon, and there was a strong family likeness between them, though Celia was a beauty on a small scale. She had the smallest feet, the smallest hands, the largest eyes, and the daintiest little figure imaginable. Her rich auburn tresses, taken back from her polished brow, were gathered in a magnificent chignon. An arch expression of countenance, a lively and somewhat coquettish manner, added to her attractions. Whenever she laughed—and she was constantly laughing—she displayed two splendid ranges of pearls. On the present occasion she was attired in vapoury tarlatane, which made her look like a fay.

Presently Mrs. Curzon entered, and both gentlemen rose to salute her. If Scrope Musgrave had been captivated by her beauty overnight, he thought her ten times more lovely now. A light silk dress of the latest Paris mode displayed her graceful figure to admiration. Since her first introduction to the reader, Sophy was somewhat changed, and if possible, improved. She was now four-and-twenty, and in the full perfection of her beauty. Her figure was a little fuller than before. A slight shade of melancholy heightened the interest of her features, and gave additional sweetness to her smile.

On entering, she apologised for not making her appearance sooner.

"I have been writing to India," she said, "and could not delay my letter, as the mail goes out to-day."

"You have not been in India, I suppose, Mrs. Curzon?" inquired Musgrave.

"No; and I have not the slightest wish to go there. I don't think the climate would suit me."

"The heat is formidable, I own; but then we have many contrivances to render it supportable. Generally ladies like India. They are made much of, and contrive to pass their time very agreeably. In all the chief towns there is delightful society. Having been in most parts of India, I can speak positively on the point."

"If you have been in Madras, you may possibly be acquainted with the gentleman to whom I have just been writing—Mr. Myddleton Pomfret?" remarked Mrs. Curzon.

"Oh yes, I know him. A merchant. He has a first-rate cook, and gives capital dinners."

"What sort of person is he?" inquired Celia quickly. "Do tell me, please, Captain Musgrave. Describe him as accurately as you can."

"I'll do my best to paint his portrait," replied Musgrave, laughing, "but I've no particular talent in that line. There really is nothing very remarkable in his appearance. In age, as well as I can guess, he must be nearly fifty."

"Dear me!" exclaimed Celia, with a look of disappointment. "Is he so old? I fancied he was under thirty. I hope he is good-looking."

"I should not call him so," replied Musgrave. "He's short and stout, with a brick-dust complexion, light grey eyes, a snub nose, and ——"

"Stop! stop! Captain Musgrave. I'm sure you are caricaturing him," cried Sophy. "It is impossible Mr. Pomfret can be such a fright."

"If you wish me to flatter, I'll do it, but if I am to speak truth I must describe him as—what he is—a common-place, good-humoured, jolly fellow."

"Not in the least sentimental?" cried Celia.

"Not a grain of sentiment in his composition. He is a very good man of business, as I understand, and knows how to turn over the rupees."

"I find it extremely difficult to reconcile your description of my unseen friend with his letters," observed Mrs. Curzon. "They appear to emanate from a person of great refinement and sensibility. I pictured to myself a younger man than you describe—not handsome, perhaps, but with a thoughtful intelligent countenance, and a frame somewhat worn and wasted from the effect of the climate. I know he has been suffering from illness lately."

"A touch of liver, no doubt," replied Musgrave, showing his fine teeth. "Not surprising from his mode of living. I'm sorry to dispel an illusion, Mrs. Curzon, and substitute reality for fancied ideal.   Myddleton Pomfret is not a bad specimen of an English merchant, and is popular enough at Madras on account of his dinners.   I never drank better claret than at his bungalow, and he don't stint it."

During this description the sisters had exchanged looks of disappointment, and Sophy exclaimed :—

"Whatever Mr. Pomfret may be personally, he has an excellent heart.   Of that I have had ample proof.   He is a true friend, and generous in the highest degree."

"He can easily be generous, for he has lots of money, and nothing to do with it," replied Musgrave.

"You are reluctant, I perceive, to allow him any merit," said Mrs. Curzon, "and I shall believe just as much as I please of your description of my excellent friend."

"I hope I haven't incurred your displeasure, Mrs. Curzon, for my frankness," said Musgrave ; "but as you will probably see Mr. Pomfret one of these days, you will then be able to judge of the accuracy of my description."

Shortly afterwards, an interruption was offered by the entrance of some ladies, and the two gentlemen rose to depart.   When they got out of the house, Captain St. Quintin remarked to the other, with a laugh :—

"I suspect you have been mystifying the fair widow with this description of her friend.   Come ! tell me candidly.   Is it not so ? "

"Don't ask me," rejoined Musgrave, with a singular smile.

CHAPTER III.

THE ENGAGEMENT.

ROM that day forward Captain Musgrave was unremitting in his attendance on the fair widow, and contrived to make himself so agreeable to her and to Celia that they could scarcely dispense with his society. He provided them with stalls at the theatres, and boxes at the Opera Houses, gave frequent pleasant little dinners at Richmond and Greenwich, and escorted them to Ascot. Though he never breathed a word of love, he was so devoted in his manner to Sophy that no doubt could be entertained of the nature of his sentiments. But so cautiously did he act, and so imperceptible was the progress he made in her regard, that she was quite unaware that she took any real interest in him, until one or two trifling circumstances revealed it to her. When she made the discovery it was almost too late to retreat, but she persuaded herself that she could shake him off, if necessary.

Sophy did not allude to Musgrave in the first letter she wrote to Myddleton Pomfret after making the captain's acquaintance, because she had an instinctive feeling that allusion to him would not be agreeable to her correspondent; but when the acquaintance had ripened into intimacy, she thought it only proper to refer to her new friend.

" I have lately seen a good deal of Captain Scrope Musgrave," she wrote. " He tells me he knows you, having partaken of your hospitality at Madras. Both Celia and I like him much. He speaks very highly of you, as he could not fail to do."

Fully two months elapsed before an answer to this letter arrived, and before that time the handsome and captivating Scrope Musgrave had declared his passion for the fair widow, and was accepted. Yes, we grieve to say, he *was* accepted. She, who had proclaimed herself inconsolable, who had almost vowed she would remain faithful to the memory of her dear Julian, had engaged herself to another. It was not certainly without much persistence that assent was wrung from her, and she reproached herself for giving it, but Captain Musgrave prevailed. By the next mail she announced her engagement to Myddelton Pomfret, and trusted he would approve of the step she had taken.

" I daresay the intelligence will surprise you," she wrote, "after my professions of unalterable attachment to Julian's memory, but you see what inconsistent creatures women are."

Captain Musgrave was strongly averse to this letter being sent. It would be time enough, he said, to announce the marriage after it had taken place. But Sophy would not be dissuaded. Her letter was crossed by another from Madras. It was shorter than any communication she had as yet received from Myddleton Pomfret, and quite startled her.

"Your letter has caused me the greatest uneasiness. Captain Musgrave is a person whom I hold in the utmost abhorrence. I will not characterise him as strongly as he deserves, but he is dangerous, and I cannot help dreading that he has a base object in view in obtaining an introduction to you. So anxious do I feel on this score, that, were it possible, I would come over to England. This I cannot do, but I entreat you at once to break off the acquaintance."

Captain Musgrave was with her when she received this letter. He saw by her emotion how profoundly she was affected, and took the letter from her trembling hand. She watched his countenance as he perused it. He muttered a deep execration, and his eyes flashed fire as he looked up.

"I wish the fellow would come to England," he cried. "He should answer to me with his life for his vile imputations. But I must not allow his slander to produce any effect upon you, sweet Sophy. From motives, for which I am sure you will give me credit, I have forborne to speak of him as he deserves, but I must now tell you that he and I were mixed up together in an unfortunate affair in Madras, in which a lady's reputation was implicated—implicated by him, not by me—and I had to chastise him for his conduct towards her. I have often intended to mention this circumstance to you, but have been deterred by fear of giving you pain. You will now comprehend the fellow's object in writing this calumnious letter. Fearing I should unmask him, he seeks to discredit my assertions. I am sorry you have ever had anything to do with such a scoundrel."

" If he is such a person as you represent him, Scrope, the sums which he has advanced me must be repaid. I ought not to be under any obligation to him."

" Don't give yourself any trouble about him. He deserves to lose the money. You knew nothing about him when you accepted his bounty, and should have known nothing had he not rendered exposure necessary."

" Had I been aware of his character, I would not have accepted the slightest favour from him. I am placed in a very painful position, and scarcely know how to act."

"Leave me to deal with him. If I deem it necessary, the money shall be returned. In your last, you told him of our engagement. Did you mention when the marriage was likely to take place?"

"I told him it would take place speedily—probably before the end of the month—as you were very anxious there should be no delay. That was exactly what I stated."

" I wish you had said nothing about it. But it doesn't signify. Since he is in India, he can give us no trouble. And now dismiss all thoughts of him from your mind."

Sophy strove to obey the injunction, but found it quite impossible. She could not help thinking a great deal about her singular correspondent; neither could she reconcile Musgrave's statements respecting him with her own preconceived notions, or even with Pomfret's conduct.

Celia, to whom she confided all her doubts and fears, was almost as much infatuated as herself by Musgrave, and did not attach any importance to Myddleton Pomfret's warning. He could only have been actuated by jealousy to write such a letter, she declared. It was quite certain he didn't want Sophy to marry at all, but meant to offer her his own hand on his return to his native country.

3

Captain Musgrave could not have found a better advocate, had he needed one, than Celia proved. She successfully combated any objections raised by her sister, and quieted her qualms of conscience.

When consulted, Mr. Leycester, though he was not altogether satisfied, offered no opposition to the match. He would have been better pleased if his daughter had united herself to a wealthier man, and of higher position; but as he himself was not required to do anything, he raised no objection. "Sophy was her own mistress, and could do as she pleased. Captain Musgrave was a very handsome fellow, and if she liked him she was quite right to marry him. For his own part, he should have preferred a plainer man, with more money; and if graced with a title, so much the better. However, Sophy was the person chiefly interested, and must please herself. He only hoped her second marriage would turn out more prosperously than the first."

This was all he said. The allusion to her first marriage brought tears to Sophy's eyes; but Celia, who was present at the time soon chased them away.

CHAPTER IV.

APTAIN MUSGRAVE'S impatience increased for the speedy celebration of his marriage with the lovely widow. Sophy would have preferred a little longer delay, but suffered herself to be over-ruled, and the day was at last fixed, and at no distant date. The interval, which was about three weeks — Musgrave would have abridged even this if he could—was spent in preparations for the happy event.

Throughout this period Sophy's irresolution continued. Her spirits drooped. One morning she informed Celia that she had dreamed of Julian, and that he had regarded her with a sad and reproachful countenance. But Celia only laughed at the relation.

As the day approached which was to link her fortunes for ever with those of Captain Musgrave, instead of becoming more cheerful Sophy became more melancholy. If she had possessed sufficient moral courage she would have broken off the engagement even then, but she had not firmness enough for the effort. Again she mentioned her mis-givings to her sister, and again was laughed at for her wavering. No word, therefore, was uttered by her.

Captain Musgrave had not failed to remark her melan-choly looks, and attributed them to the right cause; but he feigned not to notice them, and allowed her no opportunity of explanation.

Strange to say, when the expected day arrived, Sophy recovered her cheerfulness. She had passed an excellent night, and arose in good spirits. The day was splendid, and all looked bright and smiling.

An incident, however, occurred which at once threw a cloud over her liveliness, and re-awakened all her mis-givings. She had just entered her boudoir, arrayed in the

3—2

exquisite bridal-dress which had been prepared for her by one of the first modistes. Celia, who of course was one of the bridesmaids, had likewise just completed her toilette, and the two sisters were admiring each other's dresses, when the lady's-maid brought in a letter for her mistress. Sophy changed colour as she caught sight of it, and exclaimed :—

" Why, it's from Myddleton Pomfret ! "

" Never mind. Don't read it now," cried Celia.

But Sophy hurriedly opened the letter, and on perusing it became deadly pale, and appeared ready to sink.

" I'm sorry you would read it," said Celia, picking up the letter, which Sophy had dropped in her agitation. " Let us see what the troublesome creature has to say for himself."

The letter was dated Marseilles, and ran as follows :—

" This letter will serve as an avant-courrière, to announce my arrival this morning at Marseilles. Within a few hours I hope to see you. I shall start for Paris by the night express, and proceed thence, without stoppage, to London.

" The intelligence conveyed in your last letter of your engagement to Captain Musgrave, caused me such intense anxiety that I embarked by the first packet. Heaven grant I may be in time to save you from the peril by which you are threatened ! Ceaseless misery would be your portion if you were to wed this man. I have cautioned you against him ; but even if he were high-principled, and worthy of your love, as he is base and dishonourable, the marriage must not, cannot be. Unsurmountable obstacles to it exist. These you will learn when we meet, and you will then comprehend the frightful risk you have incurred. I need not be more explicit, since I shall see you so soon.

" I have a strange and startling disclosure to make, and my principal object in writing is to prepare you for the surprise, and perhaps shock, which the disclosure is likely to occasion.

" All my plans have been disconcerted by this unexpected and disastrous occurrence. I have hurried away from Madras at the greatest personal inconvenience. But my presence in London seems absolutely necessary, and may be the only means of averting irreparable mischief.

" Again I implore you to prepare yourself for our meeting.

When you know all, you may blame me ; but I am persuaded you will pardon the deception I have practised.
"MYDDLETON POMFRET."

"What can he mean?, What terrible disclosure can he
have to make?" gasped Sophy.
"I'm sure I can't tell," replied Celia, who was much
alarmed by the letter. "If he has any revelations to make,
why not speak out at once? I'm afraid there's something
wrong, as well as mysterious about him. I firmly believe
he only wants to break off your marriage with Scrope in
order to secure you for himself. But he'll be disappointed
in that anticipation."
"The marriage must be delayed, Celia. I'm too much
upset to go through the ceremony. Besides, I cannot
neglect the warning given me. I am bound to hear Mr.
Pomfret's disclosure before I take an irrevocable step,
against which he so solemnly warns me. Where is
Scrope?"
"In the drawing-room, I suppose."
"Come with me to him."
They found Captain Musgrave in the drawing-room,
capitally got up for the occasion, and looking superbly
handsome.
"What is the matter?" he inquired, startled by Sophy's
appearance. "You have just received a letter, I am told.
Has it put you out?"
"Read it," she replied.
Musgrave read the letter deliberately, and his countenance darkened. When he had finished, he laughed
bitterly.
"Didn't I tell you he was an infernal hypocrite?" he
cried. "He confesses he has deceived you, but dares not
tell you for what purpose. I could tell you, but I won't.
His effrontery, however, exceeds any notion I had formed
of it. I never supposed he would come to England on such
a fool's errand. However, he will take nothing by the
move," he added, again laughing bitterly. "He'll be rather
too late to hinder the marriage, even if he had the power."
"The ceremony must be postponed," said Sophy. "I
cannot go through with it until after I have seen him."

"Postponed!" exclaimed Musgrave. "You cannot seriously mean what you say, Sophy."

"I could not approach the altar with such a weight on my breast. I am bound to hear what Mr. Pomfret has to say, Scrope. His warning is so earnest, so impressive, that I cannot refuse to listen to it. He will be here in a few hours."

"I will consent to no delay on his account or on any other," rejoined Musgrave, angrily. "If the marriage does not take place to-day, it cannot take place at all. But wait for him, if you please. I shall be here to confront him on his arrival, and you may rely upon it," he added, fiercely, "that he will repent his audacity."

"Do consider what you are about, Sophy dear," interposed Celia, in a low persuasive tone. "If the marriage is postponed, it will infallibly cause a vast deal of unpleasant comment; and Scrope is evidently so irritated—and, as I think, so justly irritated—that if a meeting takes place between him and this provoking Mr. Pomfret, I tremble to think of the consequences."

"Have you decided, Sophy?" said Musgrave in an authoritative tone. "Will you be ruled by this fellow or by me?"

"By you, Scrope," she rejoined, gently. "Come good, come ill, I am yours for ever."

"You are an angel," he cried, embracing her tenderly.

"How delighted I am that all is satisfactorily settled!" cried Celia. "Give me that horrid letter. I'll burn it as soon as possible."

"It's lucky for Pomfret that he didn't come a day sooner," observed Musgrave, "or he would have met with a reception that he didn't expect. As it is, we shall be on our way to Paris before he turns up."

"If you should happen to meet him, Scrope, there must be no quarrel between you. Promise me this," said Sophy, earnestly. "And now," she added, on receiving the required assurance from him, "you must leave me. I must be alone for a short time in order to recover myself."

Despite the warning she had received—despite her own misgivings—Sophy was united that morning at St. George's, Hanover Square, to Captain Musgrave. She could scarcely support herself through the ceremony, and her agitation was so visible that it attracted the attention even of the clerical dignitary who officiated on the occasion. But her emotion was attributed solely to nervousness. A slight noise occurred when the awful charge was delivered, requiring the pair to confess if either of them knew of any impediment to their union, and the bride glanced round in terror, almost expecting Myddleton Pomfret to appear. But he came not. Captain Musgrave stood proudly beside her at the altar, and had quite an elated look when the ceremony was concluded.

After the nuptials there was, of course, a sumptuous breakfast; but the newly married couple did not remain long at the repast, it being their intention to proceed to Folkestone, and cross on the same evening to Boulogne. From Boulogne they proposed to proceed to Paris, and thence to the south of France. This plan, arranged by Scrope, was not altogether agreeable to Sophy, who preferred a tour in England, but she acquiesced in it.

Quitting the wedding breakfast early, as we have stated, the bride and bridegroom, accompanied by Celia and a lady's maid, crossed that evening to France. About midway in the Channel they met another steamer coming from Boulogne, and watched her as she passed by.

"I wonder whether Myddleton Pomfret is on board that boat?" remarked Musgrave to his bride.

She turned pale at the observation, but made no reply.

There was more truth in Musgrave's remark than he thought. The person alluded to *was* among the passengers in the steam-boat.

Next morning, a hansom cab drove up to the house in Hertford Street, and a tall, well-dressed man alighted from it. Though he could not be much more than five-and-thirty, this gentleman's profuse beard was tinged with grey, as were his locks. When he inquired for Mrs. Curzon, the footman who answered the door smiled. The gentleman could not be aware, he said, that she was only married yesterday to Captain Musgrave.

"They are gone to Paris to spend the honeymoon," continued the man, who did not notice the effect produced by his communication upon the stranger,

The gentleman walked away without a word, but his strength suddenly deserted him, and he caught at an iron rail for support.

"Too late !" he groaned ; "I have arrived too late to prevent the dire calamity.　She has neglected my warning. What will become of her ? "

𝔈𝔫𝔡 𝔬𝔣 𝔱𝔥𝔢 𝔉𝔦𝔯𝔰𝔱 𝔅𝔬𝔬𝔨.

BOOK II.

THE FLIGHT.

CHAPTER I.

A DINNER AT THE HOTEL DES RESERVOIRS.

CAPTAIN MUSGRAVE, with his wife and Celia, had now been nearly three weeks in Paris. They had charming rooms at the Grand Hôtel.

Neither of the ladies had been in Paris before, and both were astonished by the magnificence of the peerless city. Captain Musgrave being very well acquainted with the French capital, took care they should see the best of its multitudinous sights. One day, having ascertained that the Grandes Eaux would play, he conducted them to Versailles. After inspecting the galleries of the palace, and admiring the superb terrace, the party descended to the Allé du Tapis Vert. It was thronged by a large and gaily dressed assemblage, a portion of which was promenading to and fro, while others were seated near the quinconces on the left, listening to the strains of an admirable military band.

Sophy thought the scene enchanting. The general air of gaiety pervading the groups, the exquisite toilettes of the ladies, and the varied uniforms of the numerous officers, conspired to give a lively character to the picture.

Both sisters, from their beauty, attracted considerable attention, though the remarks of the Parisian belles were not very complimentary to them. From what cause we will not pretend to say, but certain it is, that English ladies, however beautiful, do not appear to advantage among a

crowd of French dames, even though the personal charms
of the latter may be inferior to their own. The stiffness of
our fair countrywomen, of which the French justly complain, becomes more conspicuous when brought into contrast
with the graceful and easy movements of the French dames,
and brilliant complexions, rich tresses, and regular features
do not please so much as expressive countenances, animated
looks, and piquant manner.

It is certainly rather a trying ordeal to be exposed to the
sarcastic looks and not always whispered remarks of a crowd
of sharp-eyed, sharp-tongued Parisian dames while passing
in review before them, and to feel conscious that every
particle of your dress, from boot to bonnet, is commented
upon ; that your looks and gestures are mercilessly ridiculed,
and every movement derided. Celia stood this fire with
wonderful intrepidity, but Sophy shrank from it. Though
opinions might differ as to the charms of the English women,
it was universally agreed that their companion was remarkably handsome—probably because he did not look like an
Englishman.

Though Celia's beauty was not of the same high order as
her sister's, she was more admired than Sophy, simply from
her vivacity of manner. The severest female critic could
not deny that Sophy's features were regular, that her eyes were
fine, her tresses of a beautiful blond-doré, her figure perfect,
and her toilette irreproachable. But all these attractions
were neutralised by want of expression and rigidity of
movement. Poor Sophy, it must be owned, had a singularly triste air for a bride. Yet there were some—at
least among the male portion of the beholders—who thought
that the gentle melancholy pervading her countenance was
not without a special charm.

After walking down the *allée* as far as the Bassin
d'Apollon, our friends returned to the assemblage collected
around the band. Having procured chairs for the ladies,
Captain Musgrave left them to themselves for a short time.
It was at this juncture that Celia, whose attention had been
occupied for a moment by what was going on around her,
remarked that her sister had become deadly pale, and was
gazing eagerly into the adjoining bosquet, as if in search of
some object,

"You look alarmed," cried Celia. "What is the matter?"

"I have seen him," replied Sophy, with an irrepressible shudder—"there, among those trees."

"Seen whom?"

"Him I have lost—to whose memory I have proved faithless. I have seen Julian. He was there among the trees—not fifty yards off. I saw him quite distinctly, and the reproachful look he cast upon me went to my very heart. I could not bear it; but when I raised my eyes again he was gone. You look incredulous, but I saw him as plainly as I see you."

"Absurd!" cried Celia. "You will never have done thinking of Julian. You have seen some one resembling him, that is all. This is neither the time nor the place for the indulgence of such silly fancies. Dismiss the notion at once, and compose yourself before Scrope returns, or he will wonder what has happened."

Shortly afterwards Captain Musgrave came back with a chair, and seated himself beside them. Sophy stole an occasional timorous glance towards the bosquet, but no spectre could be descried within it. Occupied by what was passing around, Captain Musgrave paid little attention to her. By-and-by the assemblage dispersed in various directions to look at the fountains, which had begun to play.

After witnessing this magnificent display, our friends repaired to the Hôtel des Réservoirs, where dinner had been ordered. Many guests, numbering among them people of all nations, English, Americans, Germans, Spaniards, and Italians, were already assembled in the airy and agreeable salle-à-manger. At a large table near the door were seated a party of Americans of both sexes, well supplied with champagne. Next to them were some Germans, who had likewise made some progress with their dinner, and who were laughing and talking loudly. In the centre of the salon were collected a party of English excursionists, who were making themselves a nuisance to all the other guests by their continuous clamour to the garçons. More English folks were scattered about the room; but there was one party seated near an open window, which afforded a glimpse of other tables set beneath the trees of the garden, and to this party we must direct attention. It consisted of five persons, and an experienced eye would have at once decided, from their looks and manner, that they were Londoners, and belonged to the eastern side of Temple Bar. There was an air about the principal personage that proclaimed him a citizen. He was no other than Mr. Flaxyard, the well-known and wealthy draper of Cheapside, who had brought his family to Paris. Mr. Flaxyard himself was 'short and stout, in age between sixty and seventy, with a bald shining head, white whiskers, ruddy complexion, common-place features, impossible to describe, because possessing no particular character, and only to be adequately represented by a photograph. Mrs. Flaxyard, of the Acacias, Clapham Common (for she wholly ignored Cheapside), was taller, and perhaps stouter than her lord, and had been accounted a very fine woman, and perhaps was so still, though rather on a large scale. She had the advantage over Flaxyard of some twenty years in point of age; and this was something. Mr. and Mrs. Flaxyard were accompanied by their only son, Hornby, a young civic swell, who was rather above the business to which he was compelled by his governor to attend, and who was dressed in rather a loud style, especially in regard to necktie and vest, wearing a superfluity of chains, breast-pins, and rings, and boasting a pair of light Dundreary whiskers, of which he was excessively vain.

To complete the character Hornby had assumed, he thought it indispensable to wear an eye-glass, except when engaged in business. Theophania Flaxyard (Tiffany she was called by the elderly parties, and Tiff by her brother) was described by Hornby as a very jolly girl. Saucy-looking features, a retroussé nose, bright blue eyes, which she used pretty freely, sunny locks, and splendid teeth, constituted Tiffany's charms. She was very fast in manner—much too fast for old Flaxyard, who frequently called her to order, but she paid very little attention to what he said, and always laughed at him. Tiffany had been brought up at a celebrated boarding-school at Clapham, and the finishing graces were imparted to her at a fashionable institution des demoiselles in the neighbourhood of the Champs-Elysées. Thus she considered herself a perfect Frenchwoman, and imagined she could talk, walk, and dress like a Parisian. If she had learnt nothing else, she had learnt to flirt and to base her notions of morals and conduct upon those expounded by French novels and French plays, to sigh for the most extravagant dresses, magnificent equipages, and a sumptuous mansion. But in spite of all the French varnish she had acquired, and which only brought out the defects of her native character more strongly, Tiffany Flaxyard was nothing more than a fast English girl.

With them was Mr. Rufus Trotter, the only son of a wealthy corn-broker, residing somewhere in the neighbour-hood of Mark Lane. Rufus was the bosom friend of Hornby, and, like that young fellow, was an astonishing swell, wearing much the same style of attire, and embellish-ing his countenance with splendid beard of a glowing hue. Rufus was a very sharp fellow in his own estimation, as well as good-looking, and had rather ambitious views, being determined to get into the best society—not the best City society, but the best society to be found in Belgrave Square or Eaton Square—and he was also determined to get into the House of Commons (as several of his City friends had recently done), where he fondly persuaded himself he should cut a figure, but he had been prevented from doing so by heavy railway losses recently sustained by Mr. Trotter, senior.

Rufus was an admirer of the bewitching Tiffany. Not that he did not raise his eyes far higher—not that he did not feel sure he could marry an earl's daughter or a duke's sister, but somehow or other Tiffany had ensnared him. On her part, the fast young lady had by no means made up her mind to accept him, but liking admiration, she encouraged him. Still, she would have thrown him over without a moment's hesitation, if any one more eligible had turned up. The Flaxyards had been in Paris about a fortnight, on the way to Switzerland, and were staying at the Grand Hôtel, where they had seen Captain and Mrs. Musgrave and Miss Leycester at the table d'hôte, and constantly encountered them in the court-yard and in the public rooms. The younger folks were anxious to make the acquaintance of such very stylish-looking people, and Captain Musgrave, who thought something might be made of them, and who, besides, was rather pleased with Tiffany's appearance, con-

descended to meet them half way. He first talked to the
young men, then to Tiffany, who was quite ready to flirt
with him, though she knew he had only just been married,
and next presented his wife and sister to Mrs. Flaxyard and
her daughter, so they all presently became good friends.
The elder people were charmed with Sophy's beauty and
amiable manner, and from various causes the younger folks
got on very well together. Though not quite so fast as
Tiffany, Celia was just as fond of flirting as that intrepid
young woman, and she very considerately divided her
attractions between Hornby and Rufus ; but Sophy pleased
them best, and young Flaxyard secretly regretted to his
friend that he had not known Mrs. Musgrave before the
captain was accepted. The new acquaintances had done
St. Cloud, and St. Germain, and talked of doing Fontain-
bleau, but meantime they had agreed to dine together at
Versailles, after witnessing the Grandes Eaux.

The ordering of the dinner had been entrusted to Hornby
and Rufus, and with the aid of the host they had contrived
to make out a tolerably good menu. After many greetings
and explanations as to why they had not met before, the
whole party took their places, Sophy being seated between
old Flaxyard and his son, Celia next to Rufus, and Captain
Musgrave between Tiffany and her mother.

The dinner was excellent, quite as good, old Flaxyard
declared, as one they had partaken of a few days before at
Durand's, and the champagne soon did its duty, and
loosened their tongues. Celia laughed and chattered gaily
with her two neighbours—now raising the hopes of one, now
of the other. Old Flaxyard did his best to amuse Sophy,
and Tiffany talked with a freedom to Captain Musgrave that
almost surprised him, accustomed as he was to fast girls.
They talked of all sorts of things ; of the charming toilettes
and superb equipages they had seen in the Bois, declaring
they preferred the Bois a thousand times to Hyde Park ;
they talked about the galleries of Versailles and the charms
of the Trianons ; they talked of the grande-monde and the
demi-monde, of high-born dames and actresses, of the
fountains they had just seen, comparing them to those of the
Crystal Palace, much to the disadvantage of the latter ; the
young men talked of Mabille and the Jardin des Fleurs, the

bouffes, and the cafés chantants, and Tiffany laughed at what they said; and as the dinner went on, and more champagne bottles were opened, the merriment of the party increased. There was one person, however, who, amid the general gaiety, continued absent and sad, ate little, declined champagne, and smiled not at the liveliest sallies.

A party of excursionists from the other side of the Channel, as we have said, occupied a central table in the salle. They likewise drank a good deal of champagne, and being probably unaccustomed to such potations, rather too lively an effect was produced upon them, and they soon became boisterous, talking and laughing so loudly as to become an annoyance to the rest of the room. The garçons looked aghast; the guests at the surrounding tables stared in astonishment, and shrugged their shoulders; and our young friends were so disgusted at this display of bad manners on the part of their compatriots, that they seriously proposed to eject the noisy fellows from the room, and were only dissuaded from the attempt by old Flaxyard who was apprehensive that a tremendous row would ensue.

"It is owing to the misconduct of such fellows as these that we have acquired such a bad name on the Continent," remarked Captain Musgrave. "No wonder the French call us a nation of shopkeepers."

"Such fellows as those ought to stay at home, since they don't know how to behave," remarked Hornby. "They make one ashamed of one's country."

"Not so loud," cried old Flaxyard. "They'll hear what you say."

"I don't care whether they hear or not," cried Hornby. "They are quite welcome to my opinion about them."

"And what may be your opinion about us, Sir, I should like to know?" demanded one of the excursionists, with a fierce look. "Not that it's of much consequence. Still I should like to know it. What say you, Jennings?—and you, Blewjones?"

"Yes, Jack Wigglesworth," rejoined the others, scowling at Hornby. "We should both like to know the fellow's opinion."

"Well, then, I've not the slightest objection to oblige you," replied the young man, in an impertinent tone, and totally disregarding his father's looks. "My opinion of you is, that you are an infernal set of ——"

"Hold your tongue, Hornby!" cried old Flaxyard. "I'll have no more of this. You'll get into a brawl."

"You were about to tell us what we are, Sir," said Wigglesworth, rising and approaching the table. "Pray, what are we?"

"Yes, what are we?" added Blewjones, and Jennings following him.

"Infernal snobs, since you want to know," rejoined Hornby.

"Perhaps a stronger term might suit you better, and if so I have one at your service," supplemented Musgrave. "It's quite clear you don't know how to conduct yourselves in public."

"We didn't come to Paris to be taught manners by fools like you," rejoined Wigglesworth, snapping his fingers. "If our society ain't agreeable, you can easily rid yourselves of it."

"We mean to do so," said Musgrave, significantly. "The sooner you make yourself scarce the better. Pay your bill and go, Wigglesworth. Garçon," he added, raising his voice, "l'addition pour ces messieurs."

"A l'instant, Messieurs," cried the garçon, enchanted at the prospect of getting rid of the troublesome guests, while all the rest of the company seemed highly diverted by what was going on.

"What does he say?" cried Wigglesworth to his friends. "By Jove! I believe the fellow has ordered our bill."

"He's a cool customer, I must say," remarked Blewjones.

"Voilà, l'addition, Messieurs," said the garçon, presenting it to them.

"Perhaps you'll pay it, since you have taken the trouble to order it," remarked Wigglesworth to Musgrave.

"Let's look at the amount?" cried the captain, snatching the bill from him. "Just sixty francs. Not dear for so much champagne, Wigglesworth. Give the garçon three naps and as much more as you please, and then you'll be free to depart," he added, tossing back the bill.

Disconcerted by Musgrave's assurance, and finding himself and his companions the laughing-stock of the whole room,

Wigglesworth paid the garçon, and the whole party of excursionists beat a hasty retreat.

"I hope nothing will come of this ridiculous incident," remarked old Flaxyard, as soon as they were gone.

"You needn't give yourself a moment's thought about it, my dear Sir," remarked Captain Musgrave, with a smile. "They're not the sort of men to fight. They'll think twice before they send us an invitation to the Bois de Boulogne."

Another bottle of Larose was ordered, and when the garçon brought it he made an observation to old Flaxyard, which was not quite intelligible to that simple Briton.

"What does he say, Tiffy?" he called out to his daughter.

"He says that a gentleman outside desires to speak with you, papa," she replied.

"Bless me! that's strange. Won't the gentleman come in?"

The garçon replied that the gentleman would not come in.

"Are you quite sure there's no mistake?"

The garçon being quite sure there was none, old Flaxyard went out with him, and remained away so long that the Larose was finished before his reappearance.

CHAPTER II.

OW to see what old Flaxyard had been about. On going forth, in compliance with the summons he had received, he found in the court-yard of the hotel a tall personage, attired in black, whom the garçon indicated as the gentleman who had sent for him. The person was an entire stranger, but on seeing Flaxyard he advanced, and bowing gravely, addressed him by name, apologising for the liberty he had taken in sending for him. The stranger then led the way through an archway at the back of the court-yard communicating with the gardens of the palace, where they could converse without fear of interruption.

" You will think it odd that I should be acquainted with your name, Mr. Flaxyard," he said, " but I ascertained it at the Grand Hotel. I have seen you with Captain Musgrave and—his wife."

It was only by a great effort that he could force himself to pronounce the last word.

Flaxyard merely bowed assent, not knowing exactly what to say.

" It is in reference to Mrs. Musgrave "—and the stranger again paused, and put his hand to his side—" it is in reference to Mrs. Musgrave, I say, that I desire to speak to you."

" Perhaps you will permit me to know whom I have the honour of addressing ? " asked Flaxyard.

" When I tell you that I am named Myddleton Pomfret, and am a Madras merchant, I shall have conveyed very little to you, I fear."

" Pardon me, Sir. If you are of the well known house of Bracebridge, Clegg, and Pomfret, I *have* heard of you."

"I belong to that house," replied the other, with a melancholy smile. "And now, Mr. Flaxyard, you can render me an important service, and though I have no title whatever to ask it of you, yet I am persuaded you won't refuse me."

"You pay me a compliment, Mr. Pomfret. Let me hear what you require."

"You can serve another as well as me, Sir. You can most materially serve a lady in whom I think you feel some interest."

"If you refer to Mrs. Musgrave, as I fancy you do, Mr. Pomfret, I can only say that I shall be delighted to be of service to her."

"I do refer to her. Before proceeding further, I must entreat you not to misconstrue what I am about to say. I must also entreat you not to ask for an explanation, which I cannot give, but to be content with my statement."

"This is asking a good deal," remarked Flaxyard, staring at him.

"I know it," rejoined Pomfret. "It is impossible for me to hold any communication with Captain Musgrave. Consequently, the message which I desire to convey to his wife through you must be made without his knowledge."

"Without the captain's knowledge, did you say, Sir?" cried Flaxyard, startled. "This appears to me an underhand proceeding—a very improper proceeding, Sir, in which I must decline to take part."

"Don't mistake me," rejoined Pomfret, almost sternly. "Circumstances render it necessary. Were a meeting to take place between myself and Captain Musgrave, it would be attended by fearful consequences. He has wronged me —wronged me deeply. I would call him to account, but my hands are tied."

"Whew! here's a pretty business!" thought Flaxyard. "I begin to perceive how matters stand. The poor gentleman has been jilted by a more fortunate rival. Well, I'm sorry for you, Mr. Pomfret—extremely sorry, I'm sure—but what do you want me to do?"

"I want you to give this letter to Mrs. Musgrave privately. You will easily find an opportunity."

"Very, likely I might. But I decline to do it, Sir," rejoined Flaxyard, with an offended air. "What do you take me for, Mr. Pomfret?"

"For a sensible, good-natured man, or I should not apply to you."

"Well, you are right so far," said Flaxyard. "I *am* sensible and good-natured, but I can't allow my good nature to drag me into a difficulty. I can't countenance an improper act. I can't deliver a letter to a married woman behind her husband's back."

"Perhaps I may remove your scruples, when I tell you it is not a letter, but simply an envelope enclosing banknotes."

"Worse and worse!" cried Flaxyard, now really horrified. "Upon my word, Mr. Pomfret, you must have a very extraordinary opinion of me to venture to make such a proposition. Give a lady money secretly. Nothing of the kind, Sir."

"Yes you will, when I tell you that the money which you will thus convey to Mrs. Musgrave is indispensable to her. If you refuse, I must find other means. But I rely on your secresy. I know I am dealing with a man of honour. You won't betray the lady."

"Betray her, certainly not," cried Flaxyard. "I shan't utter a word. But I don't choose to be made a go-between in an affair of this sort."

"Hear me before you decide. A moment may come— nay, most assuredly *will* come—when it may be necessary, as I have just hinted, that Mrs. Musgrave should not be without resources, and that her resources should be unknown to her husband. That is why I wish to send her this money. That is why I wish to employ you."

The energy of his looks and manner forced conviction of his sincerity upon his auditor.

"You seem to insinuate a great deal against Captain Musgrave," remarked Flaxyard. "Is he in difficulties?"

"Don't ask me," rejoined the other. "It is my business to protect the woman he has deceived, and I am obliged to adopt this course to accomplish my purpose."

"Well, I would willingly help you if I felt quite sure you are acting in a straightforward manner. But you must allow that your proposition is singular, to say the least of it."

" You will regret hereafter, if you don't accede to my request."

" Well, I'll run the risk. Something in your manner satisfies me of your sincerity."

" I felt I could not be mistaken in you," said Pomfret, with a look of profound gratitude. " Here is the packet. Tell her she need not fear that I will intrude upon her, but shall ever be ready to aid her in case of need."

" I will give her the packet in the manner you enjoin, Sir, and will not fail to deliver your message at the same time."

They then separated. Myddleton Pomfret walked rapidly towards the great gates opening upon the Boulevart de la Reine, and Flaxyard returned to the hotel.

" I see by your looks that you've got something strange to tell us, papa," cried Tiffany, as the old gentleman entered the salle. " Out with it."

" Something very odd and unexpected has happened to me, I must own," replied Flaxyard. " But I can't explain it just now. Indeed, I'm not sure that I can explain it at all."

" Why, what a provoking old body you are ! " cried Tiffany. " I thought you had brought a challenge from Mr. Wigglesworth, or one of those polite excursionists."

" I've seen nothing of Mr. Wigglesworth, or any of his crew," he replied. " But depend upon it I won't let you into my secret, Tiffy. Order some more Larose, Hornby. This bottle is empty, I perceive. I've something for your private ear by-and-by, Ma'am," he added in a low voice to Mrs. Musgrave.

" For me ? " she replied, startled.

Sophy had become so nervous of late that the slightest thing startled her.

" Yes, to you, Ma'am," he replied, in the same under tone. " The gentleman who called me out sent for me in reference to you."

" Who is he ? What can he possibly have to say to you about me ? You excite my curiosity very strongly, Mr. Flaxyard."

" Excuse my answering any questions just now," replied the old gentleman, aware that Captain Musgrave was looking fixedly at him. " Don't give way to any emotion if you can possibly help it. The person who sent for me just now, and who has been talking about you, is Mr. Myddleton Pomfret, of Madras."

"Gracious Heaven! Is he here? Has he followed us to Paris?"

"Be calm, I entreat of you," whispered Flaxyard. "Your husband is watching you. You needn't be afraid of encountering Mr. Pomfret. He has returned to Paris."

But Sophy found it quite impossible to control her agitation, and presently rose from the table, and Mrs. Flaxyard and the other ladies withdrew with her. Captain Musgrave did not manifest any great uneasiness, but merely remarked,—

"My wife is subject to nervous attacks, but she soon gets over them, and I have no doubt she will be · better presently."

And so it proved. In less than a quarter of an hour the ladies reappeared, and though Sophy still looked very pale, she seemed to have recovered from her sudden indisposition.

CHAPTER III

THE bill being paid, the party proceeded in a couple of carriages to the station appertaining to the Rive Droite, and shortly afterwards they were speeding towards the terminus in the Rue Saint-Lazare.

Mr. Flaxyard took charge of Sophy, and by a dexterous little manœuvre, which did the old gentleman infinite credit, contrived to place her in a carriage separate from the rest of the party. All the other occupants of this carriage appeared to be French. They were thus enabled to converse without restraint; and almost as soon as they had started the old gentleman hastened to relieve her anxiety, by explaining what had passed between himself and Myddleton Pomfret. On concluding his recital he delivered the packet to her.

" I don't want to ask an impertinent question, Ma'am," he said. " But I suppose Mr. Pomfret is an old friend? "

" I have never seen him—merely corresponded with him," she replied. " He was a friend of my first husband, Julian Curzon, and as such took a strong interest in me. But I imagined his interest would cease now that I have married again—and contrary to his wishes."

" How am I to understand you, Ma'am? "

" I owe you a full explanation, Mr. Flaxyard, and you shall have it. Mr. Pomfret returned from India for the express purpose of preventing my marriage with Captain Musgrave—but he arrived too late."

" Very strange ! And you say you have never seen him? "

" Never. From a letter which I received from him I knew he was on his way to London, but I have heard nothing since. I have no idea what sort of person he is— whether young or old—and I have reason to believe that some descriptions given me of him were incorrect."

"I don't know how he has been described to you, but, according to my notion, he has a very interesting countenance. Though his beard is tinged with grey, he cannot, I conceive, be above five-and-thirty. But he appears to have suffered much, and looks out of health. He is tall and thin, and bears himself like a gentleman. Altogether, he is a very striking-looking person."

"It must be he! I have seen him!" exclaimed Sophy, who had grown pale at this description. "I caught a glimpse of him among the trees in the gardens of Versailles this morning. I only beheld him for a moment, but I was struck by his countenance, because I thought him so like —— "

And she paused.

"So like whom, Ma'am?"

"My first husband," she replied. "He is the very image of poor Julian Curzon."

"That's strange!" exclaimed Flaxyard. "And you say they were bosom friends. Odd they should be personally alike—very odd, ain't it?"

"I tell you I only saw him for a moment, for he disappeared in the bosquet. I thought it was Julian risen from the dead."

"Pray excuse me for alluding to the subject, but I have heard, I think, that your first husband met his death by accident?"

"You have heard the truth, Sir," she rejoined. "He was drowned while bathing in the lake of Windermere."

"God bless me!—yes, now I remember the circumstance —very shocking indeed!"

"I witnessed the dreadful occurrence," said Sophy. "I saw him sink never to rise again, but I was denied the sad satisfaction of laying him in the grave."

"Am I to understand that the body was never recovered?" inquired Flaxyard.

"It was never recovered," she replied.

The old gentleman evidently wished to ask a few more questions, but he did not like to pursue the painful theme;

and Sophy, whose thoughts were occupied by the past, maintained a mournful silence. At last, Flaxyard spoke.

"Will you allow me to ask you, Ma'am, and believe that I am influenced by no idle curiosity in putting the question —but are you acquainted with Mr. Myddleton Pomfret's history?"

"I never heard of him until about a year ago," she replied, "when he wrote to me from Madras explaining that he had been poor Julian's intimate friend, and offering to pay his debts."

"Oh! then your husband was in debt at the time of the accident?" inquired Flaxyard.

"Deeply in debt," she rejoined. "But all his debts were discharged by Mr. Pomfret."

"An extraordinary act of friendship," remarked the old gentleman, dryly.

"You would indeed think Mr. Pomfret a devoted friend, if you knew all he has done for me—for no other reason save that I was Julian's widow. The interest he has taken in my welfare seems unaccountable."

"Not quite unaccountable," muttered Flaxyard. "You say Mr. Pomfret came from Madras in order to prevent your union with Captain Musgrave, but arrived too late. Didn't he write? Didn't he assign any reason for his objection to the marriage?"

"He warned me against it, but reserved all explanations till his arrival."

"And you would not wait for him!" exclaimed Flaxyard, sharply. "Madam, you were wrong—very wrong."

"I now feel that I ought to have waited. But Captain Musgrave was impatient, and I yielded. The marriage was hurried on."

"Ah! it's a sad business!" cried the old gentleman. "I mean, it's a thousand pities you didn't await Mr. Pomfret's arrival. You might then have been saved from ——"

"Saved from what? You quite frighten me, Mr. Flaxyard."

"You cannot doubt for a moment that so true a friend as Mr. Pomfret has shown himself must have had some very powerful motive to induce him to come all the way from India for such a purpose."

"Indeed I thought so. But his motive was quite unintelligible, unless he had a personal interest in me."

" Well, what's done can't be undone, and you must make the best of it. But pray satisfy me on one point. Has Captain Musgrave any acquaintance with Mr. Pomfret?"

" Yes ; they met in Madras, where Scrope was stationed. But they were not upon very good terms—in fact, they quarrelled. And it is certain that they entertain a strong antipathy to each other. This may account in some degree for Mr. Pomfret's objection to my union with one whom he regards as an enemy. Scrope was equally bitter ; but I felt he was prejudiced, and my heart refused to believe all the ill he said of my benefactor."

" Have you reason to suppose, Ma'am, that Captain Musgrave and Mr. Pomfret met for the first time at Madras ? " inquired the old gentleman, after a pause. " Had they no previous acquaintance ? "

" I believe not," replied Sophy. " Indeed, I feel certain that Scrope knew nothing whatever about Mr. Pomfret, till he met him at Madras? "

" Knew nothing of his antecedents ? "

" I fancy not. I never heard him say so. Latterly I have never ventured to speak to Scrope about Mr. Pomfret, for he detests the mention of his name."

" Madam," said Flaxyard, " I cannot disguise from you that you are placed in an embarrassing position. You ought not to have married Captain Musgrave until you had heard what Mr. Pomfret had to say. That is the mistake you have committed, and I am afraid it may prove a grave mistake. I cannot acquit Mr. Pomfret of blame. He ought to have spoken out ; but I can understand why he hesitated, and I feel persuaded that he has acted with the best intentions. I would rather not say what I think of Captain Musgrave's conduct. Though Mr. Pomfret has more reason to complain than any one, I think you have nothing to apprehend from him. Unless I greatly misjudge him, his sole desire is to serve you, and he will submit to any annoyance rather than injure you. No, no ; you have nothing to fear from *him.*"

" Mr. Flaxyard, you have made some discovery which you are unwilling to impart to me—I am sure you have."

" Do not press for any explanation, Ma'am. I may be

wrong in my suspicions, and I trust in Heaven I am so. But whatever comes and goes, I will serve you as a friend, and do my best to extricate you from difficulties, should any unhappily arise."

" You fill me with alarm. Speak plainly, I entreat of you. I would rather know the worst than be kept in suspense."

" Madam, I know nothing. Therefore I can tell you nothing. I have felt it necessary to caution you, because I have some vague suspicions, but they may amount to little."

Sophy asked no further questions, and scarcely another word passed between them till they reached the station.

The whole party drove to the Grand Hôtel, but the high spirits of the younger people were too much for Sophy in her present frame of mind. Pleading fatigue, she retired at once to her chamber.

CHAPTER IV.

ERRIBLE fancies, excited by the hints thrown out by Mr. Flaxyard, disquieted Sophy and banished sleep. One strange and painful notion possessed her. She felt as if she had unintentionally committed some crime, for which a fearful penalty would be exacted. At last, towards morning, worn out by agitation and fatigue, she fell into a profound sleep, from which she did not awaken till a late hour.

The Musgraves, as we know, occupied a charming set of apartments on the second floor of the Grand Hôtel, and on issuing forth into the principal room, Sophy found her sister alone, and seated at a table on which materials for breakfast were laid.

"Why, how late you are!" cried Celia. "Scrope has breakfasted long ago, and has gone out to see the guard relieved at the Tuileries."

"Did he leave any message for me?" inquired Sophy.

"Only that he shouldn't be back before noon. I fear, from your looks, you must have had a wretched night. Sit down, dear," she continued, anxiously; "if you can manage to eat a little breakfast it will do you good. I fear these French dinners don't agree with you. Take a cup of tea, if you can take nothing else."

Sophy drank the tea poured out by her sister, but she was quite unable to eat anything, and after a time the breakfast equipage was removed by the garçon.

About a quarter of an hour later a tap was heard at the door, and Mrs. Flaxyard and her daughter came in. As we know, they were staying at the same hotel. They had got on their bonnets, and being about to order new dresses from a fashionable modiste in the Rue Vivienne, they wanted Mrs. Musgrave and Celia to accompany them. Sophy excused herself on the plea of indisposition, so they did not press her. But Celia was enchanted at the idea. Nothing she liked so much as a visit to a milliner's, so she got ready without a moment's delay. The three ladies then sallied forth, leaving Sophy alone—quite alone, indeed, for the lady's-maid she had brought from London had been sent back, and she was now without an attendant.

Half-an-hour passed by, and Sophy was still undisturbed. She was reclining on a fauteuil, vainly essaying to read *Galignani's Messenger.* All at once she was roused by the entrance of her husband. Their greeting was not like that of a recently married pair, and there was far more of fear than of love in the look which Sophy threw at her lord as he stalked into the room. Evidently something had displeased him. He merely nodded, and ,then, without bestowing another look upon her, deliberately took off his gloves and placed them inside his hat on the table. This done, he flung himself upon a sofa opposite the fauteuil on which she was seated. For some minutes he kept silence, but at last he addressed her in an angry voice :

"How long is this sort of thing going to last? Because I don't mean to stand it, I can tell you."

"What sort of thing, Scrope?" she inquired, meekly.

"You know well enough what I mean—your sulkiness. I'm getting confoundedly tired of it. I didn't come to Paris to pass my time with a peevish and fretful woman, but to be amused. Ever since you've set foot in France you have become totally changed—changed for the worse, both in looks and manner. You don't make an attempt to be agreeable to me. Perhaps you haven't got the inclination. It appears like it. But I wouldn't advise you to carry the thing too far. I'm not the easiest-tempered fellow in the world, and may chance to retaliate."

"I've not the slightest intention to offend you, Scrope, and am pained to think I have done so," she rejoined, gently. " I know I have been dull and triste, but you must forgive me. Unhappily, my spirits are not under my control, and to-day I am far from well."

"It's a confounded bore to have married a complaining woman," said Musgrave, harshly. "I can't understand why you should be in low spirits, unless you regret the step you've taken. Most women, I fancy, contrive to look cheerful during the honeymoon."

"I don't deserve these reproaches, Scrope—indeed I don't," she rejoined, unable to repress her tears.

"No use whimpering," he said, almost savagely. "It won't have the slightest effect on me. I've told you I can't stand low spirits. To please me you must smile."

"How can I possibly smile at this moment, Scrope? You really frighten me by your looks."

"Do I? Then you're very easily frightened. Why can't you borrow a little of Celia's sprightliness? She's never peevish or out of spirits."

"Celia has not the sad things to think of that I have, Scrope," sighed Sophy. "She is thoughtless and light-hearted, and I hope may long continue so."

"Well, I can see very plainly that you expect to have your own way—but you're mistaken, I can promise you. If you have been disappointed, so have I. But we may, perhaps, get on together if we can come to a proper understanding. Of one thing you may be certain. I won't have any more nonsense."

"If you call my illness 'nonsense,' Scrope, I'm afraid I shan't be able to obey you. But I will do my best."

"I know what has caused this fit of sullens," he said, regarding her fixedly. "You have had some communication with Myddleton Pomfret. It is useless to deny it. I know you have."

She made no response, but cast down her eyes to avoid his searching glances.

"He is in Paris! Have you seen him?" he demanded, after a pause.

"I have not exchanged a word with him. But I fancy I beheld him yesterday in the gardens of Versailles."

"Ah! you own to seeing him. Of course you have heard from him. Give me his letter, I command you."

This was too much, and Sophy roused herself.

"You forget yourself, Captain Musgrave, in addressing me thus. I have received no letter from Mr. Myddleton Pomfret. But if I had, I would not show it you."

"Ah! you defy me. Well, we shall see how long you will hold out. This equivocation won't pass with me. I am certain you have had some communication with the fellow—curse him! I insist upon knowing what message he has sent."

"I decline to give an answer to the question. And I think it better we should have no further conversation together till you are in a better temper."

And she made a motion of retiring, but Captain Musgrave sprang suddenly to his feet, and detained her.

"Stop! I have not done with you yet. We must finish what we have begun. What do you know about this person?"

"Nothing more than I have told you," she replied, trembling.

"It is an infernal lie," cried Musgrave, fiercely. "You know who he is."

"I saw him only for a moment," she cried, distractedly.

"But that was enough. You could not fail to recognise him. I read your guilty knowledge in your looks. It is in vain to hide it from me. You recognised him, I say."

"Then it was not a mere fancied resemblance," she cried. "It was Julian! and living!"

"Ay, it was Julian," rejoined Musgrave.

"Oh," she exclaimed, in a tone of indescribable anguish, "this is more than I can bear. I shall go mad. But no! no!—it cannot be. Julian perished before my own eyes. I saw him plunge into the lake, and disappear for ever."

"Not for ever," rejoined Musgrave, with a sneer. "Was the body found? I ask you that. No; it was not likely to be found. The catastrophe which you thought you had witnessed, and which filled you with desolation, was nothing more than a clever device, by which Julian hoped to escape from his creditors and from his wife. It succeeded to a marvel. No one even suspected the trick. While you were weeping—while others were searching for him—he was far away, chuckling at his escape. If the affair were not too serious, it might move one's laughter."

"No more—say no more," she cried. "The frightful truth becomes clear. I see it all now. I ought to have seen it from the first. Oh, into what an abyss has my fatal blindness plunged me! By the irretrievable step which I have taken I have condemned myself to ceaseless misery.

My breast will never know peace again. Scrope, you have much to answer for. You knew the truth, but concealed it from me. No consideration for two innocent persons moved you. You allowed me to commit a crime in ignorance which you were bound to prevent. And what have you gained by your wicked act? You have destroyed my happiness for ever. You have destroyed poor Julian's happiness. If you have any feeling left, you must shudder at your own work."

"You ask me what I have gained," replied Musgrave, who remained perfectly impassive during this address. "I will tell you. I have satisfied my revenge."

"Revenge for what? What injury has the unfortunate Julian done you that you should avenge yourself upon him in this dreadful manner?"

"I sha'n't gratify your curiosity by explaining the cause of my vindictive feeling towards Myddleton Pomfret, as I shall still call him," he rejoined. "Suffice it that he affronted me—deeply affronted me—and as I never forgive an injury, I determined on revenge. No opportunity for executing my purpose occurred while I was in India. But I abided my time. Not long after my return to England, chance threw in my way what I so eagerly longed for. I saw you, and was struck with your beauty—for you were beautiful then."

"Oh, that we had never met!" she exclaimed, in accents of despair.

"It was written that we should meet," continued Musgrave. "I saw and loved you. I knew nothing whatever about you then, and no other feeling was kindled in my breast save admiration of your charms. But next day I learnt more, and soon obtained a clear insight into your position. On my way to call upon you, St. Quintin acquainted me with your history, and, to my surprise, I learnt your singular connection with the detested Myddleton Pomfret. From the first my suspicions were aroused, and though I had never heard a hint breathed on the subject while at Madras, I became convinced, on reflection, that your correspondent could be no other than Julian Curzon, whom the rest of the world—yourself among the number—supposed to have been drowned in Windermere.

Was it likely that a man would pay his friend's debts without some extraordinary motive? Was it likely he would make a friend's widow so large an allowance from purely disinterested motives? I understood his motives at once. But there was proof conclusive. Myddleton Pomfret's arrival in Madras was nearly coincident with the date of Julian Curzon's supposed death, just allowing time for the voyage out to India. All doubts, therefore, were removed from my mind. The revenge for which I thirsted was in my power. My enemy was delivered into my hands. Not only had I penetrated his secret—not only did I comprehend his motives, but I divined his plans, and I determined to defeat them—to defeat them so effectually that the mischief done should be irreparable. I saw that he intended to return to England when he had made a fortune, and avow what he had done. But he had not calculated upon what might happen in the interim. It was a pretty project—a kindly project—and deserved to succeed; but there were difficulties in the way. He had not taken my animosity into account. To be sure, he didn't think it probable that I should cross his path. But you will remember how his fears were excited when he learnt that you knew me."

"Ah! I now perceive the justice of his fears. I ought to have paid attention to his caution. But had you no compunction?"

"None. I have told you I never forgive an injury. When my enemy was in my power, was I to let him escape? Moreover, love with me is just as strong as hate; and loving you passionately, as I did at the time, I would never have surrendered you to another. These mingled feelings—either of which was strong enough to cause me to disregard all consequences—determined me to make you mine. I had no fear of a refusal on your part, for I felt sure that I had gained a sufficient influence over you, and that I had only to go on to triumph. My sole apprehension was, that Myddleton Pomfret should arrive in time to thwart my project. He nearly did so, but his evil genius stopped him on the way. My revenge was complete."

There was a pause, during which Sophy appeared overcome by emotion. At last she spoke.

5

"You have acted infamously, Scrope. You have led me into the commission of a sin which can only be expiated by a life's penitence. My own wretchedness is increased by the thought of the hopeless misery into which your vindictive cruelty has plunged a noble-hearted man. Better have killed him than inflict such pain. Had I been the only sufferer my anguish would have been more tolerable, but it is heightened by the knowledge of his suffering. Your plan has succeeded. The evil agents you have summoned have served you well. But your triumph will be short-lived. The ill you have done will recoil on your own head. Be sure that a terrible retribution awaits you."

"Bah! I laugh at such talk!" he rejoined, carelessly. "It may tell upon the stage, but it won't do in private life. If you imagine I have any fear of Myddleton Pomfret, you are egregiously mistaken. But I peremptorily forbid you to grant him an interview on any pretence, or to hold any communication with him. Take care you obey me."

"I do not desire to see him," she cried. "Of all men on earth, I would most avoid him."

"Still he may attempt to see you, and I would have you be on your guard. You need apprehend no trouble from him. Very shame will restrain him from resuming his former name. Myddleton Pomfret he must remain, and no other. Julian Curzon is dead to the world."

"I have no fear of him," she rejoined. "He is too good —too generous—to molest me."

"Talk of him no more," cried Musgrave, impatiently. "His name sickens me. I have said enough, I think, to warn you. My stay in Paris will be brief. I shall proceed almost immediately to Nice."

"You will go where you please, Scrope," she rejoined. "But you must not expect me to accompany you."

"Not expect you to accompany me! But I do," he cried, sharply. "Do you suppose I mean to leave you behind? Don't think it."

"I am not your wife, Scrope," she rejoined. "You have convinced me that my first husband is alive."

"You are a fool!" he cried, furiously. "If I choose to consider you as my wife, and to treat you as such, that ought to be enough. Your secret is in safe keeping. It is only known to me and to one other, and for good reasons he will never betray it. You *are* my wife, I tell you, so let us have no more nonsense on the subject. Go to your own room. Dry your eyes and compose yourself. Celia will be back presently, and she mustn't find you in this state. Away, I tell you."

Sophy looked at him as if she had something to say, but she left it unsaid, and withdrew into the inner room.

"I'm deuced glad it's got over," mentally ejaculated Musgrave as he was left to himself. "If I hadn't stopped the matter at the onset, there would have been no end of bother with her. Sooner or later she must have learnt the truth, and now she is aware that she is entirely in my power she'll be more manageable. If not—well, I won't think of that just yet."

Half-an-hour afterwards, when Celia returned, accompanied by Mrs. Flaxyard and Tiffany, they found him lounging on the sofa, smoking a cheroot and reading *Galignani.* To judge from his looks, no one would have suspected that anything had disturbed him. All traces of anger had disappeared from his handsome countenance. Little recked he of the anguish endured by poor Sophy, who was on her knees in the next room, praying fervently for strength and guidance. Once, feeling curious, he had gone to the door, but finding it fastened, he gave himself no further concern about her.

On the entrance of the three ladies, he entered into a lively chat with them, and listened to the details of their visit to Madame Frontin's with the greatest apparent interest. Rather surprised that Sophy did not make her appearance, as she must have heard their voices and laughter, Celia went in search of her, and, after a little unexpected delay, obtained admittance to the inner room. Here she remained some minutes, during which Captain Musgrave continued his discourse with Tiffany. When Celia came forth again her countenance was changed in its expression.

"My sister hopes you will excuse her," she said. "She feels very unwell—quite unequal to conversation."

"Dear me! I'm excessively sorry to hear it," cried Mrs.

Flaxyard, in a commiserating tone. "Is there anything we can do for her?"

"Let me go in to her," said Tiffany. "I'm sure I can manage to cheer her up."

"Thank you, my love, no," rejoined Celia. "She will be best kept perfectly quiet."

"Well, say all that's kind to her from us," observed Mrs. Flaxyard. "I hope we shall see her again later on in the day."

Hereupon the two ladies took their departure.

"Scrope," said Celia, as soon as they were gone, "I fear you and Sophy have had a quarrel."

"We have had a few words," he replied, carelessly. "That confounded Myddleton Pomfret is in Paris, and I spoke to her rather angrily about him. I hate the fellow, as you know. Go and see what you can do with her."

"Shall I tell her you're very sorry for being so cross?" remarked Celia.

"Yes, do. You had better have dinner in your own room to-day, for I'm sure Sophy won't go out. I am going to Vincennes. On my return I shall dine at Brebon's. I may look in at the Palais Royal, where they have a laughable piece. *Au revoir!*"

Putting on his hat and gloves, and lighting another cheroot, he went out, while Celia re-entered her sister's room.

CHAPTER V.

HE sisters had been alone together nearly an hour, during which scarcely a word had passed between them, when a tap was heard at the door of the principal room, and going to see who was there, Celia found Mr. Flaxyard. It was evident from his manner that the old gentleman had something important to communicate, and without preface he told Celia that he wished to see her sister.

"I am afraid you can't see her just now, Mr. Flaxyard," Celia replied. "She is very unwell. Can I convey a message to her?"

"No, thank you. I have a word to say to her in private. Pray tell her I am here. She will see me."

"I'm by no means sure of it. But we can but try," rejoined Celia, wondering what he could have to say.

With this she went into the inner room, and the result proved that the old gentleman was right, for almost immediately afterwards Sophy came forth. She looked pale as death, and it was easy to perceive she had been weeping.

"I am very sorry to intrude upon you, Mrs. Musgrave," said Flaxyard, in accents of profound commiseration, "but I know you will excuse me. I have just seen ——"

A glance of caution from Sophy caused him to lower his voice, and he added :—

"I have just seen Mr. Myddleton Pomfret."

"Has he said anything further to you?" cried Sophy.

It was now the old gentleman's turn to enjoin caution. Glancing significantly towards the inner room, he replied, in a low voice :—

"He has charged me to give this letter to you, Madam."

Sophy trembled so violently that she could scarcely hold the letter which he placed in her hand.

"I promised to bring him an answer," said the old gentleman, watching her with deep interest.

With trembling fingers Sophy opened the letter, but a film gathered before her eyes, and prevented her for a moment from distinguishing the writing. At last she read as follows :—

"I beg you to grant me an interview, and without delay. It is absolutely necessary that I should give you some explanation before leaving Paris. To-morrow I shall be far away.

"It might compromise you were I to present myself at your apartments, and there would be risk of an unpleasant encounter were I even to enter the hotel. I have therefore, made such arrangements as I trust will prevent accident, and save you trouble.

"In the court-yard of the hotel you will find a carriage waiting for you. The coachman will drive you to the Bois de Boulogne, whither I shall precede you, and will set you down at a spot in the Alée de Longchamps, which I have described to him. Arrived there, you will alight. Enter the wood on the left, and you will find me.

"Do not refuse my request. It is the last I shall prefer to you. We shall only meet to exchange an eternal adieu!"

There was no signature to the letter.

So much was Sophy overcome by its perusal, that she would have given vent to her distress if the old gentleman had not checked her.

"Recollect that your sister is in the next room," he said, "and that there is a very thin partition between us."

When Sophy had in some degree mastered her emotions, he inquired :—

"What answer shall I return to him?"

"I cannot write," she replied. "But tell him," she added, with a great effort—"tell him I will come."

"I am glad you have so decided," he replied earnestly. "I am sure you need not fear to meet him. I will convey your message to him instantly."

So saying, he bowed and withdrew.

The noise caused by shutting the door announced his

departure to Celia, who at once issued from the inner room. The liveliest curiosity was painted on her countenance.

"Well, am I to learn the meaning of this mysterious visit ? " she cried.

" I am going out immediately—that is all I have to tell you," rejoined Sophy.

"Going out ! " cried the other, in astonishment. " Where to ? "

" To the Bois de Boulogne, to meet Mr. Myddleton Pomfret," replied Sophy, calmly.

"Well, I declare I never heard of anything so shocking ! " exclaimed Celia, staring at her with the utmost astonishment. " And you look as innocent as if wholly unaware of the impropriety of the proceeding. What will Scrope say ? "

" He will know nothing about it."

" There you are mistaken. I shall make a point of telling him."

" Do as you think proper. I shall go. You may accompany me if you choose."

" That renders the step less objectionable. Mind, I protest very strongly against it. But since you are resolved to go, you shan't go alone. I may as well tell you that Scrope is gone to Vincennes, and won't return till late, as he means to dine at Brebon's, and go to the theatre in the Palais Royal afterwards, so you needn't fear meeting him."

Scarcely noticing what was said, Sophy hastily made the necessary preparations for going out. Celia used equal despatch, and both sisters were ready at the same moment.

Though she had screwed her courage to the sticking-point, Sophy felt considerable trepidation as she descended the great staircase. As usual, a number of persons were upon it, but there was not an acquaintance among them.

On gaining the court-yard she perceived a handsome dark coupé, standing a little in advance of the other equipages, and the coachman, who was evidently on the alert, seemed at once to recognise her. As she approached, he called out to a page in the livery of the hotel to open the carriage door.

No sooner were the two ladies seated inside the coupé, than without waiting for orders the coachman drove through the broad porte cochère, and then along the boulevart in the direction of the Madeleine. There is scarcely an hour in the day when this part of the Boulevart des Capucines is not crowded with carriages, omnibuses, and vehicles of all sorts, but the ladies met with no interruption, and were soon speeding along the gay Champs Elysées. Numberless carriages and equestrians were here to be seen, but Sophy was too much absorbed by her own painful reflections to pay any attention to them. She sat as far back as she could in the carriage. Celia, however, enjoyed the brilliant spectacle, and kept continually calling her sister's attention to some splendid equipage or to some marvellous toilette. But in vain ; Sophy never raised her eyes.

At length the superb Avenue de l'Impératice was traversed amid an undiminished throng of carriages, and passing through the Porte Dauphine, the ladies entered the crowded Bois.

Skirting the lower lake, they took a winding road on the right, which soon brought them to the Allée de Longchamps, along which they proceeded.

Presently they reached a thick part of the wood, and the coachman stopped at a spot on the left of the road.

"Here I am to meet him," said Sophy, looking very pale, but very determined. "This is the place of rendez-vous."

"Are you going to alight ? " inquired Celia.

"Yes," replied Sophy, opening the door of the carriage.

Both got out, and striking into a little path which lay before them, entered the wood.

They had not proceeded far, when the tall dark figure of a man could be distinguished among the trees, about fifty yards off. It was evident that he had seen them, but on perceiving that Sophy was not alone, had retreated.

"Wait for me here," said Sophy. "You cannot be present at the interview."

CHAPTER VI.

THE MEETING.

HE person whom Sophy expected to meet had re-tired into a side-path on the right, leading into a thicker part of the wood, and on reaching this path she beheld him about twenty or thirty paces off, moving slowly on in the opposite direction. The light sound of her footsteps caught his ear, and he turned.

It was he !

Yes, it was he, whom she had so long mourned as lost ; whom she never expected to behold again on earth ; and who was brought back only to be taken away.

Yes, it was he. Anxiety and the influences of a fierce climate had done their work upon him. He looked full ten years older than when he had disappeared. His lofty figure was wasted, but still symmetrical ; his countenance bore traces of suffering, and seemed stamped with settled gloom, but it had not lost its noble outline. Changed he might be to others, but to her he was unaltered. While gazing at his features, and feeling those well-remembered eyes fixed upon her with an unutterable expression of tenderness, pity, and reproach, she ceased almost to breathe, and must have fallen to the ground if he had not flown to her assistance.

Return to entire consciousness, which did not take place under a couple of minutes, was evidenced by a profound sigh proceeding from the very depths of her breast. For a moment only did she look into his face. For a moment only did she feel the contact of his arm. A thrill of horror then pervaded her frame, and collecting all her energies, she withdrew from his support.

It seemed as if the unhappy pair had only come together to mingle their tears. He had much to say, but his voice was suffocated by emotion. Sophy spoke first.

" I dare not ask your forgiveness, Julian," she said, in

accents that pierced his heart like points of steel, "for the irreparable wrong I have done you, thought it was done unwittingly. I well know that forgiveness for a fault like mine is impossible, but as I know you to be just and generous, I feel you will not utterly condemn me."

"Condemn you, Sophy!" he cried. "I do not even reproach you. How can I do so when I alone am to blame? I do not attempt to exculpate myself. I am the cause of all the misery that afflicts us both. Had it been possible, the terrible truth should have been concealed from you. But it is necessary you should be made aware of the exact position in which you are placed, in order that a worse calamity may be avoided."

"What worse calamity can there be than that which I now endure? For me there is no more hope in this world. I must expiate my offence in tears and penitence. Oh, why were you not more explicit? Why did you allow me to remain so long in ignorance of the truth? Why did you allow me to commit this crime?"

"I can offer no excuse," he rejoined, in a sombre tone. "As I am the author of the crime, so ought I to bear the punishment, and I hope Heaven will spare you, however severely it may afflict me. But I will try to explain the motives of my conduct, though I feel it to be wholly indefensible. The history of the last few years of my life will be quickly told, and it is proper you should hear it. Else you cannot judge me rightly."

He paused for a moment and then went on :—

"On that dread night which you cannot fail to remember, and which it pains me to recal, when I was environed by difficulties, and when I thought I had forfeited your love, my first desperate impulse was to end my woes by self-destruction. What, indeed had I to live for? But suddenly, and as if by some merciful interposition, my ideas changed, and I was spared this crime at least. Picturing to myself how I would act if I could begin life anew, I came at last to the determination of carrying out the plan I had conceived. You know how I executed the project, or can guess, so it is not needful to enter into details."

"You executed it so well, that you imposed upon me as upon all others," she remarked. "But if you had taken me

into your confidence, Julian, you would have spared me
frightful suffering."

"Had I done so, my project would have failed. It was
owing to your entire ignorance of the scheme that it succeeded so well. But do not imagine that I did not feel for
you profoundly. I did. Nevertheless, my resolution remained unshaken. I had taken all necessary precautions,
and concealed a change of attire in the copse bordering the
lake. I had also a sufficient sum of money for any purpose.
Within three hours after my plunge into the lake, I was
seated in an express train, and on the way to London."

"And I had given you up for lost, and was with those
who sought for your body," she rejoined. "Oh! Julian, if
you had seen me then, you would have pitied me. You
would not have left me."

"I should not. Therefore I fled. The plan I had
conceived was to go out to India—to Madras—where I had
a near relative, Mr. Bracebridge, a prosperous merchant, on
whose friendship I could depend. I was obliged to halt for
a day in London, in order to procure the necessary outfit
for my journey, but I took care to keep out of the way of my
old acquaintances. I put up at the hotel near the London
Bridge station, and assumed the name of Myddleton
Pomfret, which I have ever since retained, and which I shall
now never discontinue. As soon as I had made all
preparations, I crossed the Channel, and proceeded, without
stoppage, to Marseilles. If I had laid out my plan beforehand, it could not have been better contrived. All fell out
well. Within twenty-four hours after my arrival at Marseilles
the Overland Mail started for Alexandria. Again I was
favoured. Not one among my fellow-passengers knew me.
But the *Times* had been brought on board, and in it I read
the account of my own 'accidental death,' and heard some
comments upon it, which made me laugh bitterly. I learnt
the estimation in which I was held. The voyage was speedy
and prosperous, and in due time I arrived at Madras. I
had not miscalculated my influence with Mr. Bracebridge.
I concealed nothing from him. At first he was very angry,
pointed out the consequences of the rash and inconsiderate
step I had taken, and insisted upon my immediate return,
but in the end he yielded to my entreaties, and consented

to aid my plan. This he did most effectually by making me a partner in his house. His confidence in me was not misplaced. I wanted knowledge and experience, and, above all, habits of business, but I made up for these deficiencies by untiring industry, and soon mastered my new position. Mr. Bracebridge had reason to congratulate himself on possessing a good working partner, for in a couple of years I had helped him to double his business."

" During all this time did you bestow no thought on the unhappy wife you had deserted, and who mourned you as dead ? " asked Sophy.

" You were never absent from my thoughts," he rejoined. "It was for you that I toiled—for you that I sought to realise a fortune. And as my endeavours promised to be successful, I persuaded myself that we should not long be kept apart. Fool, madman that I was to suppose you could, or would, wait for me ! I should have returned sooner, but circumstances delayed my departure. Mr. Bracebridge was carried off suddenly by cholera, and the entire management of the business devolved upon me, for my other partner took no active interest in it. But though I could not return, I resolved no longer to defer the execution of my scheme— the first step being the payment of my debts. From a trusty correspondent, who, however, was wholly ignorant of my motives for making the inquiry, I had obtained constant information respecting you, and knew that you were residing in Yorkshire with your father in perfect retirement. I therefore wrote to you, and since you received my letters, it is not necessary to enter into further details respecting them. Neither will I attempt to describe my transports of delight at the sight of your well-known handwriting. Had you seen me press your letter to my lips, you could not have doubted my love for you."

Here he paused, and a minute or two elapsed before he could resume his narrative.

" I now come to a painful portion of my story," he said, evidently speaking with great effort ; "but it must be told. At the time of his death, Mr. Bracebridge was a widower, having lost his wife some years before. He had only one child, a daughter, to whom he was devotedly attached, and he left her all his property, appointing me her guardian, and with his last breath committing her to my charge. I promised to watch over her, and I have kept my promise."

Sophy uttered a slight exclamation.

"When she sustained this heavy bereavement, Eva Bracebridge was not much more than seventeen, but in appearance and manner she was a woman. She had not long arrived from England, where she had been educated, and her surprising beauty created an extraordinary sensation at Madras. Already she had received many offers for her hand, but she declined them. Naturally, I was thrown much into her society, and her vivacity served to dispel the gloom that frequently beset me. She often rallied me upon my melancholy, declaring that I looked like the Corsair or the Giaour, or some other of Lord Byron's moody heroes. 'Come, confess, what have you done, Mr. Pomfret?' she would say playfully. 'Something dreadful, I'm certain.' It may sound like vanity, but I know you will acquit me of any such feeling, when I say that a suspicion sometimes crossed me that, most unintentionally, I had excited a tender interest in this fair young creature's breast. Had not my heart been engaged I could not have resisted her fascinations."

"Did you resist them, Julian?" said Sophy.

"You need not ask the question," he rejoined, coldly. "Prepare yourself. You will have need of all your courage for what I am about to relate. At this juncture the Bengal Rifles were quartered at Madras. Among the officers was one who was accounted exceedingly handsome, and who plumed himself upon his successes with your sex. He had already caused two or three serious scandals, which were much talked about, but which he fancied redounded to his credit. Mr. Bracebridge, who was very hospitable, like every Indian merchant, naturally invited him, and he was introduced to Eva. He could not fail to be struck with her beauty, and was at no pains to conceal the impression it produced upon him. Mr. Bracebridge kept almost open house, and having been once invited, the enamoured officer came when he pleased, and had abundant opportunities of practising all the arts he was a master of to win Eva's affections. But she cared nothing for him, and mortified him bitterly by her indifference."

"Oh, she did well," cried Sophy. "Would I had acted so!"

"In spite of Eva's manifest coldness to him—a coldness almost amounting to aversion—he persevered," pursued Pomfret, becoming still more sombre as he proceeded. "He was unaccustomed to defeat, and persuaded himself he should triumph in the end. How was an inexperienced girl to resist him when so many artful women had succumbed? He was still occupied in the fruitless attempt when Mr. Bracebridge died, and, as I have already stated, Eva became my ward. Up to this point her beauty alone had influenced her admirer, but now she had the additional attraction of wealth, a large fortune being assured to her on coming of age, or on marriage, by her father's will. The prize must be won, but his chances of gaining it were even slighter than before, and at Eva's solicitation I begged him to desist from his suit, telling him it was utterly hopeless. He was very angry, and said, in an insolent tone, 'I see through your design. You don't like to part with the girl. You flatter yourself she loves you. But you're mistaken. I'll have her yet.' It was with difficulty that I controlled myself, but desiring, for Eva's sake, to avoid a quarrel with him, I made no reply to his taunts, and perhaps attributing my forced calmness to cowardice, he went away with a menacing and contemptuous look. I thought I had done with him. But the worst was to come. What I have now to tell will prove that I was justified in writing of him as I did to you."

"I doubt it not," said Sophy, sadly.

"Though Eva had seen but little of her father, she suffered much from his death, and I suggested her return to England, but she declined, saying she liked India, and would remain out for another year, or till such time as I could take her back, for I had often spoken to her of my own wish to return. To this I could offer no objection; but as I thought change of scene really desirable for her, I advised her to go to Ootacumand, on the Neilgherry Hills, where her poor father had possessed a charming retreat, which now, of course, belonged to her. She consented, but on the express understanding that I would shortly join her. Next day she set out on the journey, which was to occupy about a week. As it turned out, I could not have acted more unwisely than in recommending the journey. A detachment of the Bengal Rifles was stationed at a fort on the Neilgherry Hills, and the officer who had so long persecuted Eva with his addresses was proceeding in the same direction as herself, and at the same time. They travelled by the same route, stopped at the same places, but though they met daily, Eva would never exchange a word with her importunate admirer. He hovered about her palanquin, volunteered assistance when she crossed the deep bed of some mountain nullah, halted when her bearers halted, toiled up the steep ghaut by her side, but he did not succeed in winning a smile from her. On arriving at her destination she wrote to me complaining bitterly of the annoyance to which she had been subjected, and entreating me to come to her, as she did not like remaining at Ootacumand without my protection. Thus urged, I could not refuse, and set out at once, with the fixed determination of calling the obnoxious personage to strict account."

Sophy made a low and inaudible remark.

" I made so much haste on the journey, that, late on the fifth day after quitting Madras, I arrived at Ootacumand. As it was past midnight, I left my attendants to shift for themselves, and went on alone to the bungalow in which my ward was lodged. It was beautifully situated in the midst of a large compound, or enclosure, overlooking steep mountain precipices clothed with a thick jungle, which at this hour resounded with the prolonged howls, fierce yells, and savage roaring of various wild beasts. A glorious moon was shining—such a moon as can only be seen in that resplendent clime—and on entering the compound I paused to look around and admire the beauty of the scene, rendered doubly beautiful at that magic hour. I knew the place well. Twice before I had been there to seek health from the bracing air. On either side there were mango-groves, and nearer the bungalow, with its white walls and green verandahs glittering in the brilliant moonbeams, grew some tall palm-trees. The house was surrounded by a garden laid out in the Eastern style. The profound stillness of the night was only broken, as I have said, by the ceaseless howling of the wild beasts in the jungle; but I was too familiar with such sounds to allow them to disturb me. I remained standing under a tree for a few minutes, placidly contemplating the lovely scene. Suddenly my ear caught a slight sound, and I perceived a tall figure issue from the grove and proceed quickly towards the house. In another moment, and before I could recover from the surprise into which I was thrown by the unlooked-for incident, the person in question had gained the verandah and entered the house by an open window. I could not be mistaken in him. Instinctive dislike would have told me who he was, even if his military attire, tall stature, and peculiar bearing had not betrayed him. What was his object? I did not dare to ask myself, but I felt sure he was an unlicensed intruder. A thrill of fierce indignation shot through my frame. Speeding towards the bungalow, I passed through the open window and entered a room, which bore evidence from a hundred eloquent trifles that Eva had been there before retiring to rest. An inner door was open. In another instant I was in a gallery communicating with the sleeping-chambers. Hitherto I had seen no one, but the sound of my footsteps had alarmed the intruder, and just as I reached the gallery he came from out an ante-room. There we were face to face. The villain's countenance, made ghastly by the white moonlight, showed how terribly he was disconcerted by the interruption. 'For what infamous purpose have you come here?' I cried, in a voice hoarse with passion. 'Speak at once.' 'I have no explanation to give to you,' he rejoined. 'Put any construction you please on my presence. I did not come here uninvited.' Exasperated beyond all endurance by this vile insinuation, I rushed towards him, meaning to fell him to the ground.

But he was not unprepared for the attack. Stepping back he drew a small pocket-pistol, and threatened to fire if I advanced. But I threw myself upon him, and in the struggle the pistol went off, the ball grazing my arm, and inflicting a slight hurt, which added to my fury. Seizing him by the throat, I should probably have strangled him if the report of the pistol had not alarmed the house, and brought several native servants instantly to the spot. In another minute, Eva, wrapped in a robe de chamber, appeared on the scene. 'Let me go,' cried the villain, trying vainly to free himself from my grasp. 'I will give you any satisfaction you like to-morrow.' 'You shall not go till you have apologised for this outrage,' I replied. And I forced him down to Eva's feet. What he said, while in this abject posture, I know not. But she entreated me to let him go, and I released him. As he rose to his feet he turned on me with an aspect of fiercest menace, and said, in a deep voice, 'We shall have an account to settle.' 'It shall be settled now,' I replied. 'Drive this fellow forth,' I added in Hindostanee, to the native servants who were standing around. 'He is a scoundrel, and does not deserve to be treated like a sahib.' Several of them were armed with bamboos, and no sooner was the order given than a shower of blows drove him from the place."

" How could he survive this degradation ? " cried Sophy.

"He bore it meekly enough," rejoined Pomfret, with stern contempt, "for, despite his threats, I heard nothing more of him. Not one of his brother-officers would have supported him. But he felt that his secret was safe, because he knew that consideration for Eva, whose name was not to be mixed up in such an affair, would keep me silent. I thought I had done with him for ever. But I was wrong. Chance gave him an opportunity of vengeance."

"Alas! alas!" cried Sophy, "I, who would have laid down my life for you, have been made the instrument of his revenge. Oh, what a revelation you have made to me, Julian! Oh, what a weak, contemptible creature I appear in my own eyes! Oh, that I could have been the dupe of such a man !"

"Knowing what you now know, Sophy, imagine what my feelings must have been when you first informed me that you had made the acquaintance of one whom of all men I would have kept from your sight. Till then I was not aware that Captain Musgrave had returned to England, for after that night I had not concerned myself about him. A foreboding of ill struck me, but, though alarmed, I would not attend to it. Eva was unwell. The villain's infamous conduct gave her a great shock, and she had not recovered from it. Otherwise, I should have come to England at

6

once. But I had no serious apprehension, for I had too much confidence in you."

"How wofully was your confidence misplaced, Julian!" she cried.

"Your next letter tore the bandage rudely from my eyes, and showed me the imminence of the danger. My helplessness to avert the dire calamity added to the intensity of my suffering. I would almost have bartered my soul to annihilate the space between us. All my plans were destroyed in a moment, and by the hand of him I most detested. Eva chanced to be with me at the time, and was all anxiety to learn the cause of my distress, but I could not satisfy her. I told her I had received bad news—that a terrible peril threatened one very dear to me—and that my sole chance of averting it was by immediate return to England. I should start at once. She besought me to allow her to accompany me; but in that case I must have confided the secret of my life to her, and I was obliged to refuse. She taxed me with cruelty. But I was firm. I started by the first mail, and left her behind, half broken-hearted."

"She loves you, Julian," cried Sophy, with a pang keener than any she had previously experienced.

"I need not tell you of my anxieties during the voyage," he continued. "Alternately I was buoyed up by hope, or plunged into the depths of despair. My excitement was so great that I suffered from a nervous fever, which increased as I travelled from Marseilles to London. All the way I was constantly asking myself one question, 'Shall I be in time to save her?' Arrived at last at Hertford Street, I received the fatal response, and learnt that I was too late."

"Yes, too late!—too late!" cried Sophy, distractedly. "All this crushing misery might have been spared if you had but told me the truth in the letter which you sent me from Marseilles. What am I to do, Julian? In pity counsel me!"

"I dare not—cannot counsel you," he rejoined. "You must act as your own feelings dictate."

"Oh, this is cruel, Julian! I know that I am nothing to you now. I know that the fault I have committed is irreparable ; but you loved me once, and by that love I conjure you to help me."

"My heart bleeds for you, Sophy," he rejoined. "But I repeat, I cannot advise you. Think well before you take any desperate step."

"I understand," she cried, bitterly. "You fear that I am about to throw myself upon you, and you repulse me. The suspicion is unworthy of you, Julian. I have no such thought. I shall never seek to pass the bar that separates us. But in this frightful extremity I have no one to appeal to but you. You see before you a poor, bewildered, terri- fied creature, who supplicates you on her knees for aid, and yet you will not help her."

"Rise, Madam," said Pomfret, with forced coldness, and raising her as he spoke. "It is not fitting you should kneel to me."

"You rebuke me justly, Julian," she said, in a tone of resignation. "Heaven help me ! I have no friend left."

"There you are wrong," he rejoined. "You have a true friend in me, and always will have one. But even *I* shrink from the awful responsibility of counselling you at a juncture like the present."

"My resolution is taken," she said. "I have left Captain Musgrave for ever."

"I neither approve the step, nor attempt to dissuade you from it. But whatever course you resolve upon, act with prudence. A terrible fault has been committed. Do not add another to it. You will inflict no punishment upon Captain Musgrave by leaving him. He is too heartless to feel your loss, and may be glad to be freed from the restraint."

"Not even to punish him would I remain with him," she cried. "I shall try to find out some secure retreat. You have furnished me with the means of flight, and I thank you for doing so."

"The crisis has come sooner than I anticipated," he said. "But on one point you need feel no uneasiness. You shall never want resources. The income you have recently enjoyed shall be continued."

"Impossible !" she exclaimed. "I cannot accept it. Without the money you have so generously sent me, I

6—2

might be unable to carry out my design, therefore I will avail myself of it. But I can be under no further pecuniary obligation to you."

"As you will. But should occasion arise, you may depend on me. It is my intention to return almost immediately to India; but you know how to address me there, and can easily communicate with me."

"And you mean to go back to India at once?" she cried, unable to conceal her disappointment. "I thought you would have remained in England."

"What have I to do in England now?" he exclaimed, with mournful bitterness. "I have no longer any interest in the country. All whom I have known there, suppose me dead, and I do not design to undeceive them. They have long since forgotten me, and would feel little pleasure at my resurrection. Could the dearest friend we have lost come to life again, we should accord him but a cold welcome. However, I shall not try the experiment. Doubtless the change is in myself, and something may be owing to my frame of mind, but London seems strangely altered—altered for the worse—since I left it. I felt like an utter stranger in its streets. I have business to transact there which may detain me for a week or two, and then I shall set out for India —never, I think, to return.

"May you be happy there, Julian!" she sighed.

"I do not expect much happiness, unless I can purchase oblivion," he rejoined.

"But you have Eva to care for," she remarked, trembling as she spoke.

"She will leave me soon, and then I shall be utterly desolate. But this painful interview must be brought to an end. Have you aught more to say to me?"

"Nothing," she rejoined, sadly. "I will not ask you to think of me, for it were best to forget me. But be sure I shall never cease to think of you."

"You are quite resolved to leave Captain Musgrave?"

"Quite," she rejoined firmly. "I shall go—I know not whither—but I shall not return to him."

"You ought not to abandon Celia. Take her with you."

"Such is my intention," she replied. "When she is made acquainted with my sad position, I am sure she will attend me in my flight. She owes me some reparation; since, but for her persuasion, I should not have made this fatal marriage."

He heard not what she said. Without a look—without a farewell word—he was gone.

A few minutes elapsed before Sophy found her way back to her sister, who was impatiently awaiting her.

A long and earnest conversation then took place between them. At first, Celia strenuously opposed her sister's design, but eventually she yielded, and consented to accompany her.

A certain plan being agreed upon, they returned to the coupé, and, entering it, bade the coachman drive to the Parc de Monceaux. Arrived there, they alighted and dismissed him.

After remaining for a short time in this exquisite garden, they proceeded to the gates opening upon the Boulevart Malesherbes, where they engaged another coupé, and drove to the Hôtel du Chemin de Fer du Nord.

End of the Second Book.

BOOK III.

EVA BRACEBRIDGE.

CHAPTER I.

THAT NIGHT.

HAT night Captain Musgrave did not re-enter his rooms at the Grand Hôtel till late.

An evening to himself had convinced him that a bachelor's life was far more congenial to his tastes than that of a Benedict. After dining well at Brebon's, and passing two or three hours very much to his satisfaction at the lively little theatre of the Palais Royal, he repaired by way of the Rue Richelieu to the boulevarts, and thinking it too soon to return to his hotel, as the night was extremely fine, and the boulevarts still crowded, he extended his stroll.

While passing the Café Napolitain, he was hailed by our young acquaintances, Hornby and Rufus, who were seated outside the café, refreshing themselves with ices, so he stopped and took a chair beside them. They had just come from the Concert Musard, which did not offer them half as much attraction as Mabille, and then they began to narrate their adventures during the day, to which Musgrave vouchsafed to listen, while smoking an excellent cigar supplied him by Hornby.

"After all, there, is no place for amusement like Paris," remarked the captain; "but a married man is cut out of so many pleasant things that he might as well be anywhere else. I shan't prolong my stay beyond a day or two, but be off to the shores of the Mediterranean."

" Awfully dull work there, I should think. Won't suit you," said Rufus.

" It will suit my wife," replied Musgrave. " Paris don't agree with her."

" I was glad to see her out this afternoon," observed Hornby. " I had heard from Tiff that she was unwell."

" I've been at Vincennes, and wasn't aware she had been out," rejoined Musgrave, surprised. " But I'm glad to hear it. Where did you see her ? "

" In the Bois, with Miss Leycester," replied Hornby. " They were in a dark coupé. They didn't see us, but we saw them plainly enough, and tried to attract their attention, but the coachman was driving rather quickly, and had gone by in a minute."

" Later on we caught sight of them in the Parc de Monceaux," said Rufus. " But, unluckily, we were unable to join them."

The trio occupied their seats for some time longer, but neither of Captain Musgrave's companions guessed from his manner that he was angry at what they had told him.

When they returned together to the Grand Hôtel it was not far from midnight. Having made some arrangements for sight-seeing on the morrow, to conclude with a dinner at Riche's, they separated on the second landing of the great staircase, Hornby and Rufus mounting to a higher story, and Captain Musgrave proceeding to his own apartments.

No presentiment of ill crossed him as he unfastened the door and let himself in. He was rather surprised to find the room buried in darkness, but concluding that his wife and Celia had long since retired to rest, he struck a match and lighted a candle, when his eye fell upon a letter lying on the table.

It was addressed to himself, and in his wife's handwriting. He opened it with some misgiving. The very first words startled him, as well they might. Thus he read :

" We have parted for ever.

" After what passed between us this morning, when I learnt from your own lips the frightful position in which you have placed me, you could not expect me to remain with you longer. Were I to do so, I should be equally criminal with yourself. I have sinned in ignorance, but now that my eyes are opened, I will sin no more.

" The exultation which you manifested at the success of your vindictive scheme, changed the feelings which I had previously entertained for you into horror and aversion. Henceforth, I can only regard you as the destroyer of my earthly happiness.

" Since it is impossible you can make reparation for what you have done, you can never hope for my forgiveness. Still, for the sake of another who is yet more deeply injured than myself, I shall keep silence as to your infamous conduct, unless forced in self-defence to speak out.

" Every present, however trifling, that you have made me is left behind. I wish to have nothing to remind me of a period of shame and dishonour. Would I could wholly obliterate it from my memory !

" It will be useless to follow me, or to attempt to discover my retreat. Were you to find me, you would gain nothing. Neither prayers nor threats will induce me to return. I will die rather than hold further intercourse with one who has so wickedly, so cruelly betrayed me.

" If I can, I will hide my sorrows and my shame from the eyes of the world, and will strive by a life of penitence to make my peace with Heaven.

" I know it is idle to appeal to your compassion, but regard for yourself may prevent you from troubling me further. Though cruelly used and deeply wronged, I nourish no vindictive feelings against you. But desperation may make me dangerous.

" Celia knows all, and accompanies me in my flight."

Captain Musgrave read this letter with mingled emotions of alarm, vexation, and rage. Anger, however, predominated over the other feelings.

Throwing down the letter, he gave vent to a deep imprecation, which he levelled against the heads of his unfortunate wife and Myddleton Pomfret ; entertaining not a doubt in his own mind that the latter was the instigator of Sophy's flight.

" This is an infernally vexatious occurrence," he exclaimed, pacing to and fro within the room, " and upsets all my plans.

Were it not for this cursed Myddleton Pomfret, she might
have gone away and welcome, for I have quite lost my
liking for her. In the lesson I gave her this morning I
rather overdid it. I meant to frighten her, but it appears
that I roused the little spirit she possesses. A worm, they
say, will turn, and I suppose it will. Women are so difficult
to understand. My influence over her has been coun-
teracted by Pomfret, now she has found out who he is. She
has left me to return to him—that's the long and the short
of it. My only surprise is that he should be idiot enough to
take her back. That Celia should have accompanied her
surprises me more than all the rest. I didn't think the girl
had been such a confounded fool."

It then occurred to him that he ought to ascertain that his
wife and her sister were really gone. Accordingly, he went
into the inner room. Subsequently to Sophy's hasty
departure, the chamber had been put in order by the
servants of the hotel, but several dresses hanging from the
rails, various articles of feminine requirement on the toilette-
table, trinkets, caskets, boxes, large and small, piled up in a
corner—all plainly told that she had taken nothing with her.
Captain Musgrave was not easily affected by trifles. But
the sight of these objects gave him a sharp pang.

"Why the devil did she leave me?" he cried. "Or, if she
must go, why couldn't she take her dresses with her? The
sight of them makes me sick."

After enduring another pang, and persuading himself that
his sensibilities were over-acute, he repaired to the chamber
latterly occupied by Celia, and found it in much the same
state as the other—dresses lying about, articles on the
toilette-table, shoes and brodequins of most diminutive size.
She, too, had left all her things behind her.

"It's plain they've gone off in a desperate hurry," thought
Musgrave, as he gazed around. "I'm sorry to lose Celia,"
he added, heaving a sigh; "she was an uncommonly lively
girl. I fancied she would have kept her sister right. · But
women are all alike."

With this sage reflection he returned to the principal room,
and in order to calm his nerves and assist in the consideration of the best course to be pursued, he lighted a
cheroot. After weighing the matter over, he came to the

conclusion that it was not worth while disturbing the house at that time of night. So prudently resolving to defer any steps he might deem it proper to take till the morrow, he sought his couch and fell asleep much quicker than most men, similarly circumstanced, would have been able to do.

CHAPTER II.

"WHAT do you think, my dear?" cried Mrs. Flaxyard, as her husband entered the room. He had gone out before breakfast to take a bath at one of the floating establishments on the Seine. "What do you think? I'm almost afraid to tell you. Our charming friend, Mrs. Musgrave ——"

"Well, what of her?" interrupted Flaxyard, impatiently.

"Let me finish, and you shall hear. You'll scarcely believe it, though, when I tell you, for she's the very last person one would have expected to commit such a foolish act."

"What the deuce *has* she done?"

"Nothing to make such a fuss about," interposed Tiffany, with a laugh. "Only eloped from her husband—that's all."

"The deuce she has! Well, I'm not surprised at it."

"If you're not surprised, Mr. Flaxyard, I am," said his lady. "I thought them the happiest couple I ever met. Why, they haven't been married a month!"

"It's a thousand pities they were ever married at all," cried old Flaxyard, dryly.

"That's easy to say now, pa," remarked Tiffany, "but I have heard you express a very different opinion. You said Mrs. Musgrave was a most lovely and amiable creature, and the captain a most fortunate man."

"That was before I learnt—before I perceived, I mean—that they were not quite so happy as they appeared."

"I'm sure Captain Musgrave is very fascinating," said Tiffany, "and deserves a better wife than he has found. The faults must have been entirely on her side. Don't you think so, ma?"

"I'm not quite prepared to say that, my dear. But it shows how one may be deceived by appearances."

"You don't know what you are talking about, you silly girl," cried Flaxyard to his daughter. "My belief is that Mrs. Musgrave has only left her husband."

"Well, ain't that eloping from him?"

"Not exactly. She may have had good reasons for the step she has taken. Mind, I don't attempt to justify her, but it may be so. What has happened to Miss Leycester?"

"That's the strangest part of the affair," rejoined Tiffany. "She has gone with her sister."

"What, Miss Leycester eloped too! Now I'm satisfied. That confirms my view of the case."

"If I'm not greatly mistaken, pa, you could give us some explanation of this mysterious affair if you thought proper."

"Perhaps I might, but I don't choose."

Just then there was a tap at the door.

"Entrez!" vociferated the old gentleman.

Conceive his astonishment, when, in answer to the summons, Myddleton Pomfret stepped in.

The two ladies had never seen Mr. Pomfret before, but were both greatly struck by his distinguished appearance, and wondered who he possibly could be. He bowed gravely to them, but did not advance far into the room.

"Bless my soul, Sir, is it you?" cried Flaxyard. "You are the very last person I expected to see."

"I must apologise for intruding upon you at this hour," said Pomfret, again bowing to the ladies, "but I have something important to say to you."

"We'll leave you with the gentleman, my dear," said Mrs. Flaxyard, rising.

"Ay, do," replied her husband. "Go down to breakfast in the salle-à-manger, and I'll join you as soon as I can."

"Who is it, pa?" whispered Tiffany, who had never removed her eyes from the handsome stranger.

But no notice being taken of the inquiry, she was obliged to leave the room with her curiosity ungratified.

"Well, Sir," cried Flaxyard, as soon as they were alone, "I needn't tell you what has happened. She's gone. But pray understand that I won't stir another step in the matter. I am sorry I have had anything to do with it."

"You won't object, perhaps, to my assuring you that I

am not an accessory to Mrs. Musgrave's flight," rejoined Pomfret. " I shall also take it as a favour if you will signify to Captain Musgrave that I am at the Hôtel Wagram, should he desire to communicate with me."

"Sorry I can't oblige you—must decline. I won't affect to deny that I have some idea who you are. Don't be alarmed. Your secret is perfectly safe with me. I sympathise with your unfortunate position, and I sympathise yet more strongly with poor Mrs. Musgrave, but I won't be dragged into the affair. It doesn't concern me in the least. Allow me to say that I came to Paris with my family for recreation, and not to be mixed up in a painful case with which I have no concern. A fortnight ago I knew nothing whatever of Captain and Mrs. Musgrave. And you, Sir, are a still more recent acquaintance. I should like to be of service to you if I could—but I can't. However, I may tender you a little friendly advice, and since it is well meant, I hope you won't take it amiss. You're wrong to come here at this juncture. Keep out of Captain Musgrave's way. No need to provoke a quarrel—you understand."

"Keep out of his way !" cried Pomfret, so fiercely that he made the other start. " It is for him to keep out of my way. I came here for no other purpose than to let him know, through you, where I am to be found. I won't allow him to assert, as he might do, that I shun him. I will take care that he shall know where to find me—if he is so inclined."

With this he turned to depart. Just then, a key was heard in the lock, the door opened, and in came Hornby, followed by Musgrave.

The latter recoiled for a moment, but quickly recovering himself, sprang towards Pomfret, and a collision must have occurred if Flaxyard had not thrown himself between them.

" Keep the peace, gentlemen ! keep the peace ! " he cried. "No fighting in this room. Shut the door instantly, Hornby," he added to his son.

" How comes it that I find this person in your room, Sir?" said Musgrave to Flaxyard. " I did not know you were acquainted with him."

"I have only recently made Mr. Pomfret's acquaintance,"

replied the old gentleman, with a puzzled look, "and he has done me the honour to call upon me."

"For what purpose?"

"Really, I cannot answer that question, Captain."

"Tell him," interposed Pomfret.

"Well, then, since I must speak, I believe Mr. Pomfret's principal object in coming here was to beg me to let you know where he is to be found."

"He need not have taken the trouble. I am aware that he is staying at the Hôtel Wagram, and I am about to send a friend to him."

"Perhaps I may be permitted to observe that I am charged with the message," remarked Hornby. "I shall be happy to wait on Mr. Pomfret at any hour that may suit his convenience."

"Hold your tongue, Sir," said Flaxyard to his son. "Gentlemen," he added to the others, "for the poor lady's sake—for your own sakes—this matter must not proceed further. You will both understand why I urge a pacific arrangement. If you desire it, I am ready to act as umpire between you. But I must insist that the discussion be conducted temperately."

"It's all very well to talk about conducting a discussion temperately," said Hornby to his father. "Some allowance ought to be made for the feelings of an injured husband. No wonder Captain Musgrave should feel exasperated when he sees before him the individual whom he supposes to have been the instigator of his wife's flight."

"I have yet to learn that Captain Musgrave is an injured husband," said Flaxyard. "I hope not. I believe not."

"I don't know what you consider an injured husband, Sir," cried Musgrave, fiercely. "I feel certain that Mr. Pomfret is the contriver of my wife's flight, and I am almost equally certain that she has taken refuge with him."

"I shall content myself with saying that I neither counselled Mrs. Musgrave's flight, nor aided it," said Pomfret, sternly.

"Are we to understand, Mr. Pomfret, that you are entirely unacquainted with Mrs. Musgrave's retreat?" inquired Hornby.

"I am entirely ignorant of it," was the reply.

"'There, Captain, I think you ought to' be satisfied," remarked Flaxyard. "You have Mr. Pomfret's distinct denial that he knows anything about Mrs. Musgrave's disappearance."

"Pardon me, Sir, I am far from satisfied," rejoined Musgrave. "I attach little credit to the denial. Perhaps Mr. Pomfret will explain the nature of the interest that he takes in my ill-advised wife? I understand that he represents himself to be a friend of her first husband."

"Pray favour us with an explanation on this point?" added Hornby.

"Will you be quiet, Sir, and not make mischief?" said his father, in a low tone.

"I could give such an explanation as would confound him who ventures to ask for it," said Pomfret, in reply to Hornby. "He may thank me for the restraint I put upon myself."

"You talk of restraint," cried Musgrave, furiously. "What prevents me from tearing the mask from your face, and showing you as what you are?"

"Self-consideration prevents you," rejoined Pomfret, sternly.

"Pray have done with these bitter taunts and provocations, gentlemen," interposed Flaxyard. "I don't ask you to make friends. I don't ask you to do so. But consider the sad consequences of any indiscretion, and let silence be observed."

"You counsel well, Sir," said Pomfret. "And as I cannot command myself, I will withdraw."

"I applaud your determination, Sir," said Flaxyard, attending him to the door. "For Heaven's sake not another word!" he added, gently pushing him out.

"You flatter yourself you have put an end to this dispute, Mr. Flaxyard, by getting rid of the fellow?" said Musgrave, as the old gentleman re-entered the room.

"Yes, Captain, I rather think I have. Take my advice, and don't make any more fuss about the matter. Reconcile yourself to the loss of your wife as well as you can. I daresay you'll get over it in time."

"Very likely I may. There's philosophy in your counsel, at all events."

"Then my services are no longer required?" remarked Hornby, with a slight look of disappointment.

"Of course not," replied his father. "There are cogent reasons why the matter should not proceed further."

"I don't quite see them," rejoined Hornby. "Were I in Captain Musgrave's place, I shouldn't feel inclined to let Mr. Pomfret walk off so easily."

"Captain Musgrave has come to a very wise determination."

"Then if I should ever marry, and my wife should happen to run away, you would advise me to take it patiently?"

"Don't trouble me with any nonsensical questions, Sir."

"Mr. Flaxyard, you are a wise man," said Musgrave, after a moment's reflection. "If I can help it, I won't furnish any paragraphs for the newspapers; and as to the Divorce Court, that's the very last place in which I should like to figure."

"I felt sure you would come to that conclusion," remarked Flaxyard.

Just then the door opened, and Mrs. Flaxyard and Tiffany came in. On seeing Captain Musgrave, they both set up a cry.

"Oh dear!" exclaimed Mrs. Flaxyard. "How sorry we are for you, to be sure!"

"Never was there anything so dreadful!" cried Tiffany. "I haven't half recovered from the shock."

"You needn't be sorry at all. Nothing dreadful has happened," said Flaxyard, winking at Musgrave and Hornby. "An absurd story has got about which I know you've heard. Nothing can be further from the truth. Yester-afternoon, while Captain Musgrave was at Vincennes —at Vincennes, wasn't it, Captain?—Mrs. Musgrave received a telegraphic message, requiring her presence in London this morning. It was a matter of life and death. What was she to do?"

"Consult her husband, of course," replied Mrs. Flaxyard.

"But she couldn't consult him. He wasn't in the way. He wasn't expected back till late. To be in time, she must go by the night mail. So she went and took her sister with her."

"A very independent step. I rather approve of it," remarked Tiffany. " But didn't she leave any message ? "

"Of course she did!" cried Flaxyard, again winking at Musgrave. "But the garçon didn't deliver it. Those garçons are so abominably stupid and dilatory."

"She left a letter in the room, but I didn't chance to find it," said Musgrave. " She and Celia went off in such a hurry that they scarcely took anything with them. They gave me a terrible fright, and I passed a dreadful night, as you may suppose."

"No wonder at it," cried Tiffany. " Pa would have gone wild if ma and I had left him in such a manner. Wouldn't you, you dear old darling?"

"Don't try me," said the old gentleman.

"Well, I'm truly rejoiced at this satisfactory explanation," cried Mrs. Flaxyard. " I must own that it did appear to me inconceivable that so superior a woman as Mrs. Musgrave could act in such a way. But when do you expect the dear lady back?"

"I can scarcely say," rejoined Musgrave. " Her return depends on circumstances."

"How we shall laugh at the mistake when we see her!" cried Tiffany. "The idea that she should have eloped! How droll it seems! I shall never get over it."

"Well, Captain, since you're left quite by yourself, I hope you'll pass the day with us," said Mrs. Flaxyard.

Musgrave bowed, and said he should be delighted. And so it was settled, in spite of the significant looks of old Flaxyard and Hornby.

CHAPTER III.

F the many admirably-conducted hotels that now accommodate the herds of tourists who flock to Switzerland, commend us to the Beau-Rivage at Ouchy. With its great central hall, cool on the hottest day in summer; its broad stone staircases; its airy chambers, the windows of which look upon the broad expanse of Lake Leman and the stupendous range of Alps on the opposite shore; its internal comforts of all kinds, amongst which the capital cuisine and capital cellar ought to be enumerated; its gardens sloping down to the lake; its shady walks which lead you to baths, where you may plunge into Leman's dark blue waters; its ever lively little port; with all these, and many more attractions in the way of balls, concerts, sailing-matches, and the command of all sorts of excursions either by steamer or rail, to Geneva or Coppet, to Vevay or Chillon, no more delightful séjour can be found than is offered by this splendid establishment.

Generally, the Beau-Rivage is full to over-flowing. Russian princes, German nobles, wealthy Spaniards and Americans, to say nothing of our own compatriots, take possession of the best apartments, and remain there. Thus you may esteem yourself fortunate if you can secure an upper room, the casements of which command the glorious view of lake and mountain to which we have just adverted.

At the time when we are about to visit the Beau-Rivage, the Swiss season was at its height, and never had such an army of tourists invaded that picturesque country. They came from all parts, but the English far outnumbered the others, for the great Mr. Cook had marshalled his legions and led them on from Chamouni to Lucerne, from the foot of Mont Blanc to the kulm of the Rigi. The managers and

proprietors of the vast hotels at Zürich and Lucerne, at
Basle and Geneva, were driven half frantic by the countless
hosts that besieged their doors. That year Germany being
out of favour with Englishmen, Switzerland reaped the
benefit of the stream thus diverted from its channel. Had
the Beau-Rivage possessed thrice its number of rooms it
would still have been unequal to the demands upon its
space. But though there were necessarily frequent de-
partures, the hotel was always full—too full, in fact.
Crowded were all the breakfast-tables, crowded was the
early table d'hôte dinner, crowded the later repast.

Gay groups thronged the wide verandah in front of the
hotel on those fine summer evenings, or wandered about the
grassy slopes till it was time to take coffee, or collect
together to hear an impromptu concert got up by some
musical amateurs in the reading-room. Plenty of professional music there was besides. Almost every evening
an excellent band enlivened the visitors, and twice a week
a ball took place in the great hall.

Bathing betimes in the blue lake to repair the fatigues of
the evening, and procure an appetite for the ferraz and
trout and white honey that awaited them at breakfast;
boating on the lake during the day, fishing, sketching by
such as were of an artistic turn, excursions in the steamers
to either extremity of the lake, or across it to Evian, to
visit the jewellers' shops on the Grand-Quai or the Rue de
la Corraterie at Geneva, or the secluded beauties and grand
scenery of Vevay and Villeneuve. Returning in time for an
excellent table d'hôte dinner, strolling afterwards on the
gazon, or under the trees, with no end of flirting, singing,
and dancing—such was the pleasant life led by the company
at the Beau-Rivage.

Of course, the society was a good deal mixed. Amongst
the three hundred persons brought together in this way,
there must naturally be specimens of various classes, but
the majority, if not exactly of the higher ranks, consisted of
such persons as one is in the habit of meeting during a
Swiss tour—lately married couples, who were spending
the honeymoon on the Continent; English parsons with
their spouses; English country gentlemen with their wives
and blooming daughters; rich merchants with ditto, the

7—2

daughters not quite so blooming; M.P.s just set at liberty; young men of all kinds and all professions, young barristers, young officers, young mercantile men, civil engineers, clerks in government offices, and others.

The ladies, however, outnumbered the men in the proportion of three to one. Paterfamilias on his travels seems always accompanied by more daughters than sons.

Prince and Princess Woronzoff were staying at the hotel, and these illustrious personages conducted themselves with remarkable affability, dining habitually at the table d'hôte, and without the slightest form and ceremony, mixing on equal terms with the other guests, and not unfrequently taking part in the little musical soirées. The princess was an accomplished musician, and sang divinely. The prince spoke all languages, and conversed with equal ease with German, Frenchman, or Englishman.

Besides these, there were some German nobles, who were not distinguished by equal affability. Of course there were many Americans among the company, the most noticeable of whom was the great Mr. Sankey, of New York. Mr. Sankey, who was reputed to be enormously rich, was a widower, and possessed a daughter of extraordinary beauty. To all the bachelors staying at the Beau-Rivage, Melissa Sankey was an object of great attraction, and wherever she appeared she drew after her a crowd of admirers. She was attended by Mrs. Sharpe, an elderly lady, who watched her with the vigilance of a duenna. If Melissa could be said to have shown a preference for any one, it was for Sir Norman Hylton, a young English baronet, who had been staying at the Beau-Rivage for about a fortnight, having been detained there, it was thought, by the charms of the lovely American damsel.

Sir Norman was about four or five-and-twenty, and had succeeded to the baronetcy about a year ago, on the death of his uncle, Sir Langley Hylton. His property, situated in one of the most beautiful parts of Surrey, had been very much encumbered, so that he was only in possession of a very moderate income; but though by no means rich, and quite unable to maintain his title in the way he desired, Sir Norman was a perfect gentleman, pardonably proud of his ancient lineage, high-spirited, liberal-minded, and generous as far as his means would allow. Perhaps he might have some idea of repairing his fortunes by marriage. We won't pretend to say. Certes, he had a very graceful person as well as a title to offer to any heiress in exchange for her wealth.

Sir Norman Hylton was tall—very tall, indeed, for he stood above six feet—exceedingly well-proportioned, and sufficiently good-looking. He had a lofty forehead, keen grey eyes, and well-cut features. A dark brown beard heightened the manliness of his expression. Sir Norman was a keen sportsman, and fond of all athletic exercises, a bold horseman, and a first-rate shot ; he had stalked deer in the Highlands, and killed salmon in Ireland, Scotland, and Norway. For a few years he had been in a crack cavalry regiment, but had sold out on the death of his uncle. Out of the wreck of his family possessions Sir Norman had contrived to preserve a decayed old mansion, situated on a woody eminence overlooking some of the loveliest scenery in Surrey, and surrounded by a park full of magnificent timber, which its owner refused to cut down. Sir Norman was not a member of the Alpine Club, but he had come to Switzerland with the intention of doing something in the way of an ascent before repairing to the moors of Scotland to shoot grouse ; but he got detained, as we have shown, at the Beau-Rivage, and gave up scaling mountains for the present.

Sir Norman being the best-looking Englishman that Melissa had seen, she was determined to captivate him, and she succeeded. The mode of life at the Beau-Rivage was favourable to flirtation. Sir Norman was as much with Melissa as Mr. Sankey and Mrs. Sharpe would permit. He made excursions with her in the morning, sat next her or opposite to her at the table d'hôte, flirted with her in the garden, or listened enraptured to her melodious strains.

But after all this display in public, he found he had made little real progress in her regard. When he asked her if she would like to be lady of Hylton Castle, she only laughed at him, and said she never intended to leave New York.

" What is your old castle like ? " she asked, with an air of languid interest. She had not been in England, and fancied that all old castles must resemble those described in romance.

Sir Norman told her that the old mansion stood upon a woody eminence, at the base of which flowed a river. The park was not extensive, but it was picturesque and beautiful, and boasted some of the finest chestnuts in England—trees four centuries old. Moreover, there was a long double avenue of limes planted in the time of Henry VIII. He could not say much for the house. It was partly in ruins. But it had the recommendation of being haunted.

" Of course you intend to rebuild your old mansion ? " said Miss Sankey.

" Probably, when I marry," he replied. " But I don't mean to fell my trees to repair my house."

" Then you expect your wife to find the means to do it, I suppose ? "

" I don't think she could lay out her money better. I wish you could see the old place, Miss Sankey—such great, crazy, unfurnished rooms, and such a terrace overlooking the river. You'd be delighted with it."

" I should be frightened to death. I wouldn't sleep in a haunted house for the world. Your description of Hylton Castle doesn't tempt me in the least. I prefer a house in Fifth Avenue."

" Ah ! but you should see my old chestnuts ! and my grand avenue of limes ! "

" I don't care for old trees," she replied, shaking her charming head. " And I don't mean to build up an old house."

Sir Norman perceived that he had made no impression, and concealed his disappointment with a laugh. From that moment he gave up all hopes of winning the fair American girl, and he afterwards learnt that several other aspirants to her hand had been treated in like manner.

CHAPTER IV.

AN ARRIVAL.

EXED with himself for the time he had lost in this unprofitable chase, Sir Norman made up his mind to start for Interlachen, when, as he was standing in the great hall, looking on the bustling scene caused by the departure of certain guests and the arrival of others, he noticed a large number of trunks and boxes being brought in, which he felt certain, from their shape and size, had come from India, and he was wondering whom they could belong to, when his speculations were set at rest by the appearance of the owners of the luggage.

These were a tall, distinguished-looking man, and a young lady of remarkable personal attractions. She was a brunette, with a rich southern complexion, eyes of Oriental splendour, fringed with long silken lashes, splendid jetty tresses, ruddy lips, and pearly teeth—a perfect contrast, in all respects, to the late object of Sir Norman's idolatry, who was a blonde, with pale yellow hair and blue eyes. The new comer's figure was rather petite, but faultless in its symmetry, and Sir Norman, who scanned it critically as her companion was talking to the host, thought he had never beheld such tiny feet. He was puzzled to make out her relationship to the gentleman with her. She could scarcely be his daughter, for though his beard was grey, he could not be much above thirty. She might be his wife, but Sir Norman doubted it.

While traversing the hall the new comers passed near Sir Norman, who now felt almost certain that he had seen the gentleman before, though he could not recollect under what circumstances. He therefore bowed, and said :—

" Your features are quite familiar to me, Sir, though I

cannot give you a name. If the dead could come to life, I should say you were my uncle's old friend, Julian Curzon. You are certainly wonderfully like him."

"I am not aware that I had the pleasure of your uncle's acquaintance, Sir," replied the stranger. "I am Mr. Myddleton Pomfret, of Madras."

"Never heard the name before. Pray excuse my presuming to address you. Your astonishing likeness to a departed friend must plead my excuse. But since I have gone so far, allow me to introduce myself as Sir Norman Hylton."

Pomfret bowed courteously, and in return presented Sir Norman to the young lady, describing her as his ward, Miss Eva Bracebridge, who had just returned from Madras.

"Miss Bracebridge only arrived at Marseilles a few days ago," said Pomfret, "and I brought her on to Switzerland to recruit after the voyage."

"You could not have come to a more charming place than this," remarked Sir Norman, delighted to have achieved an introduction to the young lady. "But perhaps you are familiar with all the beauties of Lake Leman?"

"No, I am half ashamed to confess that I have never visited Switzerland before," she replied, smiling. "I asked Mr. Pomfret to bring me here, and though I believe he has business which ought to take him to London, he kindly consented."

"I never refuse your requests, my dear," observed Pomfret.

"Don't say that," she cried. "Sir Norman shall hear what you did, and then he will be able to judge whether you are as amiable as you pretend to be. Would you believe it?" she added to the young baronet. "My guardian, who is bound to take care of me, left me behind at Madras, though I begged and prayed of him to take me to England. Even now I can't understand why I was thus abandoned—but so it was—and you may imagine how forlorn and disconsolate I felt when deprived of my best friend. He had talked of coming back, but I wouldn't wait for him, so I started by the first mail, and here I am, as you perceive."

"I am quite sure your unexpected arrival must have been a great gratification to Mr. Pomfret," remarked Sir Norman.

"I am not quite sure of that," rejoined Eva. "He happened to be at Marseilles when the *Delta* arrived, and you may conceive his astonishment when he discovered his deserted ward among the passengers."

"Nothing astonishes me that you do, my dear," said Pomfret, smiling kindly at her. "You are giving Sir Norman a very erroneous notion of the affair, and he ought to know that I half suspected you would arrive by the *Delta*, and I therefore went to Marseilles under the conviction that I should meet you—and so I did."

"Well, I believe that's the correct version of the story," she said. "You can have no idea, Sir Norman, of the awful responsibility my guardian has incurred, and how happy he would be to be relieved of it. You see, he doesn't contradict me. He'll give me a shocking bad character, if you ask him."

"Not worse than you deserve," said Pomfret, smiling. "But come! The landlord is waiting to conduct us to our rooms."

"I hope you have got good rooms," remarked Sir Norman.

"The best in the house," interposed the landlord, who spoke English perfectly. "The apartments are on the ground floor. You know them, Sir Norman. They have just been vacated by an Austrian general."

"Oh, then you are well off," cried the young baronet.

Splendid rooms they proved, exquisitely furnished, lofty, spacious, with windows opening upon the verandah, and commanding a view of the lake and the Alps. Eva was enchanted, and ran first to the windows to look out at the view. Then surveying the charming salon, she exclaimed,—

"I cannot fail to be happy here."

Though Mr. Pomfret, as may be supposed from what we know of his history, would have preferred a secluded life, he thought it necessary, on Eva's account, to mix with society, and he therefore informed the host that they would dine that day at the table d'hôte.

As usual, the dinner was very numerously attended, two long tables being required by the guests. But very good places had been reserved for the new comers. Eva's appearance created a decided sensation. It had already been rumoured that a remarkably pretty girl had arrived at the hotel, and as she came in, leaning on the arm of her guardian, all eyes were directed towards her, and it was universally admitted that her beauty had not been over-rated.

"Who is she?" was the general inquiry. The answer was, that she was Miss Bracebridge, and that the gentleman with her was Mr. Myddleton Pomfret, but beyond these points little information could be obtained. However, her beauty was so transcendent, that it excited universal admiration, and she at once eclipsed Melissa Sankey, who had hitherto reigned supreme.

Prince Woronzoff, who, like all the rest of the company, was struck with Eva's beauty, and who formed her *vis-à-vis*, paid her particular attention. Sir Norman, who had contrived to secure a place near her, held a very animated conversation with her, and announced his intention of pro-longing his stay at the Beau-Rivage.

Totally unconscious of the sensation she had caused, and of the triumph she had achieved, Eva could not fail to be gratified by the attentions shown her, and she thought Prince Woronzoff and the princess charming, and Sir Norman extremely agreeable. The only person who did not, or would not, admire her, was Melissa. Eva, on the contrary, inquired the name of the fair American damsel from Sir Norman, and declared she was the loveliest creature she had ever beheld.

The effect produced by Eva on her first appearance was not lessened as the guests at the Beau-Rivage saw more of her, and became more familiar with her beauty. She joined in all the amusements that were going on, not perhaps because she cared for them—though she was of a very lively turn, and not indisposed to gaiety—but because Mr. Pomfret wished her to take part in them. It was soon found out that her tastes were musical, that she played on the piano quite as well as Princess Woronzoff, and her talents were called into requisition. She valsed

admirably, but she would have no other partner but Mr
Pomfret. She strolled about the gardens in the evenings
but Mr. Pomfret was always with her, and she neve
quitted his side. Still, his manner towards her was such
that it did not even excite Sir Norman's jealousy. Before
a week had elapsed, the young baronet had become
tremendously spoony.

CHAPTER V.

MEANTIME, there had been other arrivals at the Beau-Rivage. Amongst these were our acquaintances the Flaxyards, who had been making excursions among the mountains and valleys of the Bernese Oberland. Rufus Trotter, having sprained his ankle, had been left behind at Thun. Tiffany took a prodigious fancy to Eva, and an intimacy soon sprang up between the two girls, in spite of their dissimilarity of character. Tiffany spent half her time with her new acquaintance.

One morning, when they were alone together in the charming room we have described as opening upon the verandah, and looking upon the lake, Tiffany thus broke out :—

"I'm sure you must be the happiest person in the world, dearest Eva. I was only observing yesterday to Hornby—who, by-the-bye, has lost his heart to you, though you don't care a pin for him—that if there is anybody I should like to change places with, Eva Bracebridge is the person. Those are the very words I used. I won't praise you to your face, sweet girl. I won't repeat all the pretty things I hear said of you by everybody, from Prince Woronzoff downwards. I won't tell you how much you are admired. But I *will* tell you why I think you the happiest person in the world."

"Well, do tell me," replied Eva, smiling. "But before you begin, I may remark that you are quite mistaken. I am not so very, very happy as you seem to imagine."

"Then you ought to be, dearest. You know I'm a very freespoken girl, and don't mind what I say. It isn't because you are young, and rich, and beautiful enough to turn men crazy, that I set you down as the happiest person I know, but because you have got such a very handsome fiancé. Nay, don't blush, dearest, or look cross. I'm not going to take him from you. I only meant to convey to you my opinion that in choosing Sir Norman Hylton you have chosen well."

"You surprise me more than I can express," cried Eva. "How can you have got such an absurd notion into your head? I havn't the least idea of choosing Sir Norman. I never gave him a serious thought."

"Oh, indeed," exclaimed Tiffany, with a look that seemed to imply, "You expect me to believe this, don't you?"

"I see you are incredulous," said Eva. "But I cannot allow you to continue in so strange a misapprehension. I like Sir Norman very much. He is very gentlemanlike and agreeable. But as to marrying him, that is another question entirely."

"Are you serious, dear?"

"Perfectly so."

"Then I must tell you that everybody thinks you are engaged to him."

"Everybody is wrong; and I beg you will contradict them—on the best possible authority."

"Well, I can't say I'm glad to hear it. But perhaps an engagement may come about yet."

"Don't think so for a moment," rejoined Eva, gravely. "What you have said convinces me that I have allowed Sir Norman to pay me too much attention."

"Oh, a little innocent flirtation is of no consequence. I shall never forgive myself if anything I have said should occasion a coolness between you and Sir Norman."

"I certainly would break off his acquaintance if I didn't fear that I should displease Mr. Pomfret. He is extremely partial to Sir Norman, and might be hurt if I treated him coldly."

"Well, let us change the subject. How fortunate you are in your guardian! Generally speaking, one's notion of a guardian is of a stout old party, awfully ugly and ill-tempered. Now, your guardian is exceedingly handsome. I shouldn't object to be a ward under such agreeable conditions."

"Mr. Pomfret was poor dear papa's partner," said Eva; "and when papa died he appointed him my guardian. You may praise him as much as you please, and you can't praise him too highly. You don't know half his good qualities. I'm sure I cannot be sufficiently grateful for his unwearying kindness to me. I was never vexed with him, except when he left me behind at Madras. But I quickly followed him."

"Quite right. He had no business to leave you. As your guardian, he is bound to watch over you till you are fairly settled. I daresay he wants to get you married."

"Perhaps he may, but I don't intend to oblige him."

"Is he a widower? He has the air of one."

"Oh no, he has never been married. But I fancy from the melancholy to which he is subject, and which he finds it impossible to shake off, that he must have met with some great disappointment. Knowing him as well as I do, I can hardly imagine that any woman could jilt him, but I suppose something of the sort must have happened."

"Well, he's very foolish to take such a matter to heart. Pride would make me despise a man who jilted me."

"Mr. Pomfret has very acute sensibilities. I know that he suffers, but I don't know the cause of his suffering. And I am also quite sure that he does not deserve to suffer."

"Well, it's a great pity, seeing he is so amiable and handsome, and all that sort of thing, that he can't find somebody to take compassion upon him, and cure him of his griefs."

"Where there has been a profound attachment, such as Mr. Pomfret *may* have experienced, there can be no second love. A wounded heart cannot be healed."

"Excuse me if I doubt the truth of that adage, dear. Mr. Pomfret, I am persuaded, is capable of loving again. He looks like a man to inspire a great passion."

"He ought to have some one to love him. But I fear he has suffered too cruelly ever to trust our sex again. Mind, I never heard a word escape him of reproach or complaint. He is not embittered. But his heart is steeled."

"Still, I don't think his case incurable," rejoined Tiffany, with an arch look. "Somebody, I am persuaded, will find out the true remedy. And now just let me mention a circumstance, which I think you ought to know, though pa bade me not to allude to it. When we were in Paris, a few weeks ago, we made acquaintance with a newly married couple, Captain and Mrs. Musgrave, who were staying at the same hotel with us. Without the slightest reason given, they separated—or rather Mrs. Musgrave left her husband. Some explanation of the occurrence was attempted by Captain Musgrave, but I am certain that his wife left him. However, he didn't seem to mind it at all. One would almost have thought he was glad to get rid of her."

"Poor thing! How could she have married such a man?" cried Eva, who had listened with painful astonishment to this story.

"I don't think he ill-treated her," pursued Tiffany. "He seemed very fond of her ; but something extraordinary must have happened to cause such a sudden separation."

"I daresay the poor lady made some discovery. If you are not aware of it, I must tell you that Captain Musgrave has a very bad reputation in India. He has caused unhappiness in more than one family."

"Oh dear! what a dreadful man! No doubt, as you say, something shocking came to his poor wife's ears, and caused her to take this foolish step. But what I was going to tell you, dear, is, that somehow your guardian was mixed up in the matter, though in what way I can't tell. I fancy he wrote a letter to Mrs. Musgrave—at all events, Hornby told me that Captain Musgrave attributed his wife's flight to Mr. Pomfret's interference."

"Indeed!" exclaimed Eva. "Mr. Pomfret has not mentioned the matter to me."

"Then don't say anything about it to him, dear. I know I ought not to have told you."

"But since you have told me so much, pray tell me how the matter ended?"

"Why, it began and ended with the separation. There was a terrible row between Captain Musgrave and Mr. Pomfret, at which pa and Hornby assisted : but nothing came of it. I can't give you any more particulars, or I would. But both pa and Hornby thought that Mr. Pomfret came off with flying colours. Don't you think he must have had a powerful motive thus to espouse Mrs. Musgrave's cause?"

"Who was she?"

"A Mrs. Curzon—a young widow. Her sister, Miss Leycester, was with her at the time of the occurrence."

"I never heard of her, but I sincerely commiserate her; and I am quite sure Mr. Pomfret had good grounds for his interference."

"Oh, there can be no doubt about it. It is to be hoped that Captain Musgrave won't find his way here. When we left him in Paris, about ten days ago, he talked of coming on into Switzerland, but I daresay he has changed his plans."

"I hope so," said Eva, with a look of alarm.

An interruption was here offered to the conversation by the entrance of Pomfret and Sir Norman, who came to ask the girls to take a stroll in M. Haldiman's ground, and they readily complied with the invitation.

Just as the little party issued forth into the garden, the loud quick ringing of a bell proclaimed the approach of a steamer, and they walked down to the little port to witness the arrivals. Before they could reach the landing-place, the *Leman* was half-emptied of its occupants.

There were tourists of all ages, all classes, and all countries; ladies in dust-coloured dresses and hats with green veils, and men in all sorts of travelling costumes, most of them provided with alpenstocks and umbrellas, gibecières, or haversacks, and shod with stout mountain boots. Besides these, there was another class of travellers, attended by couriers and ladies'-maids, and who brought ashore with them piles of boxes and trunks. Most of them hurried off to secure seats in the omnibuses to Lausanne, though a few shaped their course to the Beau-Rivage.

Almost all the passengers had gone by, the engines had begun to work again, and the *Leman* was preparing to cast off, when a traveller, who had been giving some directions about his baggage to a porter, came forward and approached the group.

It was Captain Musgrave.

He had seen the party, and would have avoided them if he could, but since that was impossible, he marched haughtily on. Up to this moment Musgrave had not been aware of Eva's return from Madras, but he instantly recognised her, and her presence added to his confusion. On noticing him, Eva instantly turned aside and addressed Tiffany, who pretended not to observe him, though she glanced at him furtively. A dark cloud gathered over Pomfret's brow as the detested personage approached.

Musgrave raised his hat slightly while passing the group, but took no other notice of them. Curious to ascertain what he would do, Pomfret kept his eye upon him, and remarked that he mounted the garden-path leading to the hotel, and that the porter followed him with his luggage.

NTERING M. Haldiman's delightful grounds adjoining the hotel, our friends took their way along a shady path, which ever and anon afforded them glimpses of the broad expanse of the lake and the mighty range of Alps beyond it. The shade of the trees was delightful after the glare of the sunshine. Sir Norman paused for a moment to point out a lovely view to Eva, and while she was contemplating it the others passed on.

Here was an opportunity which the young baronet would not let slip. It is said that it requires more courage in a man to propose—unless perfectly certain of being accepted —than to mount a breach, and Sir Norman felt a most unwonted trepidation assail him, but he was determined to ascertain his fate.

"Forgive me, Miss Bracebridge," he said, abruptly, and in faltering accents, very different from his usual mode of address—"forgive me if I venture to put a question to you. You cannot fail, I am sure, to have observed the effect produced upon me by your charms. When I first beheld you I was struck by them, and the admiration then kindled has become passionate love."

She made no reply, but moved on.

"For pity's sake stay a moment, and hear me out," he cried, now growing really impassioned. "I love you to distraction, Eva—I must venture to address you by that adorable name—you alone can make me happy, and if I should be fortunate enough to win you, the business of my life shall be to prove my sense of the prize I have obtained. I have not the vanity to suppose that I have produced any such impression on you as your charms have produced on me, but I hope you are not entirely indifferent to me."

"I cannot allow you to delude yourself, Sir Norman," she said, with a seriousness that almost froze his blood. "Your love is thrown away upon me. Highly as I esteem you, you can never be more to me than a friend."

Again he stopped her.

"Stay!—one word more, I implore you, and I have done,". he cried. "Pardon me if I venture to ask the question, but are you—are you engaged to another?"

"This is not a fair question, but I will answer it. I am not."

"Then you do not condemn me to utter despair. If there is no obstacle in the way, let me try to win your love Your guardian approves of my suit."

"Indeed!" exclaimed Eva. "Have you spoken to him on the subject?"

"I have. And he has afforded me this opportunity of making a declaration. Since you refuse to listen to me, I must get him to plead my cause with you."

At this moment Mr. Pomfret and Tiffany were seen returning along the walk in a very leisurely manner.

Eva flew towards them, followed more slowly by Sir Norman, whose countenance, notwithstanding his efforts to conceal it, betrayed profound mortification.

An indefinable smile passed over Tiffany's face, showing that she suspected what had been taking place, and a significant glance was exchanged between Pomfret and the young baronet.

"What have you been about?" cried Tiffany, archly. "We thought we had lost you."

"An enchanting view of the lake detained us for a moment," remarked Sir Norman.

"Oh, do point it out to me!" said the young lady.

"With the greatest pleasure," he replied.

So they walked on together, leaving Eva and her guardian alone.

"I fear from appearances that Sir Norman has been unsuccessful," he said. Finding she did not contradict him, he went on. "I fancied you liked him. I know all about him, and consider him very eligible. He is of a very old family, and though not rich, has quite enough. He is far above the average of young men, and well calculated, I firmly believe, to make you happy."

"He told me you would advocate his cause," she rejoined, in a tone of pique. "To please you, Sir—mind, merely to please you—I have tolerated his attentions, but I always intended to refuse him; and if you had thought proper to consult me, I should have told you so."

"I did not desire to influence your decision, and therefore left him to take his own course. But I am really concerned to find you have refused him."

"I suppose I am able to judge what sort of person is likely to suit me," she rejoined. "I agree with you that Sir Norman is very gentlemanlike and agreeable—amiable, indeed—but I don't care enough for him to marry him."

"You are a strange, wilful creature, and I begin to think will give me a vast deal of trouble," said Pomfret, with a half smile. "A most unexceptionable person accidentally turns up, and without a moment's consideration, is rejected. I despair of meeting with another with half Sir Norman's recommendations. I may possibly find a wealthier man, but as you yourself have money enough, that is immaterial."

"Why are you in such a hurry to get me married?" she cried, reproachfully. "Are you tired of me?"

"It was your father's dying wish, when he committed you to my charge, that I should see you married to some worthy man, and I am anxious to fulfil the injunction."

"You needn't give yourself any more trouble about me. I don't intend to marry at all."

"Nonsense!" he cried. "You are far too young to come to any such determination. All that can be said is that you have not yet met with the man whom you could marry."

"I am not so certain about that," she rejoined. "But I have no desire to change my present state, and I may well be deterred from doing so when I hear of so many unhappy marriages. Apropos of unhappy unions, I have just heard of one that has excited my sympathies. I allude to the case of the unfortunate lady who was rash enough to wed that dreadful Captain Musgrave. Pray what led to the separation? I know you can inform me."

"I would have kept this painful matter from you if I could," he rejoined, becoming deathly pale, "but since you have learnt that I was forced to take some part in it, I am bound to give you an explanation. It was to prevent this ill-starred union from taking place that I hurried from Madras; but before I reached London the mischief was beyond repair. Foreseeing what would inevitably happen, and still desirous of aiding the unfortunate lady, I followed her to Paris, and communicated with her through the medium of Mr. Flaxyard. Subsequently, I had an interview with her, when she announced to me that she had determined to leave her husband for ever. I did not attempt to dissuade her from the step, but left her to act as she deemed proper. On ascertaining that she had carried out her purpose, I placed myself in Captain Musgrave's way; but little came of the meeting, and the affair was hushed up. I cannot tell you what has become of the unfortunate lady. I have made no inquiries about her. In regard to her previous history, and my own connexion with her, I must remain silent. Never again, I beg of you, let the subject be referred to."

He spoke with such unwonted sternness, that Eva felt quite frightened, regretting that she had sought the explanation.

"Forgive my indiscretion," she said. "I will never seek to penetrate your secrets. But I may breathe a prayer for the unfortunate lady."

CHAPTER VII.

EVENING.

LL sorts of stories were circulated about Captain Musgrave, but though few of them were to his advantage, he managed to get on very well with the general company at the Beau-Rivage. His remarkable coolness and assurance—some people went so far as to call it impudence—stood him in good stead. He made himself conspicuous at the table d'hôte dinners, rattled away in conversation, flirted with everybody who would flirt with him, assisted at the musical soirées, and valsed admirably at the balls. He was the horror of the elderly parties, but the admiration of the young folks, with some of whom, we regret to say, his bad reputation lent him a certain charm. Mr. Flaxyard tried to fight shy of him, but this was not an easy matter, and the old gentleman was obliged to give way, since his wife and family were against him. Musgrave, indeed, had contrived to ingratiate himself with Mrs. Flaxyard, and she refused to see any harm in him. Tiffany liked to flirt with him, and Hornby felt quite proud of being intimate with such a tremendous swell.

Ever since Musgrave's arrival, Mr. Pomfret and his beautiful ward had ceased to dine at the table d'hôte, or to take any part in the public amusements of the house, confining themselves entirely to their own rooms, where they received such society as was agreeable to them. Eva's seclusion, whatever might be its cause, was a' source of great regret to the general company. They missed her charming face at the table d'hôte, they missed her graceful figure in the garden, but, above all, they missed her at the concerts and balls. None knew the exact cause of this sudden disappearance of their brightest luminary, but everybody connected it with Captain Musgrave.

To Eva this change was no great deprivation, for she had

grown rather tired of the incessant gaiety and racket of the place. She had a piano in her own room, with plenty of music and plenty of books, and quite as much society as she cared for. Indeed, if we are not greatly mistaken, she would have been quite content with no other society than that of her guardian. Poor Sir Norman had not been altogether banished from her presence. Notwithstanding his rejection, he still persevered in his suit, probably because he received secret encouragement from Pomfret.

It was a lovely evening. After a burning hot day, the sun had set gloriously behind the mighty Alps, dyeing their snowy peaks with crimson ; and rosy patches still lingered on the summits of some of the loftiest of the range, though their sides looked spectrally white. A gentle breeze was stirring just sufficient to fill the lateen sails of the barks which were winging their way like butterflies to the little port. A steamer was seen in the distance, and the sound of its paddle-wheels could be heard in the stillness. Nearer to Ouchy, aud yet perhaps a league from shore, a crowd of gay-looking little barks might be seen decking the waters. At the rear of the hotel might be seen the cathedral and castle of Lausanne, crowning the vine-clad slopes. Numerous modern châteaux, with here and there a feudal tower, embellished the woody landscape. The background formed by the magnificent range of the Jura offered a picture wholly different, but little less beautiful, than that presented by the Savoyard shore. Mirthful talk and light laughter arose from the various groups scattered about the garden, or collected in the bosquets, or under the trees, and these were the only sounds, except distant shouts on the lake, that broke the stillness.

CHAPTER VIII.

EVA was alone.
Her guardian had gone that day to Geneva, and had not yet returned.
She had been contemplating the splendid sunset, and had noted all the wonderful changes which the giant mountains had undergone, from rose to ghastly white; had gazed upon the wide glistening expanse of the lake, had admired the picturesque effect of the old round tower near the little port, and then, satiated with these beauties, had taken up a book and seated herself in a fauteuil near the window. She had not been thus employed long, when she heard a footstep on the balcony, and the next moment the light and pretty figure of Tiffany appeared at the casement.

They had not met there before that day, and a cheerful greeting took place between them.

" Why are you standing there ? " cried Eva, noticing that Tiffany did not enter. " Come in ! "

" Not just now, darling. I want you to step out for a moment. I've something to tell you."

" Then you must contrive to tell it here," laughed the other. " I shan't go out till Mr. Pomfret returns."

" How silly you are ! " cried Tiffany. " What are you afraid of? I tell you I've something particular to say to you."

" Well, what is it ? " asked Eva, rising and approaching the window.

" I desire to be a peace-maker, dearest," rejoined Tiffany. " There is a person in this house who has offended you, and I have promised to intercede for him. He is deeply penitent, I can assure you, and will beg pardon on his bended knees, if allowed. May I tell him you forgive him ? "

"On no account," replied Eva. "I did not suppose you would undertake such an errand. I cannot be mistaken as to whom you allude, since there is only one person in this house who has offended me. With him I will never exchange another word."

"Don't be very cross with me, darling," said Tiffany. coaxingly. "Captain Musgrave really is very sorry for what he has done. I couldn't resist his piteous entreaties —and so consented to bring him here."

"You have done very wrong!" cried Eva. "But I won't see him," she added, in a determined tone.

"Grant me only a moment, angelic girl!" cried Musgrave, springing forward. He had been standing on the balcony at a short distance, listening to what was said. "Let me try to exculpate myself."

"I won't listen to a word, Sir," rejoined Eva, with a spirit that could scarcely have been expected from her. "By this inexcusable intrusion on my privacy you have added to your previous offences. I insist upon your immediate departure."

"I refuse to go till I have obtained your forgiveness!" he cried. "You cannot conceive how wretched I have been."

"Do be good-natured, darling. Say you forgive him, and I will take him away at once!" cried Tiffany.

"Never!" rejoined Eva. "If you persist in remaining here, I shall ring the bell for assistance."

"Don't be foolish, dearest!" cried Tiffany. "Say a kind word, and he shall go."

Most opportunely the door opened at this juncture, and Sir Norman came in.

"Oh! you are just in time," cried Eva, springing towards him. "I claim your protection."

"Against this fellow?" demanded the young baronet, glancing fiercely at Musgrave, who, though greatly disconcerted, still stood his ground. "What is he doing here?"

"He has come to ask Miss Bracebridge's pardon—that's all," responded Tiffany.

"Then let him go at once," cried Sir Norman, in a menacing voice, "or I will throw him out of window." Stepping up to Captain Musgrave, he added, in a low determined voice, "Don't compel me to use violence before these ladies."

"Come away!" cried Tiffany, who was now greatly alarmed. "I've been the cause of all this."

"Before I· go, will you hear my explanation, Sir Norman?" said Musgrave.

"Explanation is impossible. No gentleman would act thus. You are unworthy the name."

Musgrave's dark eyes flashed fire, and he raised his hand with the intent to strike Sir Norman, but the latter, who was a most powerful man, caught the uplifted arm, dragged him to the open casement and thrust him forth.

CHAPTER IX.

A DUEL.

ABOUT an hour after the occurrence just related, Sir Norman was quietly reclining on a divan in the large and well-appointed smoking-room of the hotel, enjoying a cup of coffee and a cigar, when Hornby Flaxyard came in. As there chanced to be no one else in the smoking-room at the time, Hornby was able to enter upon his business without difficulty.

"You can guess my errand, Sir Norman," he said, after formally saluting the young baronet, who rose at his approach. "I confess that it is not a very agreeable one to myself, but perhaps I may be able to arrange it."

"I don't see how, Sir," rejoined Sir Norman, haughtily. "I conclude you are sent to me by Captain Musgrave. I expected a message from him. Let me say at once that I refuse to make any apology."

"I am sorry for it," said Hornby. "I hoped a little reflection ——"

"Don't force me to make any remarks upon Captain Musgrave's conduct," interrupted Sir Norman, sternly. "I have treated him as he deserved."

"Since that's your opinion, Sir Norman, the difference can only be settled by an appeal to arms. Captain Musgrave, though grossly outraged, under the peculiar circumstances of the case would have been content with an apology, but since you refuse him that amende, he will require another sort of satisfaction—and with the least possible delay. A meeting must take place between you and my friend to-morrow morning."

"Be it so, Sir. Any hour and place will suit me—the sooner the better. To-night, if you wish it. Fortunately, I have a case of pistols with me."

"My principal is equally well provided. In regard to the place of rendezvous, we propose, if quite agreeable to. you, to cross over into Savoy, where the ordinances are less strict in regard to duelling than here. A steamer to Evian leaves Ouchy at nine to-morrow morning. Will that be too early for you, Sir Norman?"

"Not a whit," he replied. "It will give me plenty of time for my accustomed swim in the lake, and I can breakfast on board the steamer, or at the Hotel des Bains, at Evian, when this little affair has been adjusted. I shall ask Mr. Pomfret to accompany me, and I don't think he will refuse. You may count upon me."

Hornby then bowed and left the room.

Having finished his cigar, Sir Norman was just going out in quest of Mr. Pomfret, when that gentleman entered the smoking-room. When informed of what had occurred, he was not at all inclined to allow Sir Norman to act as principal in the affair.

"This is my quarrel," he said. "I am the person affronted. It is for me to punish the offender—not you."

"Pardon me," rejoined the young baronet. "I have clearly the priority. If I fall, you can avenge me. Meet him I must, and shall. And I calculate upon your presence."

. Pomfret made no further objection, and shortly afterwards they separated for the night.

Next morning, Captain Musgrave, who, according to his own account, had passed an excellent night, and who seemed perfectly unconcerned, breakfasted at eight o'clock in the salle-à-manger with Hornby, and did ample justice to the delicious ferraz and the other good things set before him. Hornby was not half so cool, and not feeling quite up to the mark, was obliged to fortify his coffee with a tea-spoonful of cognac.

Having finished breakfast, they went forth into the garden, taking with them a small bag, which contained a case of pistols.

As the steamer in which they intended to embark could now be descried about a mile off, coming up from Vevay, they lighted their cigars, and walked towards the landing-place. To watch them, and listen to their laughter—as Tiffany did from an upper window of the hotel—you would have thought they were bound on a pleasurable expedition.

Scarcely had they passed through the gates than Sir Norman and Pomfret came forth. The former carried a haversack, which answered the same purpose as his adversary's carpet-bag. Pomfret's countenance wore a stern and sombre expression, but the young baronet seemed perfectly easy and unconcerned. He had been up for more than a couple of hours, and had invigorated himself by a bath in the cold waters of the lake.

While crossing the gazon, Sir Norman cast a glance towards the room where the incident of the previous night had occurred, and he fancied he could discern a figure partially screened by the white muslin persiennes. By the time they had reached the place of embarkation the steamer had come up, and they immediately went on board. Captain Musgrave and his friend had posted themselves in the fore-part of the vessel, where they could smoke their cigars, so our friends went aft, and sat down beneath the awning. There were a great many passengers on board— many of whom were coming from Italy—and a lot of luggage.

The steamer having little to do at Ouchy, was soon off again, and as it rapidly receded from the shore, a beautiful view was obtained of Lausanne, with its terraces and vine-covered slopes. Sir Norman's gaze was not directed towards this charming prospect, but to the casement we have just alluded to, in front of which Eva could now be clearly distinguished. It was a lovely and most enjoyable day. The Alps were entirely free from cloud, and the snowy peaks of the Dent de Jaman, the Dent du Midi, and the more distant Mont Velan, stood out sharp and clear.

The surface of the lake was smooth and bright as a mirror, and the deep blue waters, when showering down the paddle-wheels, took most exquisite hues. On all sides the view was enchanting, and the noble Jura mountains, clothed to their summits with woods, and with their sides covered with vineyards, offered a charming contrast to the snow-crowned Alps. The only person, indeed, whose sombre looks did not harmonise with the scene, and upon

whom the bright sunshine and clear atmosphere did not
produce an exhilarating effect, was Myddleton Pomfret.

Never before had his features worn so stern an expression.
He looked not around—neither towards the stupendous
Alps, nor to the riant Jura mountains—but kept his eye
fixed upon the blue waters through which the vessel was
speeding, as if he would pierce their depths.

What were his thoughts? Was he thinking of another
lake far away amid the bleak northern hills—a lake that
could not compare in size, or beauty, or grandeur, with this
lovely inland sea, but which had charmed him in days gone
by, when his heart was light? Was he thinking of the
happy hours he had passed on that far-off lake with one
now lost to him for ever? In the bitter disappointment
caused by crushed hopes, did he now regret that when
plunging into that lake, he had only simulated self-destruction? Did he feel half prompted to throw himself into
the blue waters on which he now gazed, and so end his
woes? We shall not examine his breast, but to judge by
his looks, such might have been his thoughts.

The steamer was now half way across the lake, and the
Savoy shore was beginning to display its beauties more fully.
The picturesque little town of Evian, with its tall spire, its
garden-terraces, its chestnut-groves, its vineyards, and its
hotels near the landing-place, was now clearly distinguishable. In places the banks of the lake were rocky and
precipitous, and on the right could be seen a fine mediæval
château amidst its woods. Sir Norman now thought it
necessary to rouse his friend from the reverie into which he
had fallen.

Shortly afterwards, Hornby Flaxyard came up, and after
formally saluting them, led Pomfret to the stern of the
vessel. Here they continued in earnest discourse till the
steamer was within a short distance of Evian, when Hornby·
rejoined his principal.

In the conference which had just taken place, it was
arranged that the selection of a spot adapted to the purpose
required should be left to Hornby.

Accordingly, when the parties landed, Hornby and
Musgrave at once marched off, and the others followed
them. Instead of mounting the eminence on which Evian

is built, they pursued a road on the banks of the lake, and ere long came to a footpath leading inland. Without hesitation they took this path, which conducted them to a fine grove of chestnut-trees. Having passed through this grove they came upon the exact spot they sought — a secluded meadow watered by a clear mountain stream.

In another minute the parties had gained a retired part of the field close to the brook, and shaded by trees, and the seconds at once proceeded to make the needful preliminary arrangements. The pistols were produced, and after some little discussion it was agreed that those belonging to Sir Norman should be used. The ground was then carefully chosen, and the distance measured.

During these proceedings the principals had looked calmly on, but had scarcely made an observation. Captain Musgrave continued to smoke his cigar, and merely bowed his head in assent when his adversary's pistols were selected. Sir Norman manifested equal composure. At last, the arrangements were completed.

Then, and not till then, did Musgrave fling away his cigar, and address himself seriously to the business in hand. Taking the pistol, which was delivered to him by Hornby, he placed himself as directed. His dark frock-coat, buttoned up to the throat, displayed his fine figure to advantage.

Like formalities had been observed on the other side, and the two antagonists stood face to face. Throughout, Sir Norman had maintained an undaunted demeanour, unmarked by the levity and affected nonchalance that characterised Musgrave's deportment. On receiving his pistol, he glanced significantly at Pomfret.

The seconds then retired. It had been arranged that the signal should be given by Hornby, and that the antagonists should fire when the handkerchief was dropped.

Never, perhaps, on a similar occasion were the feelings of a second more deeply interested on behalf of his principal than were those of Pomfret in regard to Sir Norman. Willingly would he have exchanged places with him. In expectation of the signal, Sir Norman had now drawn himself up to his full height, and his lofty figure and gallant bearing excited Pomfret's admiration.

The handkerchief fell, and both pistols were discharged.

At first, the lookers-on thought that neither was hit, but they presently discovered their mistake. For a moment Sir Norman maintained his erect position. Then dropping his pistol, he put his hand to his side, and fell heavily to the ground.

Almost as much pained as if he himself had been struck, Pomfret hurried with Hornby to the young baronet's assistance.

CHAPTER X.

SIR NORMAN HYLTON, we are happy to state, was not dangerously hurt. His adversary's bullet grazed his side, inflicting a painful wound, but fortunately did not touch a vital part. By the care of Myddleton Pomfret he was transported to the Hôtel des Bains at Evian, where, later on in the day, his wound was dressed by a skilful surgeon summoned by Pomfret from Lausanne, and in less than a week he had sufficiently recovered to allow of his removal to the Beau-Rivage.

Naturally, the duel caused a vast deal of talk at the Beau-Rivage. None except those immediately concerned in it, who kept their own counsel, knew exactly how the affair originated, but everybody knew that Sir Norman had acted as Eva's champion, and by common consent agreed that she must reward him with her hand.

Much interest was felt for Sir Norman. Daily bulletins were brought from Evian by the captain of the steamer; and though these were always favourable, and showed rapid progress towards recovery, several persons crossed the lake to make inquiries at the Hôtel des Bains. Such was the curiosity excited by the affair, that a large party, under the conduct of Hornby Flaxyard, visited the scene of the encounter, and listened to that gallant young gentleman's description of the meeting.

Old Flaxyard, however, was anything but pleased by the part played by his son in the affair, and would fain have broken off all intimacy with Captain Musgrave, but such a course was no longer practicable. Wife, daughter, son were against him. They all liked Musgrave, and would not hear for a moment of giving him up. So the poor old gentleman yielded, though with a very bad grace. He grumbled

9

incessantly, and often wished himself back at Cheapside and Clapham, vowing internally that he would never again bring his family to the Continent.

Though Musgrave had come off triumphantly, and though his conduct throughout the affair was unimpeachable, the circumstances that led to the meeting, so far as they were known, were not very creditable to him, and many of the company at the Beau-Rivage began to look shy upon him. Not knowing how to resent such treatment, he thought it prudent to retreat. So he proposed a visit to Baden-Baden to the Flaxyards, and though the old gentleman was decidedly averse to the plan, he was overruled in the end, and the very next day the party started for that grand resort of gamblers and demireps.

Musgrave's departure was an immense relief both to Myddleton Pomfret and Eva. During the captain's stay at the Beau-Rivage, Eva had almost been kept a prisoner in her own apartments, and so obnoxious was he to Pomfret, that that gentleman would have quitted the hotel if anxiety for Sir Norman had not detained him. Till the young baronet was completely reinstated, Pomfret would not leave him. The kind-hearted fellow crossed over daily to Evian, accompanied by the surgeon from Lausanne, and ere a week had elapsed his care was rewarded, and he had the satisfaction of bringing back with him his friend.

Sir Norman's arrival by the steamer being expected, a crowd had collected at the landing-place to offer him a welcome, and congratulations on his recovery. A wounded man is sure to excite the sympathy of the gentle sex, and Sir Norman, feeble, pallid, and unable to walk without assistance, was far more interesting in the eyes of the young ladies than he had been when full of health and vigour.

Followed by the surgeon, and leaning on the arm of Myddleton Pomfret, he gratefully acknowledged the many kind inquiries addressed to him, and while doing so looked around—but looked in vain—for one whom he hoped might be there to greet him. Not perceiving her, he moved slowly on to the carriage which was waiting to convey him to the hotel.

His anxiety to behold Eva was not long ungratified. As soon as they alighted, Pomfret led him to those pleasant

rooms which we have already described. There he found
her, and the meeting was far more agreeable than if it had
taken place amid a throng of curious spectators.

Eva's reception of her champion was so cordial, so unlike
her previous manner towards him, that Sir Norman persuaded himself that her heart was at length touched. Never
before had she addressed him with so much warmth, never
had she regarded him with so much interest. It was worth
while to be wounded, he thought, to obtain such a com-
pensation.

The interview was brief, for the surgeon, who was present,
thought proper to abridge it, but it was in the highest degree
satisfactory to Sir Norman. Pomfret also entertained the
impression that a favourable change had been wrought in
his lovely ward's sentiments towards the young baronet.

Both were wrong. Undoubtedly, Sir Norman's gallant
conduct had raised him in Eva's estimation. He had risked
his life in her behalf, had bled for her, and she could not
be insensible to so much devotion. She felt profoundly
grateful to him, but that was all. This she told him frankly
at another interview, when, emboldened by her change of
manner towards him, he ventured to renew his suit. The
blow being unexpected, came upon him with the greater
force. His distress was so evident that she could not help
compassionating him. Yet she could not possibly excite
hopes that could never be realised.

Pomfret, who had stepped out upon the verandah, in
order to leave them alone together, now returned. A glance
at the pair sufficed to show him how unsatisfactorily matters
had been going on, and he looked reproachfully at Eva. She
did not, however, stay to be questioned by him, but, making
some slight excuse, hastily withdrew.

Seating himself on the sofa beside Sir Norman, Pomfret
expressed his annoyance at the unexpected turn which the
affair had taken, and earnestly besought his friend to desist
from a pursuit which seemed certain to end in mortification
and disappointment.

"It is plain I have failed," rejoined Sir Norman, sighing
deeply. "And yet I do not see why I should have failed
so signally. Without vanity, I may say that I have generally
contrived to make myself agreeable to any girl whom I have

particularly desired to please. But all my efforts to win Eva's love have proved ineffectual. I am just where I was when I began—a friend, but nothing more. There must be some one in the way. Tell me frankly, my dear fellow, has she an attachment?"

"I have no reason to suppose so. I have been constantly with her since her father's death—even before that sad event—and have never known any one who has seemed to engage her affections. She has had many admirers, and has refused several advantageous offers made her at Madras."

"Still I adhere to my opinion. She may have formed an attachment, and have concealed it from you."

"Why should she do so? There can be no motive for concealment from me., I am not a flinty-hearted father, but a good-natured guardian, whose consent could be easily obtained, for I will not suppose for a moment that she would fix her regards on any person whom I could not approve. I have always encouraged her to consult me. If she had any secret attachment, I must have detected it."

"My dear fellow, you give yourself credit for far more penetration than you really possess. Take my word for it, your ward is in love. That is the reason why she is insensible to my suit. Think again. You say you are constantly with her. Some one, I am convinced, has forestalled me. Who is it?"

As he put the question, he looked fixedly at Pomfret, but the latter bore the scrutiny unmoved.

"You tell me I am wanting in discernment," said Pomfret, with a half smile, "and very likely I am, for I have seen no one for whom Eva has shown a marked preference. However, whether you have a rival or not in her affections, it is clear that she does not appreciate you as she ought, and as I would have her do. Since I cannot force her inclinations, the only course left me is to take her away. I have stayed longer at this place than I intended, chiefly on your account."

"Don't let me drive you away," cried Sir Norman. "I promise you not to intrude further on Eva, or attempt to renew my hopeless suit. If I were able to travel, I would relieve you from any uneasiness on my account by instant departure, but I must, of necessity, remain here a few days longer."

"I am anxious to be off," said Pomfret. "I have business in London which ought to be attended to, and which I have neglected. I hope we shall meet again at no distant date, and under happier circumstances. It is idle for me to say that I should have been delighted to give my ward to you, but since she is obstinate, and will have her own way, my little matrimonial project, which I am certain would have tended to her happiness, must fall to the ground. Don't be downcast, my dear fellow. After all, yours is a very mild case."

"A mild case! Few men, I fancy, could suffer more than I do now. What can be harder to bear than unrequited love? What more painful than to discover that another is in possession of the heart you seek to win?"

"You are wrong, Sir Norman. There is suffering far harder to bear than that which you are compelled to endure. What is unrequited love to the loss of one bound to you by sacred ties who has been snatched from your arms by a villain? Your suffering, I grant, may be sharp for the moment, but it will pass away, and leave no trace behind. But wrongs such as I have described for ever torture the heart, and stir the brain almost to madness."

He betrayed so much excitement, and spoke with such passion, that it was evident the case he described was his own.

Sir Norman looked at him earnestly, and said,—

"I can conceive the misery of one who has been deeply injured, but at least he may have the satisfaction of revenge."

"Even that satisfaction may be denied him," cried Pomfret. "But let us not pursue the subject further. Few men escape without some laceration of the heart, and he is happiest who has least sensibility."

"Do you mean to remain in London, may I ask?" inquired Sir Norman.

"My plans are uncertain. Much depends on Eva. I am perplexed how to act for the best in regard to her. A marriageable ward is as great a plague as a marriageable daughter."

"The easiest way of getting rid of the difficulty would be to marry her yourself," said Sir Norman, with a certain intention. ". Pardon me, I did but jest," he added, startled by the effect produced by the suggestion. " I am excessively sorry that I have pained you."

" Your remark has pained me," said Pomfret, " but I am not sorry you have made it, because it affords me the opportunity of stating positively that I look upon Eva as a daughter. I have no other feeling towards her. And she regards me in the light of a father. I need scarcely add, that I should never dream of marrying her. But if none of these obstacles existed, there is yet another, to which I will not refer, but which would be sufficient to prevent my union with her."

" Say no more, my dear fellow," cried Sir Norman. " I am sorry to have forced this explanation from you. The slight insight that you have given me into your history interests me deeply, but I will make no further inquiries about it. On one point only I should like to be satisfied, but do not answer me if you have any objection to do so. Is Captain Musgrave connected with the painful circumstances to which you have adverted ? "

" He is the cause of all my misery," replied Pomfret, sternly. "And you would have done me a good turn if you had shot him."

" I meant to kill him, but his hour, I suppose, was not come, or the devil befriended him. But if he has wronged you, why do you not avenge yourself upon him ? "

" My hand is tied," rejoined Pomfret. " Don't ask me why. I cannot explain. The time will come when I shall be able to settle accounts with him, and I will then pay him off in full."

" Don't put off the settlement too long," said Sir Norman. "But we have had enough of him. Let us turn to something else. I will now explain why I asked whether you are going to stay in town. You have often heard me speak of my old tumble-down house in Surrey ? "

" Yes. Hylton Castle. I have seen it. It is just the sort of place that would suit me."

" That's lucky. I was about to offer it to you for two or three months, if you choose to occupy it. I shall probably remain upon the Continent for some time. You will find two or three old servants there who will attend to you, but I cannot promise you first-rate accommodation. I think Eva might like the place, and I should wish her to see it, though I sha'n't be there to welcome her."

" Will you let me the house as it stands till Christmas? If so, I'll take it on your own terms."

" I would far rather lend it you, but since you won't be under an obligation to me, I agree to your proposal. I'll let it you till Christmas. But before deciding, had you not better consult Eva? She mayn't like the notion."

" We'll hear what she says," replied Pomfret.

With this he summoned the young lady, and acquainted her with the plan. She looked quite surprised, and asked Sir Norman if he was really serious.

" Serious! to be sure I am," he replied. " I have agreed to let my house to Pomfret, and he may consider that I have conferred a great favour upon him, for I wouldn't let it to any one else. Don't fear any intrusion on my part. I sha'n't come near the place unless you choose to invite me, but as I have just told Pomfret, I think you will like the old house."

" Oh, I can't fail to like it. It's very kind in you to give us the opportunity of passing a few months in such a charming old place as Hylton Castle."

" I feel quite sure the park will please you, for it has great beauties—a fine grove of old chestnuts, and a magnificent double avenue of lime-trees—but you mustn't expect too much from the house. It's in a sad ruinous state."

" I don't mind that. I daresay some portion of it is habitable."

" A few rooms are in tolerable repair. But I ought to warn you that one of them is haunted."

" Delightful!" she exclaimed. " You couldn't have conferred a greater favour upon me. I shall now be able to indulge my romantic notions to the full. I have always longed to live in an old ruined castle."

" I must not allow you to deceive yourself. This is not exactly an old castle—merely an embattled mansion."

" Well it's picturesque, I'm quite sure. And then there

is a ghost—that's enchanting! Where is the haunted chamber?"

"I should spoil your pleasure if I were to give you any information on that point. I won't even tell you in what form the ghost appears."

"Have you ever seen the ghost yourself?"

"More than once; but I must positively decline to give you any particulars. I won't frighten you too much beforehand."

"You won't frighten me at all," she rejoined, gaily. "Of all things I should like to be the heroine of a ghost story. Unfortunately, I am not at all superstitious, and, therefore, am unfitted for the part."

"Perhaps your incredulity may be shaken at Hylton Castle."

"We shall see. If I should have a mysterious adventure there, Mr. Pomfret shall send you an account of it."

"And you really think you can pass a few months in quiet seclusion in the country?" remarked Pomfret.

"Certainly I can," she replied.

"Oh, you will find plenty of society in the neighbourhood if you choose to cultivate it," said Sir Norman.

"Not on my account," said Eva. "I prefer seclusion. I don't care for town-life in the country. I don't want dinners, visitors, and balls. I can amuse myself very well in the garden—if there *is* a garden—and by roaming about the park."

"Just the sort of life I should like to lead!" said Sir Norman, gazing at her tenderly.

"But you never have led it, I suppose?" she rejoined. "You never have remained for six months at your old house, I will venture to say."

"Very true; but I *could* be perfectly content to remain there under certain circumstances."

With this he arose, bade adieu to Eva, and begging Pomfret to give him his arm, returned to his own room.

He did not see her again before she left the Beau- Rivage.

CHAPTER XI.

N a few minutes Pomfret came back.
As he entered the room, Eva ran towards him,
exclaiming, " Oh, I'm so charmed with this idea
of the old house ! "

"I'm glad you think the prospect of a secluded life
agreeable. If you are tired of it, you can easily make a
change by moving up to town. It will be a great satisfaction to me that you should be quietly settled during my
absence."

"Your absence ! What do you mean, Sir?" she cried,
quickly. "Surely you are not thinking of returning to
India? If you have any such design, I beg you will let
me know it. I won't be left behind. I now begin to
suspect that this arrangement in regard to Hylton Castle is
nothing more than a device to keep me quiet. But I
won't be so taken in. If you return to Madras, I shall go
with you."

" My dear child, that would be ridiculous, and I can't
possibly allow it," returned Pomfret. "I shan't be away
more than six months, and a considerable portion of that
time will be occupied by the voyage out and the voyage
back. If you don't like Hylton Castle, I will make other
arrangements for you, but I can't consent to your return
with me to Madras—unless you will promise to stay
there."

"No, I won't give any such promise. You know very
well that I don't want to live in India. I prefer England.
But I think you are treating me very unkindly in not allowing me to do as I like."

" Only a few moments ago you declared that nothing

would please you so much as to have a few quiet months at Hylton Castle. Now you have suddenly changed your mind."

"But I didn't imagine I was to be left quite alone there."

"I don't mean that you should be left quite alone. I will take care you have an agreeable female companion."

"Some stupid old lady, I suppose. I would rather be alone than have such a companion."

"Well, you have relations. Invite some of them."

"I don't want to invite them. I have seen nothing of my relations. As you know, when I left school I came out at once to India, so I had no time to become acquainted with any of them. They are quite strangers to me."

"Still it is only right and proper that you should keep up an intimacy with your own family. There is no reason for estrangement. On your arrival in London you must call upon them, and then you can select some one among them to whose charge I can commit you during my absence."

"I will do whatever you desire. But I should infinitely prefer going with you. You seem to care nothing for leaving me behind," she added, in a reproachful tone.

"You do me an injustice. I shall be very sorry to part with you. But it cannot be helped. I am obliged to return to Madras. I have many business matters to settle there. Indeed, I have your poor father's affairs to arrange."

"You are quite sure you will come back in six months?"

"It is my fixed intention to do so now, and unless I am prevented by unforeseen circumstances shall certainly return at that time."

"I shall be wretched while you are away. I was never so miserable as when you left me at Madras, and now you are going to abandon me again. I have been so much accustomed to be near you, that I cannot bear the thought of separation. A secluded life at Hylton Castle would have been delightful to me if you had been there; but left with people whom I care nothing about, I shall be dreadfully moped."

"This is mere childish fancy," said Pomfret, gravely. "Since I cannot always be with you, you must look to others to supply my place. I really think this separation will be serviceable to you, and prepare you for the part which, ere long, you must play in life. Perhaps on my return I may find you married; or at all events, engaged to be married. I promise my consent beforehand."

"You are very cruel to tease me so," she cried, the tears springing to her eyes. "You know very well that I shall not be married, or even engaged. If you wait till I ask your consent, you will have to wait a long time."

"You think so now, and mean what you say," he rejoined, with some bitterness ; "but I have little faith in a woman's resolutions. However, you are perfectly at liberty to change your mind, and, indeed, I hope you will speedily change it. Now attend to me," he added, taking her hand. "I have a delicate question to put to you, but as your guardian I may be permitted to ask it. Sir Norman accounts for your indifference to him by the supposition that you are attached to another. I told him that I was quite sure he was mistaken, but he adhered to his opinion."

As the words were uttered, Eva flushed deeply, and then became deathly pale.

"You display unwonted emotion, my dear child," he said, regarding her with tenderness. "I begin to think Sir Norman is right in his conjecture."

"He *is* right," she rejoined, casting down her eyes, and speaking in low tremulous tones, "and I am surprised you have not made the discovery before."

"I must, indeed, have been blind. But I had no sus-picion of anything of the kind. How long have you had this attachment?"

"How long? Ever since —— I cannot tell when it first began."

"Why did you keep it a secret from me? I have ever been anxious for your happiness, and I persuaded myself that I had your entire confidence."

"You have always had my confidence, except on this

point," she replied, still without raising her eyes, "and I did not dare to disclose it to you."

"I look in vain for a motive for such constraint."

"The motive is not hard to find. But now that I have spoken," she cried, summoning up all her courage, and looking at him stedfastly, "shall I make a full confession to you?—shall I lay bare the secret of my heart?"

"No," he replied, hastily checking her. "No. I would rather not be the depository of such a secret. You say you had a motive for restraint. The motive must still exist. Do not allow yourself to be carried away by a sudden impulse—to make a disclosure which you may hereafter regret. Keep your secret. I can counsel you just as well without knowing more, and I would say to you, if you have fixed your affections on some one who is unworthy of your love ——"

"Oh no! he is not unworthy of my love," she interrupted—"far from it. He is only indifferent to me."

"In that case you must conquer your passion. To nourish affection for one who is indifferent to you is a weakness of which I should not have deemed you capable, if you had not confessed to it. Whatever the effort may cost you, stifle the feeling. Summon feminine pride to your aid. You need not despair of a cure, if you are resolute."

"Have you found it easy to pluck out a passion that has taken deep root in your breast?" she cried. "I think not. Can you assure me that you are perfectly cured? Your looks convince me to the contrary. Yet you bid me do that which you cannot yourself perform."

"I advise you for your own happiness," he said in a broken voice. "My case is not your case. I cannot obliterate the past. I cannot forget that I have loved—ay, and been beloved in return; but I love no longer."

"Are you quite sure of that?" she demanded, sceptically.

"Quite sure," he replied. But there was something in his tone that contradicted the assertion. "Promise me you will follow my advice, and conquer this silly passion," he added.

"I will do my best. At all events, I promise that you

shall hear no more of it. I regret that I have said so much."

"Nay, it is well that you have spoken," he said, regarding her with tender compassion. "When the heart is too full there must be an outlet. You will be all the easier for this partial disclosure. Whoever has unconsciously won your heart—and I do not desire to know his name—he deserves pity, for he has lost a priceless treasure. But enough has been said on the subject. This is our last day at this lovely place. Do not let us waste it."

And he led her out.

For some time they stood upon the balcony, gazing on the magnificent scene in silence. During that interval calmer thoughts succeeded to the tempest that had just agitated either breast. At last Pomfret spoke :—

"To morrow we must bid adieu to this enchanting lake, and to those mighty mountains. Perhaps I may some day return hither, but if not, the beauties of the spot are not likely to be effaced from my recollection. I shall always be able to conjure up this glorious picture in my imagination."

"Since you like the place so much, why not remain here?" said Eva.

"Because I am not destined to know repose," he rejoined. "I cannot remain inactive. Were I to do so, my thoughts would kill me. Much as I love this place— much as I admire its beauties—I cannot stay here. I should tire of that lovely lake, of those stupendous moun-tains—of all about me—of myself most of all. I must mix with active life. I must forget myself in the turmoil of business. As I have said, the recollection of these scenes will cheer me and delight me, but I must quit them."

That evening Pomfret passed an hour or two alone with Sir Norman, during which they came to a perfectly satis-factory understanding as to the rent to be paid by the former for Hylton Castle.

Sir Norman gave Pomfret a letter which he had written to his bailiff, Mr. Beecroft, and another addressed to his housekeeper, Mrs. Austin, in which he informed them both that he had let his house, grounds, and park to Mr. Myddleton Pomfret till Christmas, and enjoined them to obey Mr. Pomfret's orders, and do all in their power to contribute to his comfort during that term.

Next day, Pomfret and his fair ward proceeded to Geneva. Thence they travelled on to Paris, breaking the journey by a night's rest at the old capital of Burgundy. Three days—sadly too little, Eva thought—were devoted to Paris, and then they went on to London.

End of the Third Book.

BOOK IV.

THE FLAXYARDS.

CHAPTER I.

MR. BOOTLE BROOKE SHELMERDINE.

HEN the Flaxyards arrived at Baden-Baden, a certain Mr. Bootle Brooke Shelmerdine was staying at the Hôtel de l'Europe, where they put up. A few words must be devoted to this young gentleman, who is destined to play a little part in our story.

Bootle Brooke Shelmerdine was the only son—the only child, in fact—of a Lancashire cotton-spinner. Fifty years ago, John Shelmerdine, Bootle's worthy sire, had been a factory lad in Manchester, but he had now got a large mill of his own at Bury, with a noble mansion and grounds in the neighbourhood of that thriving but ugly town.

John Shelmerdine kept a large establishment, men-servants in livery, carriages and horses, and lived like a prince. Why should he not? He could well afford to do so, for though not exactly a millionaire, he was rich, and had only one son. Many men who have risen from nothing, and have not had the advantage of a liberal education, are narrow-minded, and don't know how to spend their money, but John Shelmerdine was an instance to the contrary. In early life he had received little or no education, but he contrived to make up for his deficiencies to a certain extent as he went on, and he fortunately possessed good sound common sense, and remarkable judgment and acuteness. He saw clearly the road that would lead to success, and steadily pursued it. Everything prospered with him.

Before he was fifty he was a wealthy man, and had purchased a large estate on the road to Haslingden, and erected the mansion called Belfield, to which we have just alluded.

In point of birth, Mrs. Shelmerdine was very superior to her husband, and rather looked down upon him. She belonged to the Bootles and Brookes of Cheshire, and had married plain John because he was rich, and could make a good settlement upon her. John Shelmerdine was very proud of his wife because she was a lady, and submitted humbly to all her whims and caprices; and he was also proud of his son, because he thought him a very fine gentleman, and because he resembled his mother.

Very lucky was Bootle in having some one to make a fortune for him, for we doubt if he would have made one for himself. He had not a tithe of old John's natural ability, and was totally wanting in the judgment and discrimination that had conduced to his father's eminent success. Bootle had no taste for business of any kind. He did not care even to have a profession. He would not go into the church, though urged to do so by his father, nor into the army to please his mother. Law and medicine equally repelled him : the first was too dry and laborious, to the second he entertained a decided aversion. He was quite content to be a cotton-spinner, provided his father would look after the business, so he was taken into the concern, and allowed to do as he pleased.

He went to the counting-house now and then, talked to the book-keepers, who laughed at him in their sleeve, and after passing an hour or two in doing little more than reading the newspapers, or conducting some stranger over the mill, he rode back to Belfield, or made some calls in the neighbourhood. But as Bury and Manchester — John Shelmerdine, being closely connected with the latter important city, was constantly there — offered no great attractions to Bootle, he passed a considerable portion of his time in town. Indeed, he might be said to live in London during the spring and early summer. He had three or four clubs to which he could resort for society. When the London season was over, he yachted ; and when tired of yachting, he went to Scotland ; when he had had enough of the moors, he went upon the Continent; and, returning towards winter, took up his quarters at Brighton, where he rode out with the harriers.

Thus it will be seen that he did not spend much of his time at Belfield, nor bestow much of his society upon his worthy father. He saw more of his mother in London in the spring, and at Brighton in the winter, than he did at home in Lancashire. Bootle Brooke Shelmerdine had received the education of a gentleman, and had been at Eton and Oxford. But he had as little ambition as energy, and did not desire to distinguish himself. Anything that gave him trouble, bored him. He would not go into parliament, because attendance at the House was a bore; he would not join the volunteers, because rifle practice was a bore. So little capable was he of mental exertion, that he thought it a bore to write a letter. Yet he was not a bad fellow, and had few of the vices into which idle young fellows are apt to fall. He was not extravagant, and his demands on the paternal exchequer were never excessive. In personal appearance, Bootle differed as much from his father, who was short, stout, and hard-featured, as he did in character. Some people thought him good-looking, and he would have been so but for the vacant expression of his features. His manner was languid and indifferent, and he spoke in a drawling, affected voice. He was rather tall than otherwise, and stooped slightly, as if it was too much trouble to hold himself erect, and sauntered rather than walked. With his blonde locks and fair complexion he looked exceedingly juvenile — almost boyish — the only evidence of his manhood being a slight silken mustache.

Within a very few weeks of his introduction to the reader, Bootle Shelmerdine had never for a moment entertained the idea of a wife. Marriage was a frightful bore, and he shuddered at the bare notion of it. He had seen plenty of pretty girls in town, at Brighton, and even at Manchester, but none of them had produced the slightest impression upon him.

It was reserved for Tiffany Flaxyard to convince him that he was not so indifferent as he supposed to the attractions of the fair sex. He saw her on her arrival, and was at once taken by her—perhaps because she was so fast, and he him-

10

self was slow. There was something about her that struck his fancy. Gazing at her at the table d'hôte, and listening to her converse, he thought her an amazingly fine girl. At the same time he became a little jealous of Captain Musgrave, who sat next her. He afterwards beheld her at a ball at the Conversations Haus, charmingly dressed, full of spirit and fun, waltzing and flirting with Musgrave. He grew more in love, and more jealous. His jealousy stirred him on, and roused him from his wonted listlessness. Thus Musgrave unintentionally aided Tiffany in her conquest. Quickly perceiving that she had found a new admirer, she put in play all her little artifices to lure him on. Bootle was entangled in her meshes before he had even exchanged a word with her. For the first time in his life he took a little trouble. He introduced himself to Hornby, and very soon got introduced to Hornby's sister. Finding that the young man was really smitten, and having ascertained that he had very good expectations, Tiffany laid herself out to complete her conquest.

As Musgrave spent all his time at the gambling-tables, the field was left open to Bootle, who was now constantly with the Flaxyards, breakfasted with them, sat next his charmer at the table d'hôte, and accompanied her to Lichtenthal, Eberstein, and the Alte Schloss. During these excursions many favourable opportunities for a declaration occurred, and Tiffany was at all times quite prepared to give it due consideration. But Bootle being a slow man, could not make up his mind. He seemed always on the point of proposing, but never did propose. Tiffany, who did not like such "shilly-shally work," as she termed it, was determined to bring him to the point; and while they were at Eberstein, gazing at the beautiful valley of the Murg, and he was hesitating in his usual style, she quite disconcerted him by laughing in his face, and telling him plainly that she knew what he meant to say.

"No use in being bashful with me," she said. "If I didn't like you I'd tell you so in a moment. But I *do* like you—so there's an answer to the question which I know you're dying to ask me."

"Then I may consider myself ——" stammered Bootle, whose confusion prevented him from going on.

"Consider yourself the happiest of men," supplied the young lady. "Speak to pa as soon as you please. Ah! here he is," she added, as the old gentleman came up, and broke out into raptures about the picturesque beauties of the Murg-thal.

"Never mind the Murg-thal just now, pa," said Tiffany. "Your consent is wanted to make two young people happy. Be so good as to perform the part of an amiable parent at the close of a farce—join our hands, and give us your blessing."

"Bless my soul! what does the girl mean?" exclaimed Flaxyard, staring at Bootle. "Am I to understand ——"

"How exceedingly dull you are, Sir," said his daughter. "You are to understand that Bootle has proposed. But of course I couldn't say 'yes' without your consent."

"I haven't exactly made the proposal in due form, Sir, but ——"

"It comes to the same thing," said Tiffany. "All now rests with you, pa. What have you to say?"

"Why, that I give my consent with all my heart," he replied. "I won't say that the announcement has taken me by surprise, because I have noticed what has been going on —ha! ha! Since you have succeeded in gaining my daughter's affections," he added to Bootle, "you shall have her. I'm sure you'll make her happy, and from my own experience, I can confidently affirm that there is no true happiness except in the married state."

"That's the correct thing to say on the occasion, but it's rather hackneyed," laughed Tiffany. "Tell Bootle you'll come down handsomely. That will be more to the purpose than a common-place observation on conjugal felicity."

"Well, so I will come down handsomely, my dear," replied her father. "I hope the arrangement will be as agreeable to your own family as it is to mine," he added to Bootle.

"I daresay it will," replied the young gentleman. "I suppose I must write and tell them about it. But it will be a confounded bore. I hate writing letters of any kind."

"I can't take this trouble off your hands, or I would," said Tiffany. "Stay! I have it. Send them a telegram, That will do as well."

"A brilliant idea, upon my soul!" exclaimed Bootle. "I should never have thought of it. By Jove! you're a wonderful girl."

"Yes, I flatter myself I am," she rejoined.

Brilliant as the plan appeared to Bootle, neither old Flaxyard nor his wife approved of it; but, in spite of their objections, it was acted upon. A telegraphic message was sent to Bury. It was necessarily brief, but to the purpose, and ran thus :—

"Engaged. Fine girl. Lots of tin. Handsome settlement expected."

To this came a prompt reply :—

"Glad to hear it. Who is she? How much tin? No difficulty as to settlement."

So far as it went this was satisfactory, but further information being required, Bootle was obliged to send another message, and enter a little more into detail.

Old Flaxyard, who was delighted with the proposed match, undertook to give his daughter thirty thousand pounds, and this liberal offer being communicated to John Shelmerdine, he telegraphed the following decisive response :—

"All right. Choice approved. Will make corresponding settlement. Love to the young lady."

Thus the preliminary arrangements of the intended marriage of the slowest man going were settled with lightning-like rapidity. Had Bootle employed the post instead of the wires of the telegraph, he would have been a month about it. We recommend a like course to other contracting parties. Besides its expedition, the telegraph saves a world of discussion. In the present instance, we will almost venture to say that if long letters had passed between Bootle and his mother, the engagement would have been interrupted, if not broken off altogether.

Mrs. Shelmerdine did not at all like the choice made by

her son. The very name of Flaxyard repelled her, though she admitted that Shelmerdine was not much better. And she was astonished that Bootle had not looked higher than a draper's daughter. The girl might have money, but in his case that was not half so important as a good connexion. With Bootle's expectations he might have married into a titled family. She could easily have arranged such an alliance for him, and would have done so, if he had consulted her, but she had never supposed he would marry in such a hurry. Tiffany Flaxyard (was there ever such a dreadful name !) must be vulgar and underbred. How could Bootle, whose tastes were refined, be captivated by such a person? The thing was inconceivable. The girl must be artful, and no doubt the girl's mother was a designing woman. Poor Bootle ! he had been nicely taken in.

In such terms as these she gave vent to her disappointment, and in such terms, though probably more at length, she would have written to her son—had time been allowed her. But the electric telegraph did the business before she could interfere. John Shelmerdine did not take the same view of the arrangement as his wife. He ascertained that Flaxyard was a highly respectable, wealthy man, and saw no reason why Flaxyard's daughter should not suit Bootle. So he gave his consent, as we have seen, and this done, no more could be said. Mrs. Shelmerdine had to reconcile herself to the match as best she could.

To save himself the trouble of description, Bootle sent his mother a photograph of his intended, taken at Baden, and very like the original. On seeing it, Mrs. Shelmerdine almost screamed.

" What a pert, disagreeable-looking creature ! " she cried " I told you she must be underbred. Look at her and judge for yourself. There, Sir—there's your precious daughter-in-law, and a nice creature she is ! "

And she tossed the portrait to him.

" Well, I can't find any fault with her," said John. " She's a smart, saucy-looking lass, and looks as if she had plenty to say for herself."

" She has talked Bootle into making her an offer, that's what she has done. I will never believe he can admire such an impudent piece of goods as this."

"Why not?" cried John. "I'm sure the girl's un-commonly pretty."

"Mere vulgar beauty. One of your odious fast girls. Talks slang, I'll be bound. I shall never be able to endure her. She's not a lady, and Bootle ought to marry a lady."

"Well, my dear, I can't say whether she's a thorough-bred lady or not, as I have never seen her; but I must maintain that she's pretty. She'll do all the talking for Bootle, and that's some recommendation."

"Yes, there's no fear of that," replied Mrs. Shelmerdine.

While this arrangement was going on, Captain Musgrave had come to grief at the roulette-tables, as will be seen from the following letter addressed by Hornby to his friend Rufus Trotter:—

"On our arrival at Baden-Baden, Musgrave could never keep away from the rouge et noir and roulette tables, and being rather lucky at first, talked of breaking the bank, and all that sort of thing. But ere long all his winnings vanished, and every stiver he possessed went with them. Being in a desperate fix, he begged me to lend him a few hundreds till he could get a remittance from England. I got him what he wanted from the governor, and off he set at once to the Conversations Haus, and lost the whole of it. Again he applied to me, and I was fool enough to lend him three hundred more. This was swept away in no time by the croupier's rake, and as I chanced to be standing near the table, watching his game, he asked me for twenty pounds. Moved by his desperate looks, I emptied my pockets for him, to give him a last chance—but he lost it. Next day, he tried it on again, but I had now had enough, and refused point blank, adding that I must trouble him to repay me the money I had already lent him. He replied very coolly that he should suit his own convenience, and walked away. Knowing he was regularly cleaned out, I fancied he couldn't leave Baden-Baden, but he did contrive somehow to discharge his bill at the Hotel de l'Europe, and started that very night for Paris. People say that a *petite dame* took compassion upon him, and helped him out of his difficulties. As far as I am concerned, I have heard nothing of him since, and conclude that I have lost my money.

"P.S.—I must tell you another thing, old fellow. You have lost your chance with Tiff. She is engaged to Mr. Bootle Brooke Shelmerdine, of Belfield Hall, Lancashire."

On his return from Baden-Baden with the Flaxyards, Bootle took the trouble to run down to Belfield, and then discovered for the first time how strongly his mother was opposed to his engagement. Her objections, however, weighed little with him, though he listened quietly enough to them. Eventually Mr. and Mrs. Shelmerdine came up to town, for the purpose of making the acquaintance of the family with whom they were to be connected, and put up at the Palace Hotel, Buckingham Gate, where rooms had been engaged for them by Bootle.

Here Mrs. Shelmerdine sat in state, and received her intended daughter-in-law and the Flaxyard family.

Sorry are we to say that the unfavourable notion that Mrs. Shelmerdine had formed of Tiffany was not removed by the young lady herself, but rather confirmed. Tiffany's manner, we may infer from the effect she produced, was better calculated to please men than women, for when Mrs. Shelmerdine asked her spouse what he thought of Bootle's choice, he replied that she was an uncommonly fine girl, and that Bootle was a lucky dog.

On the whole, John Shelmerdine was very well pleased with his new connexions, and the Flaxyards, especially the head of the family, were equally well pleased with him. The two elderly gentlemen talked over matters in a straightforward, business-like manner in the back room of the shop in Cheapside, and soon came to a perfect understanding. Old Flaxyard was delighted to learn that his son-in-law's expectations were much greater than he had supposed. If all went well, John Shelmerdine said, Bootle would one day be a rich man, and, meantime, he would not be badly off.

As a matter of course, the Shelmerdines were invited to dine at the Acacias. But the description of the entertainment must be postponed to another chapter.

CHAPTER II.

HE country residence—if Clapham Common can be properly styled the country—of our worthy friend Mr. Flaxyard was a good-sized respect-able-looking house, deriving its name from a couple of fine acacia trees with which the smooth-shaven lawn in front was ornamented.

The Acacias was not remarkable for beauty of architec-ture, but was plain, rather old-fashioned, and roomy; reared we should conjecture, about fifty years ago, when Clapham was not so much over-built as it is now, standing a little back, defended by a low wall from the road, and ap-proached by a couple of gates with a broad gravel drive leading to the door, having stables and out-buildings at the side, and a good garden at the back.

Such was the external appearance of the Acacias, and we may add that the internal accommodation of the house more than answered to its outward promise. The house was larger than it looked, and contained better rooms than might have been expected, and those rooms were hand-somely, not to say splendidly, furnished.

On the day after the arrival in town of the Shelmerdines, and about five o'clock in the afternoon, an omnibus stopped at the gate of the Acacias and set down the owner of the house. Now, Mr. Flaxyard had more than one carriage—he had a well-appointed phaeton for the ladies, and a brougham for himself—and Hornby had a dog-cart in which he always drove to Cheapside—but the old gentleman generally used the 'bus. He had peculiar notions, and did not like either phaeton or brougham to stand at his shop door. On the day in question he had come home earlier than usual, as he expected the Shel-merdines to dinner, and though he had an excellent and trustworthy butler, Mr. Burgess, he liked to look after his wine himself. The door was opened for him by a stout, respectable man-servant, not in livery—Mr. Burgess, in fact —and, after saying a few words to him in the hall, he proceeded to the drawing-room, which was on the ground floor, and here he found his wife and daughter.

"Well, ladies, what do you think?" he cried. "I've a surprise for you. I've made a slight addition to our dinner-party, and have invited a gentleman whom we met on the Continent."

"We met so many gentlemen on the Continent, that I can't pretend to guess whom you mean, my dear," remarked Mrs. Flaxyard.

"I'll tell you who it is, ma," said Tiffany. "He has invited Mr. Myddleton Pomfret. I heard Hornby say he is in town."

"Quite right, Tiff," said Flaxyard. "Mr. Pomfret is the identical person I have asked."

"And is he really coming?" inquired his wife. "I fancied, since the unpleasantness at the Beau-Rivage ——"

"Oh, that's all got over," interrupted Flaxyard. "I saw Mr. Pomfret on business to-day, and he was so very friendly that I couldn't help inviting him, and he promised to come. I told him all about your engagement to Bootle, and that he would meet your intended and his family, and at the same time I took good care to explain that we had no longer any acquaintance with Captain Musgrave. So he promised to come."

"Well, I'm very glad of it," said Tiffany. "I like Mr. Pomfret. But why didn't he bring Eva with him? I should have been delighted to show her my darling little Bootle. I wonder what she would think of the dear boy? Perhaps she would be one of my bridesmaids."

"Write and ask her. She is in the country—at Hylton Castle, near Dorking."

"Hylton Castle! Why, that's Sir Norman's place!" exclaimed Mrs. Flaxyard. "What on earth is she doing there? Is she married to Sir Norman?"

"Not yet, my dear. Mr. Pomfret, it appears, has taken Hylton Castle till Christmas, and that's the reason why his ward happens to be there."

"Well, it's the oddest thing I ever heard of," cried Tiffany. "I shouldn't wonder if she and Sir Norman do come together after all."

"Sir Norman is still on the Continent, and not likely to return. I asked Mr. Pomfret the question myself. Pray what have you done with darling Bootle? I thought I should find him here."

"The dear boy has been here all the morning, but he went up to town after luncheon," replied Tiffany. "Hornby will bring him back in his dog-cart. By-the-bye, pa, some people are coming in the evening. We mean to get up a little dance."

"Very well, my dear; it's all right."

"I shall be very glad when it's all over," said Mrs. Flaxyard. "I do feel so dreadfully nervous about Mrs. Shelmerdine."

"How silly you are, ma!" cried Tiffany. "Why need you trouble yourself about her? I know you think she snubbed you yesterday; but I'll take good care she shan't snub me."

Wishing to avoid a discussion, Flaxyard betook himself to the cellar; and from the liberal preparations which he there made, it was evident that he did not intend to stint his guests. He next took a walk round his garden, visited his greenhouses, conferred with his gardener, and then returned to the house.

Meanwhile, Hornby and darling Bootle had arrived in the dog-cart, and after a little chat with the ladies, had gone up-stairs to dress for dinner.

At a little before seven the sound of carriage-wheels on the drive in front of the house, and the loud ringing of the door-bell, announced an arrival, and shortly afterwards Mr. and Mrs. Shelmerdine were ceremoniously ushered into the drawing-room by Burgess, where the host and hostess, with Tiffany, now attired in a charming dress which she had brought from Paris, were waiting to receive them.

Mrs. Shelmerdine was very richly arrayed, and it was rather amusing to see in what a stately manner she comported herself towards her new connexions. She did not even kiss her intended daughter-in-law, and made Mrs. Flaxyard feel more nervous than ever. John Shelmerdine's

manner offered a marked contrast to that of his wife. He
was cordiality itself, shook hands warmly with Mrs. Flaxyard, clapped old Flaxyard on the back, and did not
neglect to kiss Tiffany, and very heartily too.

Other guests followed quickly, most of them being
denizens of Clapham. There were Alderman and Mrs.
Cracknall, the Rev. Mr. Barker and Mrs. Barker, Tom
Titterton, a distinguished member of the Stock Exchange,
Mrs. Pritchard and Miss Celsia Pritchard, Mr. Stone-
house, an old acquaintance of the reader, and Rufus
Trotter.

All these were presented to Mr. and Mrs. Shelmerdine,
and felicitations of course were offered on an approaching
happy event, and these felicitations were renewed when
darling Bootle made his appearance with Hornby.

At last Mr. Myddleton Pomfret was announced. His
fine figure and striking countenance could not fail to attract
attention, but there was one person upon whom he
produced a remarkable effect. This was Mr. Stonehouse.
His keen grey eyes followed Pomfret with an expression of
the strongest curiosity, and he watched him narrowly while
he was talking to Mrs. Flaxyard and Tiffany, and telling
them how much delighted Eva was with Hylton Castle. As
soon as he could manage it, Stonehouse drew his host aside,
and said to him :—

"Who is the tall gentleman just come in? I didn't
exactly catch his name."

" He is Mr. Myddleton Pomfret," replied Flaxyard.
"We met him when we were abroad."

" Are you quite sure ? "

" Why on earth do you ask such a question, Stonehouse ?
Do you think I can be mistaken on the point? Mr.
Pomfret is a Madras merchant, a partner in the well-known
house of Bracebridge, Clegg, and Pomfret."

"Bless my life! that makes it still more extraordinary,"
said Stonehouse. " I tell you what, Flaxyard, but for the
assurance you have given me, I could have sworn that this
gentleman was no other than Julian Curzon, who was
drowned some years ago in Windermere. I shall take it as
a particular favour if you will introduce me to him."

The introduction took place. Pomfret bowed courteously

but distantly. When he spoke, Stonehouse absolutely started, and exclaimed :—

"The very voice of Julian Curzon ! "

Pomfret's admirable self-possession did not desert him at this trying juncture.

"I see you are struck by my likeness to my poor friend Julian Curzon," he said. "I have often been mistaken for him."

"I don't wonder at it," cried Stonehouse, looking quite stupefied. "The likeness is astonishing. Excuse me, Mr. Pomfret. I knew Julian very well—I may say intimately— and I knew most of his friends—at least by name. But I don't recollect hearing him speak of you."

"Perhaps not," rejoined Pomfret, haughtily. "But I have often heard him speak of you, Mr. Stonehouse, and in no very complimentary terms."

"Ha! ha! ha!" laughed Flaxyard, who was listening to the discourse; "you've brought this upon yourself, Stone-house."

"Well, that wasn't particularly grateful of him," remarked Stonehouse, "seeing he was under considerable obligations to me. He always applied to me when he was in diffi-culties ; and as he was generally in difficulties, that was pretty often ; and I never refused him assistance. I lent him a good deal of money, Mr. Pomfret."

"I am quite aware of it," rejoined the other; "but I fancy you received good interest for the loans."

"Oh yes, I can't complain of that," said Stonehouse. "I had to wait some time for my money, but I got it in the end. I believe I have to thank you for the payment, Sir."

"I do not desire your thanks," said Pomfret, sternly. "I had my own reasons for paying you."

"I should like to be informed of them," observed Stone-house.

"No, no—not now," interposed Flaxyard, uneasily. "Some other time, if you please, gentlemen."

"Mr. Stonehouse shall be welcome at any time to my explanation," said Pomfret; "but I think, if he reflects a little, he will easily understand *why* I thought proper to pay him."

So saying, he turned abruptly away,

"You have offended him, I fear, Stonehouse," said Flax-yard.

"Can't help it if I have," rejoined the other. "He has been deucedly rude to me."

Very opportunely at this moment, dinner was announced by the butler, and each gentleman leading out the lady assigned him, the whole party repaired to the dining-room.

As a matter of course, the host took Mrs. Shelmerdine, and Mr. Shelmerdine had the honour of conducting the hostess to her chair. Alderman Cracknall brought out Mrs. Barker, and was placed on the left of the hostess. It is almost superfluous to say that darling Bootle sat next to dearest Tiffany. With the disposition of the other guests we do not concern ourselves.

The dinner was excellent, but served in the exploded style of some twenty years ago. Had the ladies been allowed to have their own way it would have been served à la Russe; but Flaxyard, who yielded to his wife and daughter on most points, was firm in this, and would not consent to the innovation. He would not have flowers on the table; he would see his dinner; he would compel Mr. Shelmerdine to dispense the turtle soup, and to carve the boiled turkey and the game. He would have all the entrées and the side dishes ranged before the guests, and—horror of horrors in Mrs. F.'s eyes!—he would have the cloth removed in order that the brilliancy of his table, which reflected every countenance like a mirror, might be admired.

Nevertheless, the dinner, though somewhat heavy and substantial, was excellent of its kind, and admirably cooked. The clear turtle soup, coming as it did from Mr. Paynter, was perfect; the turbot and smelts were equally good; and the saddle of mutton was in the finest possible order, done to a turn, and carved, we are bound to say, in most efficient style by the host.

Old Flaxyard piqued himself on his carving, and it was pleasant to watch him during the process. He declared that he did not like to be at the mercy of a butler. Servants never help you properly, and either give you too much fat or too little, he said. Undoubtedly, there is something to be said in favour of having the joint before you, and carving it yourself, provided you are a dexterous hand, and know what you are about. If the wing of a chicken with a slice of Montanches ham is brought you from the sideboard it is all very well, but not quite so satisfactory if you get only a drumstick. Still worse, if you are badly helped to mutton.

Excellent as were the viands, we must say that the best part of our old friend's dinner was the wine. The Johannisberg was superb, and came from the cellars of Prince Metternich; the sherry was marvellous—it had belonged to Marshal Soult, and cost three guineas a· bottle; and what shall we say of some rare old Madeira, which Mr. Burgess handed round just before the sweets? Words are wanting to praise it sufficiently.

Throughout the repast, Mr. Stonehouse, whose curiosity had been strongly excited, kept his eye upon Pomfret. He was favourably placed for this scrutiny, being seated opposite to him, and could hear all he said. The more closely he observed Pomfret, and the longer he listened to him, the more certain he became that it must be Julian Curzon. Impossible, he thought, that two persons could be so much alike. And yet how to account for Julian's reappearance! Determined to unravel the mystery, he commenced by addressing a few inquiries to Tiffany, who happened to be next him, but she was so much occupied by darling Bootle, that she scarcely attended to what he said, and the little he gleaned from her rather perplexed him than otherwise. Pomfret was by no means unconscious that he was the object of this scrutiny, but he did not seem to heed it, and regarded Stonehouse with haughty contempt.

"If he should turn out to be Julian Curzon, I'll expose him," thought Stonehouse. "His insolence deserves punishment."

Watching his opportunity, he called across the table, "We were talking just now of poor Julian Curzon, Mr. Pomfret. His widow seems to have been more unfortunate in her second marriage than in her first. I understand she was separated from Captain Musgrave within a month. One might almost say that a fatality was attached to her."

"Dear me! I hope not, Mr. Stonehouse," said Mrs.

Flaxyard. " I had the pleasure of meeting Mrs. Musgrave in Paris, and a more charming person I never beheld."

" So I thought her," said Stonehouse, keeping his eye upon Pomfret as he spoke. " I saw her at Bowness just before the sad occurrence that deprived her of her first husband, and most beautiful she looked, I can assure you. I can almost fancy I see her as she embarked one morning upon the lake with poor Julian. That was the very day before the accident."

" Perhaps you won't dwell too much upon that, Mr. Stonehouse," remarked Pomfret. " The subject is painful to me."

" Then I'll drop it, of course," said Stonehouse. " But pray can you inform me what has become of Mrs. Musgrave ? I understand she has not returned to her father."

" I can give you no information concerning her," replied Pomfret, coldly.

" Mrs. Musgrave is greatly to be pitied," remarked Mrs. Flaxyard. " But I must say she was lucky in getting rid of the captain. He's a confirmed gambler. Have you heard that he lost all his money at the gaming-tables at Baden-Baden, Mr. Pomfret ? "

" Yes, I have heard something about it," he replied.

" Everybody abuses Captain Musgrave now," said Tiffany, " but I can't help taking his part. I must say that I thought him very agreeable."

" I rather think you did," remarked darling Bootle, in a low tone. " I thought you would have broken your heart when he went away. For my part, I shouldn't have grieved if he had blown out his brains, as that German baron did."

" He had too much sense for that," laughed Tiffany. " You are still jealous of him, I perceive, darling boy."

" Jealous ! not I. But I could never understand what you could find to admire in him. To my thinking, he is about as handsome as a nigger, though not half so well bred."

" He has acquired the art of pleasing, and practises it with tolerable success," rejoined Tiffany. But seeing that her lover looked annoyed, she added, " I won't tease you about him any more, darling boy. So far from caring for his society, I thought him a bore, and I shouldn't have tolerated him at all if he hadn't been Hornby's friend."

" I'm glad to hear you say so," returned Bootle. " I certainly didn't like his attentions."

" He wouldn't be kept at a distance. But if you hadn't been as blind as a bat you would have perceived that I was only amusing myself with him. I couldn't have a serious thought about him. It was a very different case when a certain person addressed me," she said, significantly; " then I felt serious enough, because I knew *he* was in earnest."

" I should never have proposed to you at Eberstein if Musgrave had been there. Perhaps *you* recollect that occasion ? "

" Perfectly," she replied, with a secret laugh. " My pleasantest memories will always be associated with Eberstein. After that pretty speech, I hope you'll be content, and not exhibit any more jealousy."

Just then Mrs. Flaxyard made a move, and the ladies arose and prepared to withdraw.

" I wish you would take me with you," said Bootle, gallantly, to Tiffany. " I shall count the minutes till I rejoin you."

" Amuse yourself by thinking of Eberstein and the Murg-thal in the interim, darling boy," she said, as she retired.

CHAPTER III.

HEN the gentlemen reappeared in the drawing-room, they found it full of company. Tiffany had just played a brilliant piece on the piano, but she sat down again to please Mr. Shelmerdine, who was enraptured by her performance, though Mrs. Shelmerdine told him she played too much like a professional. The rest of the company, however, were loud in their applause. After a little more music, vocal as well as instrumental, Hornby proposed a waltz, and the motion meeting with general concurrence, Miss Celsia Pritchard sat down at the piano, and played a lively little prelude, while Hornby, Rufus, and several other young gentlemen were engaging their partners.

It was at this juncture, when a buzz of lively conversation, intermingled with light laughter, resounded though the room; when old Flaxyard and John Shelmerdine—both of whom had drank a good deal of '34 port—were expressing the warm regard they felt for each other; when Mrs. Flaxyard was vainly trying to conciliate the haughty Mrs. Shelmerdine, who did not attempt to conceal her weariness, and had just inquired whether her carriage was come; when darling Bootle was standing by the piano chatting to Tiffany, and looking supremely happy—it was at this moment, we say, that the butler announced Captain Musgrave.

11

Captain Musgrave! Impossible! Old Flaxyard, his wife, Tiffany, above all, Hornby and Bootle, thought ·they could not have heard aright. But their doubts were dispelled the next moment, as Musgrave entered the room. His appearance caused an extraordinary sensation among the company, as well it might. Luckily, Myddleton Pomfret was not exposed to the annoyance, having left earlier in the evening. Mr. Stonehouse also was gone. The cup of happiness was dashed in an instant from Bootle's lips, and bitter rage succeeded.

Musgrave did not seem in the slightest degree embarrassed by the glances of astonishment directed towards him, or by the observations made. He was got up in faultless style, and looked exceedingly well. With inimitable coolness he crossed the room and made his bow to the hostess, who was so confounded that she could hardly find words to address him.

"I am afraid you will think this visit an intrusion on my part, Mrs. Flaxyard," he hastened to say, "and perhaps I have presumed too much upon our intimacy at Baden-Baden, where you were good enough to receive me at all hours ; but I have only just returned from Paris, and having accidentally learnt that you had friends dining with you, I ventured to present myself in Continental fashion."

"Your visit is certainly unexpected," she rejoined, scarcely knowing what to say.

Having gone through this ceremony, Musgrave approached the piano, bowed to Tiffany, smiled at Bootle, who replied by an angry scowl, and then proceeded to shake hands with old Flaxyard, who was so astounded that he was unable to draw back.

"What confounded assurance the fellow must have," remarked Bootle to Tiffany. "I hope Hornby will kick him out."

"I don't know what brings him here," she replied, laughing. "But I think it great fun."

"I can't see the slightest fun in it," rejoined Bootle. "I think it an infernally impudent trick."

By this time Hornby had recovered from the surprise into which he was thrown by Musgrave's unlooked-for appearance, and now advanced towards him. But even he was not proof against the captain's coolness.

"Charmed to see you, my dear Hornby!" said Musgrave. "I owe you ten thousand apologies. You know why I left Baden so abruptly? Couldn't help it. Quite ashamed to have been so long in your debt. My chief object in coming here this evening is to repay you."

"Indeed!" exclaimed Hornby, still more surprised, and quite disarmed by the other's wonderful assurance.

"Yes, indeed! I called at your place of business this morning, but wasn't fortunate enough to find you within. Hearing that you would certainly be at home in the evening, and being most anxious to discharge my debt, which has really weighed on my conscience, I came here. In this pocket-book," he added, giving him one, "you will find bank-notes to the amount of the sum I owe you."

Hornby was now quite overcome.

"Upon my soul, my dear fellow, I have done you a great injustice," he cried.

"I know you have looked upon me as a swindler," -laughed Musgrave, "but I am not quite so bad as you thought. I never left a debt of honour unpaid."

"Well, I am bound to say you have acted most honourably in my case," said Hornby.

Proceeding to the piano, Musgrave then addressed himself to Tiffany, who, in spite of Bootle's dark looks, received him very smilingly, and began to laugh and chat with him as of old.

Darling Bootle had now become frightfully jealous. He walked away from the piano, and sat down beside his mother. Apparently, Tiffany was so much amused that she paid no attention to the dear boy.

"Do let me have the pleasure of waltzing with you once more," said Musgrave to Tiffany.

"I don't know what to say," she replied. "I should like it. But Bootle is very jealous."

"Oh, you must teach him betimes what he may expect as a married man."

Several couples now began to whirl round the room. Tiffany enjoyed a waltz of all things, and she was so excited by the spectacle that she yielded to Musgrave's solicitations. His arm had just encircled her waist, and they were about to start off, when Bootle came up, looking very red and very angry.

"Sit down, Tiff," he said, authoritatively.

But the injunction was disregarded, and he was driven aside by Musgrave, who had started off with Tiffany.

"That girl will never suit you, Bootle," said his mother, as he returned to his seat.

"I don't think she will," he rejoined. "I wish I hadn't gone so far with her."

"If she cared for you, she wouldn't dance with that man," continued Mrs. Shelmerdine.

"I won't stand it. She knows I hate him. The fellow has a mocking grin upon his countenance. I believe they're laughing at me. I was a fool to propose to her."

"It's not too late to retreat," said Mrs. Shelmerdine. "And it's the wisest step you can take. Seize the opportunity given you. Leave the management of the matter to me. I'll get you out of the scrape."

As soon as the waltz was over, Musgrave, who foresaw that a scene was likely to occur, bade good-night to his partner, bowed to Mrs. Flaxyard, nodded to Hornby, and disappeared.

Seeing Mrs. Shelmerdine rise with the evident intention of taking her departure, Tiffany hurried towards her, and said :—

"Dear me! you're not going to run away? It's quite early. I must have a galoppe with you, Bootle."

"Not to-night," he rejoined, sternly. "I'm going."

"Why, you silly fellow, you're not angry with me for waltzing with Captain Musgrave, surely? You shan't go till we have had a dance together of some sort."

But Bootle would not be appeased.

By this time Mrs. Flaxyard had come up, and vainly sought to induce Mrs. Shelmerdine to stay a little longer. Mr. Flaxyard was then summoned, and offered his arm to the lady to conduct her to her carriage.

"Well, this is very naughty of you, Bootle," said Tiffany, detaining him. "I shan't forgive you, unless you make a very humble apology to-morrow."

"I don't know that you will see me to-morrow," he re-joined, with a cutting look. "I should say it's not very likely."

"Do you hear that, ma?" cried Tiffany. "Darling Bootle says we shan't see him to-morrow."

"Good gracious! Why not?" cried Mrs. Flaxyard.

"I fear I shall be obliged to detain him during the morning," remarked Mrs. Shelmerdine.

"But you'll all come and dine here," said Flaxyard, "quite in a friendly way."

"I see nothing to prevent it," said John Shelmerdine, with a cheery laugh. "We shall be very happy—shan't we, dear?"

"I hope Mrs. Flaxyard will be kind enough to excuse us. We have an engagement."

"An engagement!" cried John, surprised. "I know nothing about it."

"Oh yes we have," rejoined his better-half. "You've forgotten it. I'll remind you of it presently."

"But Bootle won't like to stay away."

"The darling boy has just said he can't come," remarked Tiffany.

"Can't come! How's this?" cried his father, looking at him in surprise.

"My dear, the carriage is waiting," observed Mrs. Shelmerdine.

"Let it wait," rejoined John, bluntly. "Something is amiss, I perceive.. What is it, my love?" he added to Tiffany.

"I really can't tell, Sir. You had better ask Bootle."

"Well, Bootle, my boy, what is it?" said his father, turning to him.

"Nothing material," he replied. "I've changed my mind, that's all. I don't mean to be married just yet."

"Oh! good gracious, Bootle! what have I done to deserve this?" cried Tiffany. "How have I incurred your displeasure, darling boy?"

"By waltzing when I told you not," he rejoined, in a severe voice.

"Don't make yourself ridiculous, Sir," said his father. "This is the silliest lovers' quarrel I ever heard of. Make it up directly."

"I don't think it a silly quarrel," observed Mrs. Shelmerdine, in her stateliest manner. "I entirely approve of Bootle's conduct. He objected to Miss Flaxyard's waltzing with a particular gentleman, but, in spite of his objection, she persisted. I don't wonder he is offended."

"Yes, I *am* deeply offended," said Bootle.

"You are a fool," cried his father. "Go and waltz with her yourself, and let us hear no more about it."

"Excuse me, Mr. Shelmerdine," said Tiffany, in a faint voice. "I don't feel equal to another waltz—even with darling Bootle."

"Be firm," whispered Mrs. Shelmerdine to her son, fearing he might give way. "I must wish you good-night, Mrs. Flaxyard."

"Stay a minute, my dear Madam," said old Flaxyard. "Do let us set these young folks right. A word will do it. I'm sure Tiff's very sorry."

"Well, if she will admit that," said Mrs. Shelmerdine.

"No, I won't say I'm sorry, simply because you ask me," rejoined the young lady, sharply. "I think if any one ought to beg pardon, it's Bootle, not me."

"I think so too," laughed John Shelmerdine.

"If Bootle does, he's no son of mine," said Mrs. Shelmerdine, with dignity.

"Bootle has no such intention," said that young gentleman.

"Well, I'm exceedingly sorry that an evening so pleasant as I have found it should terminate in this manner," said John Shelmerdine; "but let us hope that all will be amicably settled in the morning."

"I entirely echo that wish," said old Flaxyard, "and I only regret that we cannot arrange the little difference now. But I daresay they both will have come to their senses in the morning."

Poor Mrs. Flaxyard was very much distressed by the occurrence, and tried to interfere, but in vain. Hornby was equally unsuccessful in the attempt he made to pacify Bootle, who was as obstinate as he was stupid.

While taking leave of Tiffany, John Shelmerdine told her that his son was a silly fellow, but she needn't have the slightest uneasiness; he was sure to come round. Old

Flaxyard conducted Mrs. Shelmerdine to her carriage, and Bootle, after making a formal bow to Tiffany, followed them out of the room.

No sooner were the Shelmerdines gone than Hornby observed to his sister :—

" I tell you what it is, Tiff—that waltz with Musgrave has lost you a husband."

" Don't think it," she replied. " I shall have him here to-morrow morning to beg pardon."

CHAPTER IV.

TWO NOTES FROM TIFFANY.

N the morning after the untoward event describeu in the last chapter, Mr. and Mrs. Shelmerdine sat at breakfast in a private room at the Palace Hotel. The lady looked elated, but John was evidently much put out by the occurrence of the previous evening.

Always late, Bootle had not yet made his appearance, nor did he turn up until long after his father had finished breakfast, and got deep into the leading article of the leading journal. John scarcely returned his son's salutation, but Mrs. Shelmerdine was all smiles and sweetness, and begged Bootle to ring for hot toast, hot coffee, and a broil. Bootle complied with the suggestion; but as there were plenty of other things on the table, he set to work at once upon the wing of a chicken and a slice of tongue. While he was thus employed, his father, who had been watching him for some time with suppressed wrath, at last broke out :—

"A pretty business you made of it last night, Sir. You placed me in a most unpleasant position. Never in my life did I hear of so silly a quarrel! What was it all about? A mere trifle, of which no sensible man would have taken the slightest notice. The whole thing would have been absurd, if it had not ended seriously. I felt heartily ashamed of you, Sir. I fancied you were really attached to Miss Flaxyard, but I can scarcely believe so after your ridiculous conduct. Even admitting that you had some reasonable grounds for annoyance—and I can't admit anything of the sort—you ought to have acted like a gentleman."

"I hope I did act like a gentleman, Sir," pleaded Bootle.

"Your father did not see all that passed, and refuses to lend credence to my explanation," said Mrs. Shelmerdine with an approving smile at her son. "I watched Miss Flaxyard narrowly, and highly disapproved of her manner towards that impudent Captain What's-his-name. Since she was foolish enough to waltz with him, after your prohibition, delivered, I must say—for I heard it—in a very gentlemanlike, proper manner, I think you were perfectly justified in the course you pursued—perfectly justified, I repeat. Your father takes a widely different view of the matter, but never mind. You are in the right. Now that the thing is over, I may candidly confess that I could never have tolerated Miss Flaxyard as a daughter-in-law."

"Ha! well! I don't exactly like giving her up," said Bootle. "I was in a deuced passion last night, but a little soda and brandy has calmed me this morning. Perhaps I was rather too impetuous. What do you think, Sir?" he added to his father.

"Don't appeal to me. I've already given you my opinion," replied John, gruffly. "I think you behaved absurdly."

"Be ruled by me, Bootle," said Mrs. Shelmerdine, beginning to be alarmed. "In a case of this kind, a mother is the best judge; in fact, the only judge. Having got entangled by a vulgar, designing girl, you may esteem yourself singularly fortunate that she has furnished you, by her conduct, with a pretext for breaking off the engagement. As soon as you have finished breakfast, write to inform her that the affair is at an end."

"Think twice before you take that step, my boy," said his father. "Recollect that this designing girl, as your mother describes her, happens to have thirty thousand pounds."

At this moment the waiter came in with a broiled whiting, and at the same time placed a note in a pink envelope before Bootle.

"Just been left for you, Sir."

"Any answer required?" asked Bootle, turning pale as he recognised Tiffany's handwriting.

The waiter replied in the negative, and withdrew.

"From Miss Flaxyard, I presume?" remarked Mrs. Shelmerdine, glancing scornfully at the note. "Give it to me, and I'll read it aloud, while you go on with your breakfast."

Bootle not venturing to make any objection, she opened the note, and read as follows :—

"'DARLING BOOTLE,—How very, very sorry I am that I annoyed you. It was very thoughtless in me to valse with that horrid Captain Musgrave, but I have been sufficiently punished for my folly. I couldn't sleep a wink last night.'"

"D'ye hear that?" cried John. "'She couldn't sleep a wink.'"

"Neither could I," added Bootle, sympathetically.

"'I am the more vexed with myself, because I feel that, besides annoying you, I have offended dearest Mrs. Shelmerdine. I should be grieved, indeed, if I thought that I had forfeited *her* good opinion. But you must set me right with her, dearest boy. Though awfully afraid of her, as she must have perceived, I love her and respect her; and you may confidently assure her, dearest boy, that she will ever find me a dutiful daughter.'

"Well, if I felt certain she would act up to this I might change my opinion of her," remarked Mrs. Shelmerdine. "I fancy she does stand in awe of me."

"She thinks you a very superior woman," observed Bootle. "But finish the letter."

"'As to dear Mr. Shelmerdine, I am not the least bit afraid of *him*. He's the nicest man I ever met, not excepting my own darling Bootle. Pray tell him so.'"

Here Mrs. Shelmerdine coughed rather incredulously.

"'What I have said will convince you of my earnest desire to render myself agreeable to your family. It won't be my fault if they don't like me. Dearest Mrs. Shelmerdine shan't have to complain of me again—neither shall you, dearest boy. Dear Mr. S., I am sure, has forgiven me already. So let the silly affair be forgotten. Bring them both to luncheon, and we will drive afterwards to the Crystal Palace. Adieu, dearest boy !

" ' Your ever affectionate

" ' THEOPHANIA FLAXYARD.' "

" A very nice amiable letter," said John, as his wife concluded. "Of course we must go to luncheon, my dear. We can't do otherwise."

" Hum! I don't know about that !" cried Mrs. Shelmerdine. " The letter appears creditable to the girl, but I think it has been written with an eye to effect. Eh day ! here's more of it," she added, as a thin leaf of paper, which had been placed inside the note, dropped out.

" Better let Bootle read that to himself, my dear," said John, rather uneasily. " That's private."

But his wife's quick eye had caught a few words that incited her to go on. After scanning the letter for a few moments with looks that scared both Bootle and his father, she read it aloud with bitter emphasis, pausing occasionally to make a sarcastic observation.

" ' This is your letter, dearest boy. The other, as you will readily guess, is for the benefit of the elderly party, who has the enviable privilege of calling you her son. If mischief has been made, that malicious old woman—I am sorry to speak so disrespectfully of my darling Bootle's mamma, but I can't help it—if mischief has been made, I say, *she* is the cause of it. I valsed with that odious man merely to show how little I cared for her, and for no other reason. You had prepared me for the sort of person I should find her, but I didn't expect ——'

" What have you been saying of me, Bootle ?" demanded his mother, pausing, and looking severely at him.

Very much confused, Bootle made no direct reply, but merely begged her not to read more.

" I *shall* go on," she observed, with lofty scorn. " It is perfectly immaterial what such a girl as this may say of me, but it is *not* immaterial that I should be disparaged by my son."

Clearing her voice, she continued :—

" I didn't expect such a terrible old Tartar. She soon let

us see that she looked down upon us all, and didn't think
me half good enough for you. I fancy I have a little spirit.
At all events, I can't stand this sort of thing. So, when she
sent you to bid me sit down, I wouldn't. Now you have
the truth, dearest boy.'

"A very nice young lady, I must say," remarked Mrs.
Shelmerdine in a contemptuous parenthesis. "'As to your
governor, I dote upon him. Hornby calls him a regular
brick, and so he is. After this explanation, darling Bootle
I am sure, will forgive his devoted and truly penitent Tiff,
and come to luncheon.'

"Come to luncheon, indeed !" exclaimed the incensed
lady, throwing down the letter. "After indulging in all this
vulgar slang, after calling me 'a terrible old Tartar,' does
she suppose I will ever enter her father's doors again ?"

"Consider, my dear," said John, who had been laughing
to himself, "that the letter you have just read was not meant
for your eye. She would have never called you a terrible old
Tartar to your face."

"I trust not," rejoined Mrs. Shelmerdine. "But I
suppose you are gratified by the elegant epithet she has
applied to you ? You like being called a 'regular brick,' I
make no doubt ?"

"I don't mind it in the least, my dear," he replied,
laughing. "But whether we approve of slang or not neither
you nor myself can take umbrage at anything contained in
that second letter, which was not meant to be shown us.
And allow me to add, that there is a good deal of force in
what Miss Flaxyard says—namely, that you yourself have
been the cause of this disturbance. You were certainly
very rude to her family, and no wonder she should resent
such treatment."

"I dislike her. I dislike her family, and I made no
attempt to dissemble my feelings. They are a vulgar set,
but she is worst of all, and it would have been an inexpressible grief to me if Bootle had been linked to her for
life. How he could ever have engaged himself to such a
creature passes my comprehension. I can really discover
nothing in her, either in mind or person."

"I thought her—and, for that matter, still think her—
remarkably pretty," said Bootle.

"So she is," observed his father. "A little fast, and rather too fond of slang, but she'll mend when she's married. I'll warrant she has the making of a good wife."

"Good or bad, she shall never be Bootle's wife with my consent. Luckily, the engagement has been broken off. There must be no renewal of it. Bootle shall immediately despatch a note, which I will dictate for him, informing Miss Flaxyard that we cannot possibly have the honour of taking luncheon at the Acacias this morning, since we are leaving town at once for Lancashire."

John uttered an exclamation of disapproval, and, getting up from his seat, moved towards the window.

"Do as I tell you, Bootle," said his mother, in a low voice, and with a significant look at him. "She won't suit you."

"Well, I don't know that," he rejoined doubtfully. "I rather think she would."

Here John turned round, and, leaning against the back of a sofa, addressed his wife.

"Why won't you allow Bootle to please himself, my dear? He doesn't regard the girl and her family with your eyes. You allow your prejudices to interfere with your judgment. The lass is not half so bad as you represent her. In fact, I can't find any fault with her, except that, as I just now observed, she is rather fast. But she'll soon lower the pace, especially if you will take the reins in hand."

"*I* take the reins in hand!" exclaimed Mrs. Shelmerdine, scornfully. "Don't expect it, Sir!"

"Well, she would go quieter if you did. But allow me to finish what I have begun. If you deny Miss Flaxyard every other recommendation, you must at least admit that she has an important one—a good fortune. Bootle will do well to consider that before he writes the letter you suggest."

"Her fortune need be no temptation to Bootle. Let him marry a lady, even if she has nothing."

"He cannot honourably retreat from the engagement he has entered into; neither can I support him in withdrawing from it. However, he must decide for himself. What do you say, Bootle?" he demanded, almost sure, from his son's looks, of the answer he should receive. "Will you be guided

by your mother or by me ?   Are you for the train to Bury,
or for luncheon at Clapham ? "

" Upon my soul, I can't make up my mind," replied
Bootle, glancing undecidedly from one to the other.

At this moment the waiter entered the room, and, to
the surprise of all present, announced Mr. Flaxyard.

" Mr. Flaxyard!   Good   gracious ! "   exclaimed   Mrs.
Shelmerdine.   " Let me get out of the room."

But a graceful retreat being impossible, she kept her
seat.

CHAPTER V.

MR. FLAXYARD was ushered in, and his manifest nervousness was not dissipated by the looks of the haughty dame.

John, however, shook hands with him, and inquired after the ladies, and so did Bootle, though less cordially.

"Have you breakfasted?" asked John, pointing to the table.

"Thank you! yes," rejoined Flaxyard. "I must apologise to you, Ma'am, for this early visit," he added to Mrs. Shelmerdine, "but we have all been so much distressed by what took place last night, that I could not rest till I had seen you. I am charged by my daughter to say how much she regrets the occurrence. She would not offend you for the world."

Mrs. Shelmerdine, who looked very dignified, inclined her head slightly, but made no reply. Poor Flaxyard was rather abashed, but recovering himself, he went on :—

"Without meaning to flatter, you, Ma'am, I must take leave to state that my wife and myself, impressed by your distinguished manner, have recommended you as an object of imitation to Tiffany, and she has promised to take you as a pattern. May I be permitted to tell you what she said of you this morning?"

"No, I thank you," rejoined Mrs. Shelmerdine, haughtily. "I am quite aware of Miss Flaxyard's opinion of me."

"She entertains the very highest opinion of you, Ma'am; that I can unhesitatingly declare," said Flaxyard. "Over and over again, with tears in her eyes, did she reproach herself in such terms as these: 'What will dear Mrs. Shelmerdine think of me? How shocked she must be at conduct so different from her own! How thoughtless and silly I was, to be sure—but I meant no harm! I shall never feel happy till I obtain her forgiveness. Darling Bootle understands me, and will overlook my fault—but his mother, whose standard of propriety is so very high, will condemn me, I fear, without listening to my defence.' These were her exact expressions, Ma'am, and I think they will convince you of the sincerity of her regret, as well as of her anxiety to please you."

Mrs. Shelmerdine listened with a smile of incredulity.

"Either you are trifling with me, Mr. Flaxyard, or your daughter has imposed upon you," she said. "I have proof, under her own hand, of the opinion she entertains of me. Read that, Sir, and you will see in what respectful terms I am mentioned."

And she gave him the enclosure which had just caused so much confusion. As he cast his eye over it, he turned crimson, and glancing angrily at Bootle, said,—

"Did you give this to your mother, Sir? If so, I consider you have been guilty of ——"

"Hold! my dear Mr. Flaxyard," interposed John. "I must exculpate Bootle. The letter fell accidentally into my wife's hands. I am very sorry she has read it—that is all I can say."

"Well, Ma'am, the most sensible plan will be to treat the matter as a bad joke," remarked Flaxyard. "Men of business like Mr. Shelmerdine and myself always write in a plain straight-forward way; but ladies—especially young ladies—are not so guarded, and sometimes, as in this case, mistake smartness for wit. Bootle must accept some of the responsibility of this unlucky letter, since it evidently represents his sentiments quite as much as Tiff's. But I regard it as a mere joke, and if he were to write about me in the same style, and describe me as a stout old party, I should merely laugh."

" I never write letters," remarked the young man.

" I cannot accept your explanation, Sir," said Mrs. Shelmerdine, maintaining a haughty and inflexible look, " if your daughter can speak of me in such terms ——"

" Why, my dear Madam," interrupted Flaxyard, " your son must have spoken of you in precisely similar terms. Ask him. He can't deny it."

Bootle offered no contradiction.

Here John, much to his wife's disgust, burst into a hearty laugh, in which Flaxyard could not help joining.

" Mr. Shelmerdine," said his wife, reproachfully, " I think you might show a little more consideration for my feelings. I have been grossly insulted."

" Pardon me, Madam, I do not think so," rejoined Flaxyard, becoming suddenly grave. " We have all the greatest regard and respect for you."

" Your daughter has a strange way of showing her respect."

" Come, my dear, you have said quite enough," remarked John. " When no offence is intended, none should be taken. Bootle is the cause of it all."

" I !" exclaimed the young gentleman.

" Take it upon your own shoulders," whispered his father.

" Well, I am certainly bound to admit that Tiffany wrote that letter to amuse me ; and no doubt it would have amused me, if ——"

" Enough," cried his mother. " You are just as bad as she is."

" Well, then, they'll make a nice pair," laughed John. " I think the difficulty is got over," he whispered to Flaxyard. But he was mistaken.

" Mr. Flaxyard," said the lady, " it would be improper to disguise from you that I disapprove—strongly disapprove—of my son's marriage with your daughter. You may imagine that my dislike to the match originated in Miss Flaxyard's conduct last night, and has been increased by her letter this morning. No such thing. All along, as Mr. Shelmerdine will tell you if he speaks the truth, I have been opposed to the union. On what particular grounds, it is unnecessary for me to say. But, for fear of misapprehension, I will state plainly that I think the match in every respect unsuitable to my son."

"My dear, do, pray, consider," said John.

"I will not qualify my expressions in the slightest degree," rejoined Mrs. Shelmerdine. "I think the match wholly unsuitable to Bootle."

Poor Mr. Flaxyard looked confounded, and utterly at a loss what to say.

"I wish Tiff were here to answer her," he mentally ejaculated; "I cannot."

However, he roused himself, and said, with some spirit,—

"I must at least admit, Madam, that you are plain-spoken. No mistaking what you mean. But I should like to hear what Bootle has to say on the subject."

"Bootle will write to your daughter," said Mrs. Shelmer-dine, apprehensive lest the young gentleman should commit himself by a reply.

"No, that won't do," said Flaxyard, encouraged by a slight wink addressed to him by John. "I must have an answer now. I will say nothing of my daughter's feelings— of her mother's feelings—of my own feelings—since they appear to be entirely disregarded. An engagement is formed, carried on almost to the last point, and then on a trivial pretext is to be broken off. Permit me to say, Ma'am, that it is now too late to signify your disapproval. Mr. Shelmerdine, who ought to have some voice in the matter, has given his full consent, and only yesterday we discussed and agreed upon the terms of the settlements. I was perfectly satisfied with Mr. Shelmerdine's intentions, as I believe he was with mine. Our solicitors are to meet at noon to-day in Lincoln's Inn Fields. Am I to tell them that their services are not required?—that the affair is at an end? I trust not. I cannot think that Bootle, who has professed so strong an attachment for my daughter, to whom she is so much devoted, and whom I and my wife have begun to regard as a son—I cannot think, I say, that *he* will attempt to retreat from his engagement. Naturally, I am sorry to learn, Ma'am—and I learn it now for the first time—that the engagement which has met with Mr. Shelmerdine's sanction has not met with yours ; but though that circumstance may cause me deep regret, I cannot allow it to weigh with me. My daughter's happiness is at stake—and she must be my first consideration."

A series of winks, delivered from time to time, conveyed to Mr. Flaxyard John's entire approval of this speech.

Mrs. Shelmerdine was far from impressed by the oration, but perceiving, to her dismay, that it had produced an effect on her son, she held up her finger to him. But Bootle disregarded the hint.

"Now, Bootle, speak out like a man," said his father. "Do you mean marriage ?"

"Yes, I do," he replied, firmly.

On this, Mrs. Shelmerdine instantly quitted the room.

Both the elderly gentlemen complimented him on his courage, and told him he had done right.

"I have got myself into a nice scrape," remarked John, laughing. "But I don't mind that."

"I may now tell you that the ladies are in the carriage below," said Flaxyard to Bootle. "They'll drive you to the Acacias at once, if you like to go with them."

"Go, my boy—go," urged his father. "You will be better out of the way."

Bootle required no second bidding, but taking up his hat, hurried down-stairs.

He found Tiffany and her mother seated in the phaeton, which was drawn up at the door of the hotel. Tiffany uttered a little cry of delight as she beheld him. She looked so bewitching, that he wondered how he could have quarrelled with her.

Needless to say, he was rapturously received. After a few exclamations of delight, he got into the phaeton, and his mother, who witnessed the scene from an upper window of the hotel, saw him carried off in triumph.

Mrs. Flaxyard was dreadfully shocked when she heard that her daughter's private letter had fallen into Mrs. Shelmerdine's hands, but Tiffany screamed with laughter, and thought it the best joke possible.

"Oh, how I should have liked to see her when she read the letter," she exclaimed.

"I don't think you would," rejoined Bootle. "Neither I

nor the governor found the situation agreeable, I can tell you."

"I'm afraid she'll never forgive you, Tiff," remarked Mrs. Flaxyard.

"Well, I must bear her displeasure as well as I can," said the young lady. "Since I've got my darling boy back again, I don't care for anything else."

Meanwhile, the two old gentlemen remained laughing and talking together. At last Flaxyard took out his watch.

"By Jove!" he exclaimed, "it only wants a quarter to twelve. We mustn't forget our appointment with the lawyers. We must be off to Lincoln's Inn Fields at once."

"A word to the old lady, and I'm with you," replied John.

He disappeared, but presently returned, looking rather blank. Flaxyard, however, made no observation.

The two gentlemen then got into a hansom cab, and drove to Lincoln's Inn Fields.

CHAPTER VI.

FTER a very satisfactory interview with the lawyers, who undertook that no delay should occur on their part, John drove off to Clapham to join the party at luncheon, and Flaxyard proceeded to the City. Arrived at his place of business, he found Myddleton Pomfret waiting for him in his back room.

"I want to have a word with you, Mr. Flaxyard," said Pomfret, "in reference to a gentleman whom I met at your house last evening."

"Mr. Stonehouse! Yes, I understand. I am very sorry I invited him, but I had not the slightest idea there was any risk in doing so. He declares you are no other than Julian Curzon, and that he will prove his assertion."

"In what way can he prove it? None of Julian's relations can be produced. At the time of his disappearance, I don't think he had a single near relative. He was an orphan, left to the care of an uncle, who brought him up, provided for him, and died some years ago, leaving his nephew a considerable sum of money, all of which, I am sorry to say, the careless fellow spent. Julian had plenty of friends, or persons calling themselves friends, but they have long since forgotten him."

"Let me ask you a simple question. Are you able to prove that you are actually Myddleton Pomfret? If so, the point can be disposed of without difficulty."

"I am not required to give any such proof. And I shall certainly not furnish it at the instance of Mr. Stonehouse."

"You do not consider, my dear Sir, that he may place you in such a position that you will be compelled to rebut the charge. Of course, if you can show conclusively that you are the person you represent yourself there will be an end of the matter. But, I repeat, *can* you do this?"

Pomfret made no reply.

"You will believe that I am influenced by the most friendly feelings in giving you this caution," pursued Flaxyard. "I do not ask to be taken into your confidence, though you may place the most perfect reliance on my discretion. But I have an opinion on the matter—and I see danger. Stonehouse can do you personally no harm; but if he can persuade people that you are really Julian Curzon —that the story of your death was fictitious—see what a position your unfortunate wife will be placed in. For her sake—if not for your own—this disclosure must be prevented."

"I could frighten him into silence, but I don't like resorting to that method," said Pomfret.

"There is one way of silencing him," observed Flaxyard. "Convince him that you are not the supposed defunct Julian Curzon. A plan has occurred to me, that, successfully carried out, might mystify him. Are you aware that Mr. Leycester is in town?"

"Sophy's father!" exclaimed Pomfret. "No, I was not aware of it."

"Stonehouse intends calling upon him this afternoon, and has asked me to accompany him."

"Where is Mr. Leycester staying?—at an hotel?"

"No, at No. 80 Upper Baker Street. His daughter Celia is with him. Thus much I learnt from Stonehouse. Now, my notion is that you should see Mr. Leycester beforehand, and prepare him for our visit."

"I don't think the scheme practicable," said Pomfret, after a short consideration. "I could not impose upon Mr. Leycester, and it would be a most painful task to me to enter into explanations with him. Besides, I do not know what effect the disclosures might have upon the poor old gentleman, who, I understand, is in a very infirm state of health, and nearly broken by the last calamity that has befallen him. What will he say when he learns the cruel position in which his unfortunate daughter is placed?"

"Her position may be made still worse if care be not taken," said Flaxyard. "However painful it may be to make the necessary avowal to Mr. Leycester, and however much distressed the poor old gentleman may be by what you will have to tell him, the disclosure must be made. Better anything than that the real facts should come out."

"Well, I will follow your advice. I will see him without delay. Celia, you say, is with him?"

"So Stonehouse informed me. I am glad you have come to this determination. There is no other way of saving one, who I feel—notwithstanding all that has passed —must be still dear to you."

"She *is* still dear to me," exclaimed Pomfret, in broken accents, "and for her sake I will endure this trial."

"Where is the unfortunate lady?" said Flaxyard. "You know that I take a deep interest in her, and will allow me, therefore, to make the inquiry."

"I cannot answer the question," replied Pomfret. "I am wholly unacquainted with her retreat. She has not written to me since her flight from Paris. Possibly she may be still in France, though I should conjecture, from the fact of Celia having returned to her father, that she must be in this country. I told her to address me at my bankers', in case she had any communication to make to me, but I have not heard from her. If I thought she was with her father, I would not hazard a meeting. But no! no! I am quite sure she has not returned to him."

"I am also of that opinion," said Flaxyard. "About the business at once. There is no time to lose. I will take care of Stonehouse."

Warmly thanking the old gentleman, Pomfret left him, and getting into a hansom cab told the driver to make the best of his way to Upper Baker Street.

Not without trepidation did Pomfret knock at the door of the house to which he had been directed. The summons was answered by a female servant, who informed him that

Mr. Leycester was very unwell—suffering from his eyes—and she didn't think he would like to be disturbed, but Miss Leycester was ·within, and would probably see him if he would be good enough to send up his name.

Pomfret complied with the request, and was presently conducted to the drawing-room, where he found Celia. She was alone, and as soon as the servant disappeared, gave vent to her feelings of astonishment and delight on beholding him again. Of course she had been made ac, quainted by Sophy with all the particulars of his strange story ; but prepared as she was, she could scarcely believe that he stood before her.

Pomfret hastened to explain the nature of his errand, and she saw at once how important it was that his incognito should be preserved. And she was of opinion that this might be readily accomplished, so far as Mr. Leycester was concerned.

" Had poor papa the perfect use of his eyes, he could not fail to recognise you, Julian," she said. " But at present he is suffering from a severe attack of opthalmia, and, indeed, has come to town to consult an oculist, so that he will not be able to distinguish your features. I am sure you may safely pass with him for Myddleton Pomfret. Shall I tell him you are here ? "

" Yes. But before you go, one word about Sophy. How is she ?—where is she ? "

" I can give you no information," she replied sadly. " I have heard nothing from her since we parted at Dover."

With this she quitted the room, and shortly afterwards returned with her father, whom she led by the hand.

Mr. Leycester had once been·a tall, fine-looking man, but he now stooped a good deal. Over his eyes he wore a large green shade. Pomfret was very much moved at the sight of him, and advanced to meet him as he entered the room.

" Mr. Pomfret, papa," said Celia.

" Very happy to make your acquaintance, Sir," said Mr. Leycester, warmly grasping the hand which the other extended to him. " Pray be seated, Sir. Set me a chair next Mr. Pomfret, Celia." This being done, he went on; " I am beyond expression indebted to you, Mr. Pomfret, for your unparalleled generosity to my daughter Sophy. It distresses me to allude to her, as you may conceive, but I would not appear wanting to you in gratitude. You were a great friend of poor Julian Curzon, Sir. Poor fellow! I felt his loss very severely—and so must you, Sir, to judge by your noble conduct. I always cite you as a model of friendship."

"You very much overrate what I have done," remarked Pomfret.

"Actions like yours cannot be overrated," said Mr. Leycester. "I am very sorry the condition of my eyes prevents me from distinguishing the features of a gentleman whom I so much esteem, but I can imagine what you are like."

"Indeed, Sir!" exclaimed Pomfret, glancing at Celia.

"Mr. Pomfret is very like poor Julian, papa," observed the cunning young lady.

"Then he is like a very handsome fellow," rejoined Mr. Leycester. "But it is odd you should resemble my ill-fated son-in-law in features, Mr. Pomfret, for your voice is so like poor Julian's that I could almost fancy I was talking to him."

"My resemblance to Julian has given rise to more than one curious incident," remarked Pomfret, with a slight laugh. "At dinner yesterday I met a Mr. Stonehouse, who insisted upon it that I must be Julian come to life again."

"Ah! that's very droll," cried Mr. Leycester, laughing.

"Did you succeed in convincing Mr. Stonehouse of his error!" inquired Celia.

"Scarcely, I think," replied Pomfret. "But it matters very little to me whether I convinced him or not."

"I hope he won't propagate the ridiculous story," remarked Celia. "It is calculated to do a deal of harm."

"In what way, my dear?" said Mr. Leycester. "What possible harm can it do Mr. Pomfret to be thought like his poor friend Julian Curzon?"

"Why, the world is prone to believe strange stories, and the more improbable the story, the more easily will it obtain credit. If Mr. Stonehouse asserts publicly that Mr. Myddleton Pomfret is no other than Julian Curzon, people will be sure to believe him."

"Well, suppose they do. Mr. Pomfret will laugh at them —that's all."

"He may laugh at them, papa. But it will be a serious matter to us. What will people say if they believe that Sophy's first husband was alive when she married again ? "

"Bless me ! that did not occur to me. We must stop such mischievous talk. Such a report would give me the greatest annoyance. Already I have endured affliction . enough on poor Sophy's account," he added, with a groan. "This would be more than I could bear. Ah, Sir, do you recollect Sophy before her marriage with Julian ? "

" I do," faltered the other.

"How beautiful she was, and how greatly she was admired ! She might have made a splendid match, but she wouldn't be advised ——"

"Never mind that, papa," interrupted Celia. "She loved Julian, and of course wouldn't marry any one else."

"More's the pity ! Nothing but calamity has attended her ever since. Julian lost within a month—years of grief, during which she appeared inconsolable. Then a brief season of happiness, for which she was entirely indebted to you, Mr. Pomfret. Then a second marriage, luckless as the first, and a sudden separation from a worthless husband. Can a woman be more unfortunate than Sophy has been ? Twice unlucky in marriage ! And now what would she be if Mr. Stonehouse's notion were correct ! "

"Don't think of that, papa. Mr. Pomfret is here to contradict it."

" I have never seen her since the separation from Captain Musgrave," pursued Mr. Leycester, addressing Pomfret, "for she refuses to return to her family, and won't even acquaint me with her retreat, so that I am unable to write to her. I sometimes think Celia knows where she is, but won't tell me."

"Indeed I don't, papa. Before we parted at Dover, Sophy exacted a promise from me, which, as you know, I have religiously kept, that I would say nothing about her. I would willingly have remained with her if she would have allowed me, but she was resolved to live alone."

"I trust I shall embrace her once more before I die,"

ejaculated Mr. Leycester. "I am sure her separation from Captain Musgrave was occasioned by no fault of her own. I never liked the man, and would not have consented to her marriage with him, had it not been for Celia's representations."

"We were all completely deceived by him," said Celia; "and if I had had the slightest idea —— But let us change the conversation. It can't be very agreeable to Mr. Pomfret."

Making a great effort to control his emotion, which would infallibly have betrayed him to Mr. Leycester if that gentleman could have perused his countenance, Pomfret turned the discourse into another channel, and began to talk about Miss Flaxyard's approaching marriage. In this event, owing to her acquaintance with Tiffany, Celia took the liveliest interest, and wanted to know all about Bootle. They were still occupied with the subject, when a knock was heard at the door. Celia flew to the window and exclaimed:—

"Why, I declare there is Mr. Flaxyard himself getting out of a cab, and another gentleman with him."

"It is Stonehouse," said Pomfret, reconnoitring them through the window. "No doubt he has come to tell you of the discovery he has made," he added to Mr. Leycester.

"I am glad of it," rejoined the old gentleman. "He shall have my opinion as to his sagacity."

"Pray step into papa's room," said Celia to Pomfret. "It will be best that Mr. Stonehouse should not find you here. If necessary, I will summon you."

Pomfret assented, and Celia showed him into a back parlour, and then returned quickly to her father. Next moment the new comers were ushered in by the servant.

After presenting Mr. Flaxyard to her father, who received him with great cordiality, Celia took the old gentleman aside to make inquiries about his family, and especially about Tiffany's approaching nuptials, while Stonehouse seized the opportunity of opening his business.

"I have a very singular circumstance to relate to you, Mr. Leycester," he said, "and I think it right to prepare you for a great surprise. I had the pleasure of dining yesterday

with my old friend Mr. Flaxyard, and among the guests was
a gentleman whom I certainly did not expect to meet."
" Ah, who was it ? " asked Mr. Leycester.
" You shall hear anon. But before proceeding, let me
remind you that I was extremely intimate with your son-in-
law, Julian Curzon."
" I am quite aware of that, Mr. Stonehouse. I fear his
intimacy with you led him to the commission of the rash
act which deprived my daughter of a husband."
" My dear Sir, the rash act, as you call it, was never
committed at all. That's the very point I'm coming to.
What will you say when I tell you that Julian Curzon is still
alive ? "
" Alive, ridiculous ! Is this the great surprise you have
been preparing for me ? "
" I solemnly declare to you that I saw him last night, and
conversed with him. Julian Curzon is no more dead than
you and I are, Mr. Leycester. He is living and flourishing,
and has made a fortune at Madras. He goes by an assumed
name, of course ; but any one who knew him as intimately as
I did, cannot fail to recognise him. You would know him
in an instant. I have thought it right to tell you this, Sir,
that you may take such steps as you may deem proper
under the circumstances. Rest assured he is alive."
" All a mistake, Stonehouse. You met Mr. Myddleton
Pomfret last night."
" Yes, that is the name Julian goes by—but it won't pass
with me."
" But it must pass with you, Stonehouse, since it happens
to be the gentleman's real name. Myddleton Pomfret is
Myddleton Pomfret, and no other. He is no more Julian
Curzon than you are."
" Well, · if he is not Julian, his resemblance to him is
marvellous," said Stonehouse, rather staggered. " Am I to
understand that you know this self-styled Mr. Pomfret ? "
" Yes, we know all about him," interposed Celia, quickly.
" We know who he is and what he is—all his pedigree—
and can satisfy you in every particular. He is one of the
Pomfrets of Burton Constable, in Yorkshire. The Pomfrets
are neighbours of ours in that country. Myddleton is a
younger son, that is why he has gone into business. He

has just been here—in fact he is still in the house—and came purposely to tell us what occurred last evening at Mr. Flaxyard's dinner. He is extremely offended with you, Mr. Stonehouse, and I think with good reason."

" I told Mr. Stonehouse that he was entirely mistaken," remarked Flaxyard. But he wouldn't believe me. Now, perhaps, he's satisfied."

" Not exactly satisfied, but a good deal shaken," said Stonehouse.

At this moment the servant brought in a piece of folded paper, saying, as she delivered it to Celia :—

" From Mr. Pomfret, Miss."

Celia glanced at the note. It contained only a couple of lines, and ran thus :—

" Have you anything further to say to me? I am unable to stay longer.—M. P."

" Tell Mr. Pomfret I'll come to him in a minute," said the young lady. Then turning to Stonehouse, she added, " Did you know poor Julian's handwriting? "

" Perfectly well. I've seen it often enough."

" Is that like it? " she inquired.

" I can't say it is," he rejoined, examining the note.

" All doubts must be removed," said Celia.

And she hurried out of the room, but returned the next minute accompanied by Pomfret, who very haughtily saluted Stonehouse.

" Now, Mr. Stonehouse, what do you say? " cried Celia. " Do you still maintain your opinion ? "

" Look me in the face, Sir," cried Pomfret, sternly ; " and declare before this company whether you really believe me to be Julian Curzon."

" I'm rather puzzled about it," replied the other, uneasily.

" It is lucky for you, Sir, that my poor friend is no more," continued Pomfret. " Had he been living he would have had an account to settle with you. Some documents in my possession prove that your transactions with him were not quite straightforward."

" My dealings with him were all strictly correct, and will bear investigation," interrupted Stonehouse, evidently alarmed.

"I am inclined to think that if Julian were alive, he could and would give you trouble," said Pomfret, with stern significance. "If you doubt what I say, I will show the documents in question to Mr. Flaxyard."

"That is not necessary, Sir," said the gentleman referred to. "I am sure Mr. Stonehouse will not persist in his assertion."

"No, I am ready to admit that I was in error," said Stonehouse. "I now discern a great difference between Mr. Pomfret and my late friend Julian. I beg to apologise for my mistake."

"This is something, but not enough," rejoined Pomfret. "Wherever this erroneous statement has been made, there must be a contradiction. I insist upon that."

"I have said nothing as yet," rejoined Stonehouse. "I came here first, wishing to talk over the matter with Mr. Leycester."

"Lucky for yourself you did," observed that gentleman. "However, I think you have behaved very properly in owning yourself in the wrong."

Stonehouse, who felt himself in a very humiliating position, bowed around, and made his way to the door. Flaxyard followed him, and, while passing Pomfret, observed, with a laugh,—

"That was a very dexterous manœuvre. You have silenced him effectually."

Pomfret did not remain long after the others. He dreaded further conversation with Mr. Leycester.

CHAPTER VII.

THE MARRIAGE AT CLAPHAM.

DARLING BOOTLE now reigned supreme at the Acacias, and was supremely happy. No more jealousy; no more quarrels; constant smiles from Tiffany; lively talk and merry laughter with Hornby; cheerful discourse with the elderly folk; drives to Wimbledon, Richmond, Kew, Hampton Court, in the morning; nice little dinners, and very often a private box at a theatre in the evening.

Tiffany had received a lesson, and profited by it. The Flaxyard family generally being fully sensible of the advantage of the match, did their best to further it. Hornby was assiduous in his attentions to Bootle, and took care that he should experience no further annoyance from Musgrave. Even Hornby's bosom friend, Rufus Trotter, was kept away, lest his presence should prove detrimental. Mr. and Mrs. Flaxyard likewise studied all Bootle's peculiarities, and made an extraordinary fuss of the young man, consulting his tastes upon all points, and bowing to all his opinions.

Meantime, preparations were actively made for the approaching nuptials. The bride's trousseau, on which one of the most fashionable West End modistes was employed, was almost completed. The wedding-day was fixed, and the bridesmaids were chosen. Eva was asked to be one of them, but declined. Her refusal was no great disappointment to Tiffany. She had plenty of young friends, who would be delighted to assist on the occasion, and she selected the prettiest among them. Bootle's best man was Captain Standish, a relation of his own on his mother's side. The captain had been introduced at the Acacias, where everybody found him particularly gentlemanlike and agreeable. Business matters, to which old Flaxyard attended, had likewise been completed. The settlements had only to be signed.

But what about Mrs. Shelmerdine ? What was she doing all this time ? After signifying her strong disapproval of the match, and her firm determination not to countenance it with her presence, she returned to Belfield. There she remained ; but John came up to town again for the express purpose of attending the wedding.

At last the auspicious day arrived.

All Clapham was astir to see the lovely bride drive to church from her father's house. The young couple would have liked to be married at St. George's, or St. James's, or some fashionable church, but they were overruled by Tiff's mamma, who was quite resolved that the marriage should take place at their own church on the Common. The Rev. Mr. Barker must perform the ceremony, and no one else. This was the only point on which Mrs. Flaxyard made a decided stand, and as she was supported by her husband, the young people were compelled to give way. Better be married at Clapham than not be married at all, thought Tiff; and so reconciled herself to the arrangement. Moreover, it was settled that the display should be just as grand as if the marriage had taken place at the most aristocratic church in town. Two new carriages were brought out on the occasion, one of which was presented to the bride by Mr. Shelmerdine. Besides these, there were several other handsome equipages, which, when drawn up in a long line after setting down their occupants, excited the admiration of the beholders. The Common road was quite in commotion. Omnibuses and all other vehicles went slowly past, and a crowd collected in front of the Acacias was with difficulty kept out by the policemen stationed at the gates.

The marriage of old Mr. Flaxyard's daughter, a reputed heiress, and considered the belle of Clapham, had been much discussed among the tradesfolk of that populous suburb, and everybody wanted to see how she was dressed, how she looked, and what sort of person she was about to espouse. Rumour asserted that the fortunate youth who had won the prize was handsome as well as rich. It remained to be seen whether rumour was correct.

At last the carriages were called, and the excitement of the crowd became intense. The omnibuses would not move on despite the shouts of the police, and numerous butchers', bakers', greengrocers', and fishmongers' carts blocked the way. Boys climbed the walls, gazing through the iron railings at the scene taking place at the door, and screaming information to those below. The bridesmaids, we have said, were chosen for their beauty, and, as they all belonged to Clapham, Clapham, as represented by the little boys at the railings and the crowd at the gates, hailed them with shouts. Opinions varied as to the bridegroom. Captain Standish rode with Bootle in a brougham belonging to the latter, and some uncertainty prevailed as to which of the two was the fortunate individual. When it became known that the boyish-looking personage with the blonde mustache was the hero of the day, some foolish people shook their heads, and said Miss Flaxyard had chosen the wrong man.

Bootle's demeanour towards the throng did not improve their opinion of him. Yet Bootle flattered himself he looked remarkably well, and no doubt he was remarkably well got up. However, nobody thought more about him when the bride appeared. Tiffany never looked prettier than she did in her charming bridal attire and veil of Honiton lace. Excitement imparted brilliancy to her complexion and lustre to her eyes, and as she smiled complacently at the crowd, and displayed her pearly teeth, there was a genuine burst of admiration.

A host of little boys and grown-up people ran across the Common to have another look at her. At the church door a scene almost similar to that we have just described took place; only the bridal party could be better seen as they descended from their carriages. Again an audible titter pervaded the throng as Bootle marched slowly towards the church door, and a fresh burst of admiration greeted Tiffany

13

as she alighted from her carriage and was conducted into the sacred edifice.

The church was full, and the presence of so many spectators, instead of agitating the timid bride, inspired her with confidence. She went through the ceremony admirably. Her worthy old father was much affected when he gave her away, but his real feeling was not so effective as her feigned sensibility. John Shelmerdine was completely imposed upon, and thought his son had, indeed, got a treasure. Ah! if he could have read Tiffany's breast! If he could have seen what emotions were really passing within it! If he could have perceived how, under that guise of timidity, she secretly exulted, he would have formed a very different estimate of her character.

The ceremony was over, and Tiffany was now what she had long desired to be, a married woman. She was Mrs. Bootle Shelmerdine. She could not repress her delight. Bootle remarked her triumphant look, and was gratified rather than displeased by it. It seemed perfectly natural to him—perfectly natural to his father—perfectly natural to everybody who witnessed the ceremony, that she should be elated.

There was a splendid wedding-breakfast at the Acacias. But we cannot assist at it, and shall merely mention that the happy pair proceeded to Folkstone, on their way to Paris.

End of the Fourth Book.

BOOK V.

HYLTON CASTLE.

———◆———

CHAPTER I.

THE ARRIVAL AT THE CASTLE.

A MORE picturesque old structure than Hylton Castle cannot be imagined. Standing upon a hill,. the slopes of which are clothed with trees, only the upper part of the ancient edifice, with its mullioned windows, embattled roof, and lofty chimneys, can be discerned from the charming valley that lies at the foot of the eminence. The mansion, however, cannot be approached on this side. The proper entrance will be found at the farther end of the park, nearly two miles off.

But before quitting the valley, through which wanders a lethargic little river, not unknown to fame, and dear to the angler, let us bestow another look on the antique mansion. Not much of it can be seen, as we have intimated, for it is literally buried in trees, and its broad terrace is screened by a row of yew-trees that cast a funereal shade on the walk, and darken the lower windows of the habitation; but a good idea can be gained of the place, and imagination will.

readily complete the picture. Those grand old trees—oak, chestnut, ash, elm, beech—impart a romantic character to the pile, which would be lost if they were removed. The timber, indeed, is magnificent, and constitutes the chief beauty of the picture. Nobler groves cannot be seen than crown the summit of the hill, and extend over the whole of the lordly domain. The mansion, when examined as we propose to do anon, is the mere wreck of its former grandeur, neglected, decaying, desolate; but thus seen, the ravages are hidden that time and neglect have caused. The mighty trees that have grown old with the building, but yet exult in their full strength, stretch their arms lovingly around it, and shield from observation its gloomy terrace, its crumbling walls, its deserted courts, and dilapidated chambers. Shrouded by these contemporaries and friends, it looks haughty as of yore—haughty as when reared by the first Hylton, upwards of three centuries ago.

And what a matchless situation did that proud Hylton choose for his castellated mansion! Heights overlooking a region of almost unequalled beauty—a lovely vale shut in by chalky downs, with a castle and priory in the distance; on the right, a wide expanse of heath, forest, and fertile plain; on the left, and divided only from the eminence by a valley, another hill clothed with mysterious and immemorial groves. Such was the view commanded by Hylton Castle in former days, and the main features of the scene are still unchanged. But the builder of the castle heightened the natural beauty of the spot; converting the forest land into a park, opening glades, and thinning the timber, but carefully preserving all the finest trees—among others, a grove of chestnuts, even in *his* time of great size and age—and planted a long avenue of lime trees in triple rows, which has now not its equal in the kingdom.

Eva was charmed with the old mansion, as she first caught a glimpse of it, while flying past on the railway, which conveyed her to a small station close to the farther end of the park. Nor was she less delighted when, passing through the lodge gates, and entering on the domain, she came at once upon a row of gigantic chestnut trees, with enormous twisted trunks and fantastic branches. None of these remarkable trees were exactly alike—some being so strange in shape that they looked like antediluvian monsters reared on end—but each tree in succession excited her wonder and almost awe. She counted more than fifty of the giants. Who planted those enormous trees? Pomfret, who was in the carriage with her, could not answer the question—could not even guess at their age.

Independently of the fine timber which it disclosed to their view, the drive through the lower part of the park was striking. Immediately beneath, on the left, through breaks in the trees, could be seen the river to which we have alluded— now crossed by an ancient stone bridge with pointed arches —now dammed near picturesque water-mill, so as to form a large pool, while beyond it rose a down, the summit of which was covered with ancient box-trees. Eva was quite enchanted by the beauty of the scene. On whichever side she gazed fresh, points of attraction caught her eye. The slopes and hollows were clad with gorse and ferns, and studded with ancient thorns, and the uplands crested with noble trees.

But the incomparable avenue had yet to be seen. In order fully to enjoy its beauty, Pomfret alighted with his ward, and sent the carriage on by a lower road. On entering the avenue they both stood still, almost in awe. Graceful and majestic trees, springing like slender columns from the ground, and forming a lofty arch overhead, extended in long lines to the brow of the eminence on which stood the ancient mansion, its grey portal being just distinguishable. Marvellous was the beauty of those lime- trees. Lofty, straight, clean-stemmed, vigorous, not a single tree manifested the slightest symptom of decay. As the eye swept along the beautiful and extensive arcade, regular as the aisle of a cathedral, not a single vacancy could be described. The picture was perfect in all its details. Exquisite was the effect of the sunshine on the overarching boughs—delicious the screen they afforded. Not a single ray penetrated through the foliage, and yet there was no gloom. The stillness, though impressive, did not awaken melancholy thoughts. On the contrary, the mind was completely absorbed in admiration of the grace and lightness of the trees.

Such was the impression produced by this glorious

avenue upon Pomfret and his ward as they slowly tracked it, ever and anon pausing to look back.

When they emerged from the avenue, and approached the mansion, evidences of neglect became manifest. The road was grass-grown and almost obliterated. The iron hurdles, which ought to have defended the lawn, were rusty and broken; the lawn itself was ragged, and unconscious of the scythe. The parterres had become a wilderness of weeds. Flowers were choked; shrubs had grown wild; and roses had become little better than briars. The mansion, which at a distance looked so stately and imposing, had a strange deserted look. No guest, it was clear, had lately entered by that porch, the rich decorations of which were encrusted with lichens and moss.

Still, in spite of all this neglect, the aspect of the mansion was exceedingly striking. Quadrangular, solidly constructed of stone, parapeted and embattled, with turrets at the angles, a superb portal in the centre, large projecting bay-windows with stone transoms, the structure presented a grand façade. Unluckily, the turrets and battlements were ruinous, and the noble portal sadly dilapidated.

Though Pomfret and Eva had been prepared for a partially dismantled neglected house, they scarcely expected to find it in such a lamentable condition, and they were contemplating it with some feelings of dismay, when an elderly woman, of very respectable appearance, issued from the portal.

This was Sir Norman's old housekeeper. Mrs. Austin had heard of their arrival from the coachman who had brought them from the station, and now came forth to greet them. Apologising for the state of the place, she explained, as indeed was only too apparent, that it had been greatly neglected, but promised to make them as comfortable as circumstances would permit. She then ushered them into the mansion, and Pomfret expected they would be taken into one of the large rooms with bow-windows, but Mrs. Austin told him that this part of the house was disused, and conducting him and Eva across a court, which did not appear so much neglected as the external part of the mansion, brought them to a suite of apartments, fitted up with old oak furniture. This wing, Mrs. Austin observed, was the only part of the castle that had been occupied of late years. Sir Norman, she said, talked of furnishing the other rooms, and of repairing the place generally, but nothing had been done as yet.

Pomfret now began to take heart, especially when he found that Eva was perfectly satisfied with the place. Later on in the day, when the young lady's own attendant arrived, with other servants, and when general arrangements both for Eva's comfort and his own were made, he became quite reconciled to the house; but he promised his ward that before many weeks had elapsed a transformation should take place in its appearance.

And he fulfilled his promise. In a marvellously short space of time the old place underwent a change; the garden was put in order, and a considerable portion of the interior of the mansion rendered not only habitable, but agreeable. The superintendence of these changes afforded Eva occupation and amusement, and this was what Pomfret desired, for during the greater part of the time he was necessarily absent.

There was a strange interest attached to the old mansion, which perhaps in its palmier days it did not excite. Accompanied by the housekeeper, Eva visited all the deserted rooms. Many of them were noble apartments, with deep bay-windows and richly carved chimney-pieces, but all were dismantled and dilapidated. One entire wing was shut up. All the old furniture had been removed many years ago, Mrs. Austin said, and there was not even a picture left upon the dark oak panels.

After they had inspected all the upper rooms, she asked the young lady if she would like to see the prison-chamber, and, upon being answered in the affirmative, conducted her to a vault of considerable size, the solid stone walls, grated windows, and ponderous door of which seemed to indicate that it might have been used as a strong-room. Were no legends connected with the vault? Tiresome Mrs. Austin could relate none. And the old lady rather destroyed the romance of the place by declaring it would make an excellent beer-cellar, and that she had recommended Sir Langley Hylton to use it for that purpose.

Now was the opportunity for questioning the old housekeeper about the haunted room. Eva seized it.

"Sir Norman told me there is a haunted room," she said. "Show it me, please."

"You have seen it already, Miss," replied Mrs. Austin, after some hesitation.

"Indeed! Is it one of those deserted chambers which we have just visited? I fancied so at the time."

"No, I won't tell you an untruth, Miss; it is not one of those rooms. I would rather you didn't ask me where it is —not that I believe in ghosts or anything of the sort, but you yourself might be frightened."

"I must insist upon knowing," cried Eva. "I don't believe in ghosts any more than you do, so I shan't be alarmed if you tell me that mine is the haunted chamber."

"A very good guess, Miss," replied Mrs. Austin, a smile lighting up her wintry features. "Yours *is* the haunted room. But you needn't trouble yourself about the ghost. Many a night have I slept in that room, and have never seen it. It's the best room in the wing; but you can have another, if you desire it."

"Oh dear no! I am perfectly content with the room. It is charming. But don't say a word to Susan. She is dreadfully timid, and I'm sure she won't sleep in the dressing-room if you tell her about the ghost."

"Don't fear me, Miss," said the austere dame. "I know what ladies'-maids are."

The chamber occupied by Eva, and correctly described by Mrs. Austin as the best bed-room in the house, was spacious, situated at an angle of the edifice, and commanded the lovely valley we have described. The room retained much of its original character; it was wainscoted with oak, and had furniture to correspond. Its most noticeable feature was a massive bedstead, with curiously carved posts, black as ebony from age, and richly embroidered silk curtains, though now, of course, faded and tarnished. Adjoining the chamber, and communicating with it by a side-door, was a small room, in which Susan slept.

Never since she occupied it had Eva heard the slightest sound to occasion alarm. But on the first night after she had obtained this piece of information from Mrs. Austin, she was too much excited to sleep. No spectre, however, appeared—no noise was heard. And after a few more tranquil nights, she forgot all about the ghost.

But though Eva liked the old mansion, neither Susan nor any of the other servants, who had been engaged in town by Pomfret, liked it, and would greatly have preferred a mansion similar to those adorning the neighbouring hills.

Eva had everything to make the country enjoyable—saddle-horses, carriage-horses, a well-appointed barouche, and a pony-carriage, which she herself could drive. In other respects her establishment was complete, and she had Mrs. Austin to manage the servants, and take all trouble off her hands.

With such an establishment, and with all else conducted upon a corresponding scale, a country residence could not fail to be pleasant, even though that residence should be as tumble-down as Hylton Castle. But the dilapidations did not annoy Eva. Half such a large old house was enough for her, and more than half was now habitable. Ample room, and to spare, was there for her household and for her guests, for she had always some of her relatives staying with her, and her aunt, Mrs. Daventry, a very agreeable, well-informed person, had agreed to reside with her for a few months. Thus she was never alone, and she might have had plenty of general society if she had cared for it.

There was one material drawback to her happiness. Hylton Castle was charming, the yew-tree terrace sombre and mysterious, the park delightful, the avenue exquisite, the neighbourhood beautiful, the rides and drives inexhaustible, but the one person whose society she preferred to all other was rarely—far too rarely—with her.

Pomfret was chiefly in town, occupied by business, he said, and only ran down now and then, and never stayed more than a day when he did come. Besides, he was making arrangements to return to Madras, and then she should lose him altogether for a time.

CHAPTER II.

LONG had Pomfret been without any intelligence of Sophy, but calling one day at his banker's to inquire for letters, a bulky packet was delivered to him.

He recognised the handwriting at once, and, hurrying to his hotel, repaired to his own room, fastened the door, and broke open the seals of the packet.

Enclosed was the following letter. It was closely written, in Sophy's beautiful hand, and occupied several sides of paper.

"Perhaps this letter may never meet your eyes, but it will relieve my heart to write it. Mental torture could scarcely be more acute than that which I experienced after my interview with you in the Bois de Boulogne. I felt that I was on the verge of madness. Unavailing regret for the happiness I had for ever lost, horror at my dreadful position, and despair of escape from it, these were the feelings that beset me. Hope I had none. For a time Heaven seemed deaf to my prayers, and denied me the relief rarely refused to the heart-broken.

"A fearful night was that on which I fled from Paris, hoping, but vainly, to leave my cares behind me. The train was crowded, and the carriage in which Celia and I were placed was full. Perhaps this was fortunate, since it compelled me to restrain my emotion. None of those with me, except Celia, could have been aware of the anguish I endured; but they must have thought me unsociable, for I uttered not a word.

" The night was wild and tempestuous, and soon after quitting Amiens a terrible thunderstorm came on, accompanied by vivid lighting, but though usually terrified by a storm of this kind, I felt no terror then. Celia afterwards told me that she was alarmed at the expression of my features, as revealed by the flashes of lightning. I know that I felt fearfully excited, though I did not betray myself by a single exclamation.

" Before we reached Calais the thunderstorm had ceased, but the wind was still violent, and Celia was very unwilling to cross, but I would not remain another hour in France, and of course she went with me. It was an awful passage, but we got safely to Dover, and as Celia, who was utterly prostrated, was unable to proceed farther, we stopped there.

" Next day, the excitement, which had given me false strength, forsook me. I could not leave my bed, and was slightly delirious, but Celia kept careful watch over me. A large and bustling hotel like the Lord Warden is ill suited to a nervous sufferer. I was removed to quiet lodgings, where I was undisturbed, and where I speedily began to recover strength.

" One fear had assailed me during my illness, and increased my nervous irritation. It was the fear lest he who had been guilty of such infamous perfidy towards me should follow me, and find me out. I constantly expected him to appear, and the sound of a footstep filled me with dread. Before leaving Paris I had written to him, forbidding him to come nigh me, but he might not regard my injunctions.

" My alarm, however, was groundless. He came not, and I now do not think he had any intention of following me. Without consulting me, Celia had written to him, requesting him to send to Dover all the wearing apparel and other articles that we had left behind at the Grand Hotel. They were sent without a word.

" Celia was most anxious that I should return to my poor father, but I refused. I could not return to him a second

time—now not a widow, not a wife. I could not explain
my frightful position to him. I could not look him in the
face with such a secret in my breast. I was determined to
live in absolute retirement, among strangers who could
known nothing of my sad story and who neither would shun
me nor condemn me. In such a plan it would be impossible
that Celia could take part. A life of seclusion was unsuited to
her. She would be speedily tired of it. Besides, her
presence would infallibly lead to a discovery, which I was
anxious to avoid.

"It was therefore agreed that Celia should leave me and
return home, and give such explanation as she might deem
proper to my dear father. It was a painful parting with her,
and she tried to make me change my resolution. But I
remained firm. I was left alone.

"I must now pass over a week:
"While seeking a retreat, I chanced upon a pretty little
old-fashioned village, which I will try to describe to you. The
village in question has a large green, such as you rarely meet
with now-a-days, round which quaint old houses are gathered,
intermingled with magnificent elm-trees. At one end of the
green stands a picturesque little inn, with an extraordinary
chimney, a fine porch, a bay-window, and a charming garden.
An artist would fall in love with that little inn.

"Close to the inn is a smithy—also a picture. Nothing
prettier or more peaceful can be conceived than this out-of-
the-way little village. It seems to belong to the middle of
the last century. Not a modern house in it, or near it.
Not one of the habitations would rank above a farm-house
or a cottage, yet many of them have crofts and large apple-
orchards, and all have gardens. The country around is
beautiful. Close at hand there are hills and heights
covered with timber. Large mansions, surrounded by parks,
crown some of these eminences.

"I had never heard of this sequestered little village
before—had never been in this part of the country. Chance,
or some beneficent power that took compassion upon me,
brought me hither. I was going farther—much farther,
indeed—but I at once decided upon remaining here, and
alighting from the vehicle which had brought me from the

railway station, a few miles off, caused my luggage to be taken into the little inn I have described, and went in search of lodgings.

"Thinking I might find some retired cottage, I took a path which led me, through a meadow skirted by enormous oak-trees, to the church—a grey and ancient pile, almost surrounded by trees, with a little avenue of clipped lime-trees conducting to the porch. A churchyard full of rounded hillocks, headstones, and old monuments, showed how many generations were resting there.

"The church door being open, I entered. The interior presented such an aspect as might be expected from an old country church. In partsit bore traces of great antiquity, but many reparations had been made, and not always in the best taste. Still, there were vestiges of the original stained glass in the pointed windows, and some fine brasses in the nave that belonged to the fifteenth century.

"Noticing some monuments in the chancel, I walked down to look at them. Almost all belonged to one family. Amongst them was a little tablet of white marble that fixed my attention. It bore the name of Sophia, and recorded her death at the early age of seventeen. As I read the simple but touching inscription, I envied the fate of the poor girl, who, though cut off like a flower, was perhaps saved from much sorrow.

"'Would I had died at seventeen!' I murmured.

"So engrossed was I by painful thoughts, that I did not remark that an elderly lady had silently approached me, and had overheard the exclamation. On perceiving her, I was about to retire in some confusion, but she stopped me gently, and said, in a low voice:—

"'She was my daughter, and a sweeter creature never blessed a mother. I have never ceased to mourn for her."

"We then quitted the church together, and as we stood outside the porch, she questioned me in the kindest manner possible as to the cause of the exclamation she had overheard.

"I could not enter into particulars, but I told her that I had endured so much unhappiness of late, that I was almost weary of life, and that my own name being Sophia had led me into a train of thought that had given rise to the exclamation.

" Her interest was evidently excited in me, and we had a long conversation together, in the course of which I explained that I was looking out for a quiet retreat, and thought I might find one in the adjoining village. On hearing this, she reflected for a short time, and then said :—

" 'You have inspired me with a strong interest in you, for which I can only account by the circumstances under which we have met. You tell me that your name is the same as that of my lost child, and had she lived she would have been about your age. My house is not far hence. Come and see it. If you like the place, I will ask you to stay with me. The house is quiet and secluded enough to suit any taste.'

" I could not refuse an invitation given with so much kindness. From the moment I beheld her I had been attracted as by a potent mesmeric influence towards Mrs. Carew. I had learned her name from the tablet. I never saw a more pleasing countenance than hers, nor one more strongly indicative of goodness and genuine kindness of heart. Her manner is pleasing, and the tone of her voice delightful. I have no doubt she was once beautiful, for her features are still good, and her eyes fine, but time and sorrow have left their traces.

" As we walked together in the direction of her house, along a charming road skirted by fine trees, and passed several homesteads, each boasting a large apple-orchard, she gave me an outline of her history.

" Mrs. Carew had been a widow for several years. She was the second wife of Mr. Morton Carew, a country gentleman of good property, but whose estates went to his son by a former marriage. She herself has no family. Her daughter, who bore the luckless name of Sophy, died early of consumption.

" Ere long we came in sight of her house, and she had not prepared me in the least for the singular structure that met my view. Nothing more curious and picturesque can be imagined. It is an old house, but in excellent preservation, and the walls, roof, and chimneys—the latter being of immense size—are covered with ivy. But the singularity of the place, and that which constitutes its chief charm in my eyes, is, that it is entirely surrounded by a wide deep moat, and can only be approached by a drawbridge. I have dreamed of such a romantic habitation, but never saw one before. Outside the moat there is a large garden, laid out in the old style, and house and garden are buried in a grove of trees tenanted by rooks.

" Mrs. Carew read my surprise and delight in my looks, and smiling kindly asked me how I liked the old place. I told her I was enchanted with it, but all seemed so strange that I was not quite sure that I was not in a dream.

" As we crossed the drawbridge, I paused for a moment to gaze at the moat, which lost none of its beauty on closer inspection, being supplied with clear water from a brook hard by. Mrs. Carew showed me over her house. None of the rooms are very large, or very lofty, but they are all comfortable, and fitted up with old furniture. One bed-room, with windows looking across the moat upon the garden, particularly took my fancy, and remarking that I was pleased with it, she said :—

" ' This room shall be yours if you like to occupy it. Do not hesitate. I make the offer with all my heart. But I ought to tell you,' she added, and the tears sprang to her eyes and her voice faltered as she spoke, ' that this was my dear Sophy's room. In it she passed the last few months of her brief life, and never quitted it till she was taken to the churchyard we have just visited.' After a pause, she pointed to a few books on a shelf near the fireplace. ' There is her little library. And that is her portrait over the chimney-piece.'

" Glancing in the direction indicated, I beheld the portrait of a beautiful fair-haired girl, whose frame and features bespoke extreme delicacy.

" ' Perhaps you may prefer another chamber,' pursued the kind old lady. ' But despite its melancholy associations, I am fond of this room, and it is close to my own chamber."

" I told her that I liked the room better than any I had seen.

" ' Then take possession of it at once,' she cried. ' Nay, I will have no denial.'

" Need I say that I gratefully accepted the offer. No

time was lost in making me at home in my new abode.
My luggage was brought from the little inn where I had
left it.

" Before leaving Dover, I had taken the precaution of
putting the name of Mrs. Montfort on the trunks, and by
that denomination I am now known. The initials on my
linen could betray nothing. Mrs. Carew's establishment
consists of old and attached servants. They believe me to
be a niece of their mistress, and are perfectly satisfied, for
they are not inquisitive.

" The extreme kindliness of Mrs. Carew's disposition is
manifested in a hundred ways—not merely to me, but to all
with whom she comes in contact. I do not think there can
be a more amiable person. Benevolent almost to a fault,
she seems to live for others rather than for herself. She is
profoundly religious, but hers is a cheerful, hopeful faith.
Without knowing the cause of my sorrow, she affords me
the greatest consolation. I shall never be happy again, but
she has chased away the despair that haunted me.

" Such is the friend I have obtained! such the asylum I
have found! Ought I not to esteem myself fortunate ?
Ought I to repine ?

" Behold me, then, in the little chamber assigned to me
by dear Mrs. Carew ! There is nothing gloomy about the
room, though it has witnessed sad scenes. On the contrary,
it has an air of great cheerfulness. From the window,
which would be darkened by ivy were not the intrusive
leaves carefully trimmed, I enjoy the prettiest prospect
imaginable. Immediately beneath me is the moat ; beyond
it the garden ; and beyond that a grove of splendid trees.
I might be in a convent, shut out from all the world. The
quietude is indescribable. To some people the place might
appear lonely, but to me it is delightful. Mrs. Carew loves
tranquillity, and her servants carry out her wishes. All goes
on regularly and systematically, but there is no bustle, not
the slightest disturbance of any kind.

" We have rarely any visitors, for Mrs. Carew has almost
given up society since her daughter's death, but occasionally
the vicar and his wife dine with her. Both are elderly
people, and both very agreeable. On such occasions I am
allowed to remain in my own room. The calmness I have

described—a calmness almost monastic, as I have stated—has produced a beneficial effect upon me. Allowed to do just what I like, I pass most of my time in reading and meditation, and seldom or ever stray beyond the precincts of the place. On her return from a walk or drive, Mrs. Carew generally finds me in the garden.

" Thus time flows on, and if it will only continue to flow on thus tranquilly, I shall be content. My mode of life is so uniform, that in describing one day I describe all.

" I have not taken up my pen for some days, but an event has just occurred which I must relate.

" Yester-afternoon I was walking in the garden with Mrs. Carew, when a remarkably beautiful girl made her appearance. Old Nathan presented her to his mistress, but he mumbled so that I could not catch the name of the lovely visitor. However, I understood that she had recently come to reside in the neighbourhood, and was now returning a call made upon her by Mrs. Carew. I was greatly struck by the young lady's appearance. Her beauty was not of a common order, and her manner graceful and refined. As she addressed me occasionally, I was forced to join in the conversation. She spoke in raptures of an old mansion which her guardian had taken in the neighbourhood, and pressed me to come with Mrs. Carew to see it.

" Pursuing the conversation, she informed me that she had only recently returned from India, and mentioned that she had been at Madras. My suspicions being then excited, I put some questions to her, though with caution, and soon found out that she was no other than Eva Bracebridge.

" Here, then, was an unlooked-for meeting ! A girl whom I would have shunned—whom I supposed was in India—stood before me.

" Instantaneously I felt a revulsion of feeling towards her. I did not now think her so lovely as I had done previously. I fancied I could detect faults in her which I had not perceived before. I almost forgot myself, and gave impatient answers when she spoke to me. Yet I was wrong to indulge such feelings. Eva Bracebridge is charming—charming alike in person and manner—but I regarded her with a jaundiced eye.   ·

14

"She stayed some time, and during that time I learned much, for she talked a great deal about you, and about circumstances that had occurred at the Beau Rivage at Ouchy, all of which were of the most painful interest to me. During this part of the conversation I was on the rack, but I bore it with firmness. But *you* will understand the effect which these details produced upon me.

"At last, to my inexpressible relief, she took her departure. While bidding adieu, she again pressed me to visit Hylton Castle, which she told me is the name of the place you have taken for her, but I declined.

"This visit quite upset me, but I pleaded sudden indisposition to account to Mrs. Carew for my changed manner, and retired early to rest. The calmness that had surrounded me in my retreat seemed violently disturbed. All my anxieties were revived. I had a sleepless night, and thought over all the occurrences that had been related to me. Nothing distressed and distracted me more than the thought that I should have to flee from this place. Mrs. Carew is so kind to me, and would grieve sorely at my departure. But is it necessary that I should go? Now you know where I am, you can avoid me.

"Some days have elapsed, and Eva Bracebridge has been here again.

"This time she came accompanied by her aunt, Mrs. Daventry, who is staying at Hylton Castle. There is no resisting Eva, she is so extremely amiable and ingenuous, and my unreasonable dislike has vanished. You can read her heart like a book. She has now no secrets from me. I did not seek to learn her secrets, but she would make me her confidante. She spoke to me about you, and told me a great deal more than I choose to repeat. She says you are rarely at Hylton Castle, and are soon about to return to Madras. The thought of losing you for so long a period seems to distress her much, and she says she shall be quite disconsolate when you are gone.

"Poor girl! I pity her from my soul. I offered her the best consolation in my power. Little does she dream that I am the main obstacle to her happiness.

"She spoke of Sir Norman Hylton, and told me *why* she

had refused him. I do not think she will ever marry,—unless—but we cannot penetrate the future. When you go to Madras, I shall probably see a good deal of this charming girl, in whom I begin to take a warm interest. Perhaps we have been brought together in this unaccountable manner for some mysterious purpose.

" Eva sat with me in my little room for several hours, while her aunt partook of luncheon with Mrs. Carew. She seemed as if she could not tear herself away. She evidently wished to know something of my history, but finding it pained me to talk about it, she desisted. I daresay she has many speculations about me, but I trust they are all wide of the truth. I now tremble more than ever lest she should learn who I am. She left me far happier than she found me. At all events, she has succeeded in strongly exciting my sympathies towards her. Heaven grant I may be of some service to her! I would make any sacrifice in my power to ensure her happiness.

" Again I must pass by some uneventful days without notice. I should have little but my own feelings to record. Eva has been here again, and again has passed a few hours *tête-à-tête* with me in my little room. But it is not of her I am now about to speak. A strange and most unpleasant incident has occurred. This place is no longer a secure asylum for me, and I fear I shall be obliged to quit it. But you shall hear what has happened.

" Last night I sat up late, writing this very letter. All the house had been long since at rest, but, feeling no inclination for sleep, I occupied myself as I have mentioned. It was a calm moonlight night, and from time to time I looked out at the exquisite scene before me. A thin gauzy mist hung over the surface of the moat, and partially obscured the shrubs in the garden, but the summits of the larger trees were silvered by the moonbeams. The dreamy beauty of the picture enchanted me. It was like a fairy vision. The drawbridge was scarcely distinguishable through the vapour. I fancied however, that a figure was standing upon it, but, as the person remained motionless, I concluded I must be mistaken.

" After contemplating the ravishing scene I have de-

14—2

cribed for some minutes, I sat down, and again occupied myself with my letter. I was thus employed when I heard a rustling noise among the leaves of the ivy with which, as I have said, the walls of the house are completely covered. Instantly springing up, I flew to the window, which unluckily, I had left open. But before reaching it, I recoiled. A man's head appeared at the casement. I should have shrieked aloud at the sight, but the white moonlight revealed well-known features, and terror struck me dumb.

"He was there—the dreaded, the detested;—he from whom I had striven to hide myself, had found me out. The next moment he had gained the room, and closed the window. I was so paralysed by fright that I could not stir. But he seemed perfectly easy, and said, with a slight laugh, but in a low voice,—

" ' Ivy serves as well as a rope-ladder to gain a fair lady's chamber.'

"Before I could prevent him, he stepped lightly and quickly to the door, fastened it, and took out the key.

" ' Don't make a row, my charmer—you will gain nothing by it,' he said, as he came back, fearing, perhaps, that I was about to alarm the house by my cries. ' Sit down quietly. We must have a little chat together. You will be surprised that I have found you out, after the precautions you have taken, but in reality I had no difficulty. I quickly discovered your lodgings at Dover, and followed you, step by step, to this place.'

" ' What do you want?' I gasped, sinking into the chair to which he pointed. ' Why do you add to the misery you have inflicted upon me by thus invading my retreat?'

" ' Pooh! pooh! I am not come here to annoy you,' he rejoined. ' Had such been my design, I should have knocked at the door, and insisted upon seeing my wife, Mrs. Musgrave. Not wishing to betray you, I have sought admittance in this way. After studying the premises, I found your room accessible by means of that good-natured ivy. Plan instantly adopted. Me voilà ! How very considerate in you to leave the window open !'

"I said nothing, but I bitterly reproached myself with my want of caution.

" 'Allow me to congratulate you upon your quarters,' he remarked, looking complacently round. 'What a charming little room you have got, and how nicely furnished! You could not possibly be more comfortable. And then the old house—how quaint it is, with its ivied walls and chimneys. To-night it looks wonderfully picturesque. I've seen nothing better on the stage. I'm glad they don't think it necessary to raise the drawbridge, or I should have had to swim the moat. Your friend Mrs. Carew, I'm told, is quite as pleasing a piece of antiquity as her house. How on earth did you contrive to make her acquaintance?'

" 'Torment me no more,' I cried; 'or, at all hazards, I will alarm the house. If you have any business with me, state it'

" 'You are in a desperate hurry, my charmer. Consider how long it is since we met,' he rejoined, with the same provoking calmness. 'I suppose you have no particular desire to return to me?'

" 'Return to you! Never!' I exclaimed.

" 'Well, I think you are very well off where you are,' he said. 'Your reluctance to leave old Madam Carew is natural. I won't disturb you, provided we can come to an understanding.'

" 'To what kind of understanding?' I asked. 'What do your require?"

" 'Money—money, my charmer—that's the burden of my song. After you so cruelly deserted me, I sought distraction in play, and lost heavily at Baden-Baden. I'm hard up. I am sure you have money, and equally sure you can get more if you require it.'

" I felt so indignant, that I was determined to refuse him, and I suppose he divined my attention from my looks, for he hastened to add, in an altered tone :—

" 'Refuse—and you shall see me to-morrow under a very different aspect.'

" At his sudden change of aspect, my courage quite forsook me, and gave place to abject terror.

" 'I will give you all I possess,' I said, 'if you will go instantly, and promise sacredly never to molest me again.'

" 'How much have you got?' he inquired,

"'A few hundreds. I don't exactly know how much. But you shall have all.'

"'Ah! now you are reasonable. If I have good luck on the turf, or in any other way, I will repay you.'

"'Never come near me again. That is all I ask. It will be useless to repeat the visit. You now deprive me of all my resources."

"I unlocked a drawer, and taking out a little pocket-book containing the greater part of the money which you sent me through Mr. Flaxyard, gave it to him. I know that I ought not to have done this, but I could not help it. I was so terrified, that I wished to get rid of him at any price.

"'Bien obligé, ma belle,' he said securing the pocket-book. 'Voici le clef de la porte. Maintenant pour l'échelle de lierre. Adieu, pour toujours!'

"Opening the window noiselessly, he passed out. He accomplished his descent quickly and carefully, and, hurrying towards the drawbridge, almost instantly dis-appeared.

"I remember nothing more distinctly, but when I awoke next morning, I thought I must have had a hideous dream. The truth soon dawned upon me, and all my terrors returned.

"How shall I act? Shall I disclose what has occurred to dear kind Mrs. Carew? Shall I tell her all my sad story? I feel sure of her sympathy. But no—I cannot do this without betraying your secret. I cannot fly from the place —I cannot seek another asylum—all my resources are gone."

Mingled emotions agitated Pomfret during the perusal of this letter—sympathy, surprise, indignation, exciting him by turns. That Sophy should have accidentally found an asylum near Hylton Castle, and have formed an ac-quaintance with Eva, filled him with astonishment and perplexity. But when he learnt that the unhappy fugitive's retreat had been discovered by her betrayer—when the base motives that had incited Musgrave to the quest were revealed to him—he became fearfully incensed. Conduct so infamous could not be tolerated, and he determined at any cost to call the villain to immediate account. But how could redress be obtained? Musgrave would laugh at any threats of exposure. But poor Sophy must not be left without resources. At the same time she must be guarded against further plunder. Pomfret was long occupied in considering how this could be effected.

That night he left town for Hylton Castle.

CHAPTER III.

AN ACCIDENT.

NEXT morning, after breakfast, he walked out on the terrace with Eva, and at once brought up the subject of Mrs. Montfort.

"I have heard that the poor lady is in great distress," he said. "I mean to assist her, but it must be through you."

"I do not know that she requires aid," replied Eva. "I have no idea that her distress arises from pecuniary misfortunes."

"I will tell you what has happened to her," he rejoined. "She has been stripped of her all by a worthless husband. Imagine the distress of a lady under such painful and humiliating circumstances. And there are frightful complications in her case that prevent her from seeking assistance from her own relations."

"A light suddenly breaks upon me!" exclaimed Eva. "I think I know who is her husband. I did not intend to mention the circumstance to you, feeling sure it would annoy you, but about a week ago, as I was driving through the pretty village near which Mrs. Carew resides, I saw Captain Musgrave. He was standing at the door of a little inn, and as soon as he perceived me hurried into the house. But I am certain it was he. And now I feel convinced that this poor lady of whom we have been speaking is his unfortunate wife. The strange and inexplicable interest I felt in her is accounted for. I now understand why she exhibited such aversion when I spoke of Captain Musgrave—and why her colour changed when I spoke of you. The so-called Mrs. Montfort is no other than Mrs. Musgrave. I am sure I have divined the truth."

"You have. It is the unfortunate lady you suppose. Since her flight from her unprincipled husband, she had found a safe asylum, as she believed, with good Mrs. Carew, who, I must warn you, is totally unacquainted with her history. Unluckily, Musgrave discovered her retreat, and, managing to obtain a secret interview with her, forced her to give up all her funds. She is now without resources."

"But not without friends," cried Eva. "I will help her."

"Assistance must be given with caution, or she will again become a prey to her infamous husband."

"Cannot she be freed from his toils?"

"I see not how her deliverance can be accomplished. But let her find a friend in you."

"She shall," cried Eva, earnestly.

At this juncture, a man-servant appeared on the terrace bearing a note, which he delivered to the young lady; stating, at the same time, that the messenger waited for an answer.

Eva glanced at the note, and then, without a word, handed it to Pomfret, who turned pale as he perused it.

"DEAR MISS BRACEBRIDGE,—If Mr. Pomfret should have returned, pray tell him that I have something important to communicate to him, if he will kindly favour me with a call this morning. You may think this a strange request, but I trust Mr. Pomfret will comply with it, if it should be in his power to do so.

"Yours sincerely,
"SOPHIE M."

"What shall I do?" he said, consulting Eva with a look,

"Go, of course," she replied. "Say that Mr. Pomfret will come," she added to the servant.

"And tell Bilton to bring round · the horses," said Pomfret.

Charged with these messages, the footman returned to the house.

"I could not refuse this summons," said Pomfret, in a sombre voice. "But it shall be my last interview with her."

"Why the last?" she inquired.

"Do not ask me to explain," he rejoined. "Enough that I dread the meeting, and would avoid it were it possible. Hereafter you must take my place."

Half an hour later the horses were brought to the door. Mounted on a splendid bay horse, almost thorough-bred, and full of fire and spirit, and followed by a groom also very well mounted, Pomfret rode slowly down the lime-tree avenue, and when he had gained its extremity he indulged his horse with a gallop across the park. Under other circumstances, he would have enjoyed the ride, but he was too much occupied by his own sombre thoughts to heed the beauty of the landscape.

On reaching Mrs. Carew's picturesque residence, he was about to alight, when his horse started, dashed through the open gate, clattered across the drawbridge, and then stumbling, threw his rider at the very threshold of the house. Sophy, who witnessed the accident from her window, uttered a piercing shriek.

At first it was thought by old Nathan and the gardener, who, alarmed by the noise of the fall and by Sophy's screams, rushed to the spot, that the unfortunate gentleman was killed outright, since he did not move; but this supposition was contradicted by the groan that burst from him when an attempt was made to raise him. Whether his skull was fractured the men could not, of course, decide, but it was clear that he had sustained very severe injuries, since his head had come into violent contact with the post of the drawbridge. The horse was uninjured, and after dashing back over the drawbridge, was caught by the groom. Poor Sophy was in such a state of distraction that she could give no directions, and, indeed, could scarcely command herself;

but Mrs. Carew fortunately did not lose her presence of mind, but enjoining the servants to bring the unfortunate gentleman into the house, sent the groom in quest of a surgeon.

As the old lady's directions were obeyed, and Pomfret was carefully raised from the spot where he had fallen, and carried into a room on the ground floor, where there was a bed on which he was laid, a very painful scene occurred. Sophy, who had witnessed the proceeding with indescribable horror, crept after the men into the room, and when they withdrew, flung herself on her knees beside the bed, and gave way to frenzied exclamations of despair, anguish, and self-reproach, which, had they been intelligible, must have betrayed the innermost secrets of her heart. But though her language was wild and incoherent, Mrs. Carew easily gathered enough from it to learn that deep attachment to Pomfret was the cause of her distress; and apprehensive lest the servants should make the same discovery, she closed the door, and strove to calm the distracted lady.

Shortly afterwards the surgeon made his appearance, and yielding to Mrs. Carew's earnest entreaties, Sophy withdrew to her own chamber, and promised to remain there till the old lady should come to her and bring her the surgeon's opinion. Sophy passed the time in prayer, and was still on her knees when a tap was heard at the door. Mrs. Carew's looks reassured her.

" I bring you good news, my dear," said the old lady. " Mr. Pomfret will recover. He is very much hurt, but there is no serious injury. At the same time, Mr. Southwood says that it will not be safe to move him—at least, for some days—so of course he will remain here, where he can have every attention. I have despatched the groom with a note to Miss Bracebridge, acquainting her with the surgeon's opinion, and telling her that all possible care shall be taken of her guardian, and everything done that can conduce to his speedy recovery. There seems a fatality in this accident."

" If you knew all, you would indeed think so," rejoined Sophy, with a shudder. " Many strange things have happened to me, but the strangest of all is, perhaps, this last occurrence."

"Let us hope that it may lead to good," said kind-hearted Mrs. Carew. "Indeed, I believe that in the end it will be conducive in some way to your happiness. Without wishing to penetrate your secrets, and without seeking for any information beyond what you may desire to impart, I may say that I am certain, from some expressions which you let fall just now, that you take the deepest interest in Mr. Pomfret."

"It is true," she rejoined. "Had this accident proved fatal, I could not have survived it. But I neither hope nor expect that the feelings that he once entertained for me can be revived."

"There is no saying. It cannot be denied that you are brought together in a most mysterious manner, and it will surprise me very much if a reconciliation should not ensue. You must not shrink from the task before you. You may have to go through a painful ordeal, but I retain my opinion that all will come right in the end. But let us go down-stairs, and ascertain how he is going on."

Notwithstanding Mr. Southwood's favourable prognostications, Pomfret had a hard struggle for life, and for several days even the surgeon despaired of his recovery.

During the access of the fever which came on, he talked so wildly, ,that Sophy, fearing he might betray himself, remained constantly with him, hovering about his couch like a ministering angel. She soothed him by all means in her power during his delirium, and though he could give no distinct expression to his thoughts, he seemed to be conscious of her presence.

So far as Sophy could gather, various scenes of his troubled existence passed confusedly before him, but his disordered brain could not fix them. Her own name was constantly on his lips. Sometimes he spoke of her with passionate tenderness, that recalled their brief season of happiness, and touched her to the heart. Sometimes he spoke of her with a fierceness of indignation that showed how terribly his feelings had been outraged. At other times he mourned her as dead.

It is almost needless to say how acutely Sophy suffered while listening to these ravings. They convinced her of his undying love, but the conviction only sharpened her anguish,

As the.fever abated, apprehensions of a different kind began to assail Sophy. What would he say when he recognised her? Should she leave him? No, she could not abandon her post now. Be the consequences what they might, she would remain near him.

After several nights and days of restlessness, during which his brain had been in a ceaseless turmoil, he enjoyed a few hours of placid slumber, and when he awoke, his eyes rested upon the gentle watcher near his couch. She neither spoke nor stirred, and he gazed at her long and earnestly, as if he beheld a vision which he thought would disappear. At last, he murmured her name, but not in accents of displeasure, and she rose and went nearer to him.

"Yes, I am here," she said. "Can I give you anything?"

"Where am I?" he inquired, trying to regain his faculties. "What has happened?"

"You have been ill—very ill," she replied. "But al danger is now over."

"Raise me a little," he said.

But as she endeavoured to obey him, the pain caused by the movement was so great that he sank back with a groan.

"You have had a severe accident—a fall from a horse," she remarked, in answer to his inquiring looks.

"How long ago?" he asked. "I can recollect nothing about it. Where am I?"

She answered his questions briefly, and then motioning him to be silent, sat down again.

CHAPTER IV.

PROGRESS TOWARDS RECOVERY.

N obedience to Sophy's injunctions, Pomfret remained for some time silent. He then made an effort to raise himself, and fixed his eyes inquiringly upon her.

"I now remember what brought me here," he said. "You had sent for me. You had some communication to make to me. What is it?"

"Do not trouble yourself about me," she replied. "Let your first thoughts be directed to Heaven, for the merciful preservation of your life."

"It might have been a greater mercy if Heaven had taken me," he rejoined. "I have no desire to live."

"Oh, say not so!" she cried. "Much happiness may yet be in store for you. Brighter days, I cannot doubt, will soon dawn upon you. Can you forgive me for causing you this accident? It was in compliance with my request that you came here—to meet this dreadful disaster, which might have proved fatal."

"I have nothing to forgive you," he replied. "On the contrary, I ought to feel deep gratitude, since no doubt I owe my life to your watchfulness. I now begin to comprehend who it is that has been constantly near my couch. But tell me," he added, after a pause, "why you sent for me? What are your plans? Do not fear agitating me. I shall suffer more from my own thoughts than from anything you can say."

"I have no plans," she replied. "All my notions have been scattered by the accident that has befallen you, and I have not yet been able to collect them again."

"But in your note to Eva you said you had an important communication to make to me. What is it?"

"I would rather defer the explanation till you are better able to listen to it. I may be the means of causing you further mischief."

"Speak! You will do me no harm."

"I shall stop instantly, if I perceive any excitement. My object in sending for you was to consult you before taking another decisive step. But my position is now worse than it was, and explanation to Mrs. Carew is unavoidable. When you were brought into the house, dangerously injured, I quite lost my presence of mind, and gave utterance to expressions that betrayed the state of my feelings in regard to you. Mrs. Carew believes you to be my husband—she supposes we have been separated—but she is utterly unacquainted with my real history. She must now know all. She must know exactly how I am circumstanced."

"Tell her all. I authorise you to do so."

"Oh! thank you for the permission. However she may act in regard to me, you may be sure she will keep your secret inviolate. It may be, when she learns how I am situated, that she will no longer think it right to offer me an asylum. In that case I must go."

"Do not take any step till I am able to counsel you and assist you. As yet, I do not feel equal to the effort. But you have not spoken to me of Eva. Has she been here?"

"No. I have written to her fully. She knows who I am."

He alarmed her, and she again enjoined silence.

He had just got composed when the door was gently opened, and the surgeon came in, followed by Mrs. Carew. As Mr. Southwood approached the bed, Sophy whispered to him,—

"He is better—much better."

The surgeon proceeded to feel the patient's pulse.

"Yes, a great improvement has taken place since yesterday," he said. "The fever is quite gone. You will do

now, my dear Sir," he added, in a cheerful voice to Pomfret.
" You will soon be out of my hands."

Mrs. Carew, who was standing near, uttered an exclamation of satisfaction which attracted the patient's attention.

" Is not that Mrs. Carew ? " he inquired.

Mr. Southwood replied in the affirmative, adding, in a low
voice,—

" The good lady has been unremitting in her attentions to
you since your accident."

" I am quite aware of it," replied Pomfret.   " Pray accept
my heartfelt thanks for the extraordinary kindness you have
shown me, Madam," he added to her—" kindness which I
shall never forget."

" Your gratitude is not due to me," she rejoined, " but to
the lady who has nursed you.   If any one has preserved
your life, it is Mrs. Montfort."

" Yes, I don't know what we should have done without
her," observed the surgeon.   " Mrs. Montfort has been a
most excellent nurse."

" Say no more, if you please, Sir," interposed Sophy.
" Mr. Pomfret has already expressed his gratitude to me."

Pomfret again addressed himself to Mrs. Carew.

" If you decline to accept my thanks, Madam," he said,
" you must allow me, at least, to express my concern for
the inconvenience to which I have put you.   A wounded
man is a great trouble in a house."

" You have been no trouble to me, I can assure you, Sir,"
she replied.   " My only anxiety has been for your recovery.
You must not think of leaving me till you are quite well."

" What do you say, Sir ? " inquired Pomfret of the
surgeon.   " I fancy I am strong enough to be moved to
Hylton Castle to-day."

Mr. Southwood shook his head.

" You are not so strong as you imagine, my dear Sir,"
he replied.   " I hope shortly to authorise your removal.
Meantime, you must keep quiet.   You cannot be better off
than here."

Signing to the ladies to follow him, he then left the room.

" Mr. Pomfret has talked rather too much, and is somewhat over-excited," he observed to Sophy, as they gained
the passage.   " He will be best left alone awhile."

"Is there still any danger?" she inquired, anxiously.

"None whatever. He is doing as well as possible. In a few days I shall be able to send him home perfectly cured."

From that day Pomfret gradually but slowly mended. His recovery would have been more rapid, but he missed Sophy's attendance at his couch. She came near him no more.

He learnt from old Nathan, the butler, who supplied her place, that she was not well, and confined to her room.

He did not even see Mrs. Carew, and this circumstance added to his uneasiness.

CHAPTER V.

HE groom who brought intelligence of the accident to Hylton Castle, said that he believed his master was killed, or, at all events, so seriously injured that he could not survive many hours.

On receiving this alarming news, Eva fainted away, and continued in such a nervous excitable state for some time afterwards, that neither her aunt nor Mrs. Austin liked to leave her for a moment.

Very little improvement took place in her condition until Mr. Southwood himself came to inform her that the dangerous crisis was past, and that Mr. Pomfret would recover. Her nervous excitement then subsided. The surgeon had assured her that his patient was most carefully nursed by Mrs. Montfort, and was doing as well as could be expected. Though rejoicing that her guardian was so well tended, Eva could not repress a slight feeling of jealousy that another should occupy the place which she would have given worlds to fill.

A long explanatory letter, which she subsequently received from Sophy, cause a complete revulsion of feeling, and satisfied her that her guardian ought to be left entirely to the care of that devoted lady.

Thenceforward, she was content with the surgeon's daily report, and with the frequent messages which she received from Mrs. Carew.

During this trying time, her walks were restricted in the park, which was now in its full autumnal beauty. Beneath the gigantic chestnuts the yellow leaves lay thick, and the long glades were carpeted in like manner. The red leaves of the beeches contrasted with the embrowned tints of the oaks, the bright gold of the chestnuts, and the paler yellow of the limes. Fresh contrasts were offered between the russet hue of the fern clothing the sides of the hill and the lively green of gorse. Perhaps the avenue had been robbed of some of its beauty by the loss of a portion of its delicate foliage, but if the leaves were gone, the exquisite tracery of the overarching branches was fully displayed.

One morning, after a lengthened stroll in the park, Eva and her aunt were returning homewards through the avenue, when a sound arrested their attention, and looking back, they descried a horseman riding in the direction of the mansion. On seeing them he quickened his pace, and Eva soon perceived, to her great surprise, that it was Sir Norman Hylton.

In another moment the young baronet came up. Instantly dismounting, he explained to Eva that he was staying in the neighbourhood with his friend Lord Huntercombe, and having accidentally learnt that very morning, to his great regret, that Mr. Myddleton Pomfret had met with a serious accident, he had ridden over to inquire after him.

Eva was able to give him the very satisfactory assurance that his friend was recovering rapidly—indeed, was almost well.

She then introduced him to her aunt, and felt constrained to invite him to enter the house.

The party then moved on in that direction, Sir Norman leading his horse, and conversing with Eva as he walked by her side.

" I hear you have done a great deal to the old place," he remarked, "and I am sure much was needed to render it habitable. There was a sort of understanding that I should not come here during your stay, but my anxiety about Pomfret must plead my excuse for breaking the compact. If I had not chanced upon you, I should merely have made inquiries at the door."

" Your old housekeeper would never have forgiven my

15—2

niece if you had done so, Sir Norman," observed Mrs. Daventry. "She is constantly wishing you could see the place."

"I hope you like it," he rejoined, smiling. "I am very proud of this avenue. I believe it to be the finest in England. But all the timber in the park looks to advantage just now, with the autumn tints upon the leaves. Don't you think so?"

"I am enchanted both with the park and the castle," replied Eva. "I was perfectly happy here till this disaster befel my guardian."

"Mr. Pomfret's accident was a great shock to my niece, Sir Norman," remarked Mrs. Daventry.

"It must have been," he rejoined. "Miss Bracebridge is not looking quite so blooming as when I last saw her in Switzerland. But the roses will soon return, I make no doubt."

They seemed to return at once, for Eva's pale cheek flushed at the observation.

They were now approaching the mansion, and as Sir Norman gazed around, he acknowledged that a wonderful improvement had been made in the place. Perceiving a man at work in the garden, he gave his horse to him, and entered the house with the ladies.

CHAPTER VI.

GREAT was Mrs. Austin's delight on beholding her young master, and he appeared equally well pleased to see the good old dame, and shook hands with her very cordially. Eva then desired the old housekeeper to take Sir Norman over the house, adding, that by the time he had completed the survey, luncheon would be served.

Needless to say that the young baronet would much rather have stayed with Eva. However, he resigned himself to the old housekeeper, and commenced an inspection of the place.

While looking over one of the lower rooms, and showing him what had been done, Mrs. Austin, who had been accustomed to make free with him when he was younger, began to descant on Eva's amiability and beauty, and found the young baronet a very willing listener.

"Ah! Sir Norman, I wish you would cast your eyes in this direction," she cried. "Miss Bracebridge has everything to recommend her. Of her beauty I need say nothing, and she must be rich, for you see what an establishment she keeps up. I say *she* keeps up, for Mr. Pomfret takes good care to let the servants understand that she is their mistress. Now, Sir Norman, with all these recommendations, don't you think she would suit you?"

"Most certainly she would, Austin," he replied, with a forced laugh. "Unluckily, her affections are otherwise engaged."

"I think you must be mistaken. Ever since she has been here I have not seen a single suitor, or heard of one; nor has her maid Susan—and we've had a little confidential chat on the subject."

"And you have both come to the conclusion that Miss Bracebridge has no attachment, eh?"

"Well, I can't say that exactly, Sir Norman. Susan will have it that the young lady is in love with her guardian, but I'm sure she's wrong."

"Susan is more quick-sighted than you, Austin," said Sir Norman gravely. "Sit down for a moment," he added, flinging himself into a chair. "I want to have a little confidential chat with you, myself. So Susan thinks Miss Bracebridge is in love with her guardian, eh?"

"I can't see it, Sir Norman," rejoined the housekeeper, taking a seat as requested. "But if it is so—as I very much doubt—her affection is not reciprocated. Mr. Pomfret is a very handsome gentleman, and likely enough to win a young lady's affections if he were inclined, but his manner towards his ward is quite that of a father. Susan herself has made the same remark. You needn't fear him. He has no idea of marrying his ward. He is very seldom here, and leaves the management of the house entirely to Miss Bracebridge and to me."

"She must have been greatly shocked by the accident that has befallen him?" remarked Sir Norman. "She still looks ill."

"Yes, we heard that the poor gentleman was so dangerously hurt that he couldn't survive, and the shock was too much for her. Poor dear young lady! she took on sadly. If her guardian had been really killed, I believe she would have died."

"What does that prove, Austin?"

"That she loves him like a daughter."

"Not exactly. Has she seen him since the accident?"

"No. Circumstances have prevented her. She prefers keeping away from the house."

"Indeed!" exclaimed Sir Norman, surprised. "Why?"

"I can't tell you," she replied. Though she looked as if she could.

He then desired her to give him full particulars of the

accident, and listened to what she told him with deep interest. He was well acquainted with Mrs. Carew, but had never heard of Mrs. Montfort. The old housekeeper, however, could give him no information respecting the latter.

The questions he asked about Eva, combined with his manner, convinced Mrs. Austin that he was greatly interested in the young lady.

"I am quite sure you need not despair of winning Miss Bracebridge's hand, Sir Norman," she said.

"Shall I let you into a secret, Austin?" he rejoined. "I know I can trust you. I have been refused already. And the cause of my refusal, I ascertained beyond a doubt, was that Miss Bracebridge is attached to her guardian."

"When did this occur, Sir Norman, may I venture to ask?" she inquired.

"When I was in Switzerland—only six weeks ago," he replied. "So you see my case is hopeless."

"I don't think so," she returned. "I advise you to renew your suit. You have a much better chance now. Possibly, Miss Bracebridge may have been secretly attached to her guardian at that time. I won't pretend to say. But of this I am certain, she had no encouragement from him. He is far too honourable to have deceived her."

"What on earth do you mean, Austin?"

"I can't explain myself more clearly. Whatever Miss Bracebridge's sentiments towards her guardian may have been at that time, they have changed since."

"Are you quite certain of what you state?"

"Quite certain. Since Mr. Pomfret's accident she has made a discovery that must have completely extinguished any foolish notions she may have entertained. I call them 'foolish notions,' because, as I have just said, she could never have had the slightest encouragement from Mr. Pomfret. You must not ask me to give you any further explanation. But circumstances have come to my know-that enable me to declare positively that Miss Bracebridge can never think of Mr. Pomfret as a husband. If your supposition, therefore, is correct, and he is the person who stood in your way, you need have no fear."

"You amaze me!" cried Sir Norman, unable to conceal his satisfaction. "I fancy I understand the discovery that

Eva has made.   No doubt her sentiments have undergone a complete change.   You have indeed revived my hopes."

"You must act with caution, and on no account allow Miss Bracebridge to suspect that you have obtained any information from me.   I am betraying no confidence, but still ——"

" Fear no imprudence on my part, Austin," he interrupted, joyfully.   " When I came here I had not a hope, but I now feel sanguine of success.   You can serve me most materially in the matter."

"You know that you can calculate on me, Sir Norman ; and I hope I may be instrumental in obtaining you a charming wife.   You have certainly come at the right moment."

"Yes, I begin to think that this time fate will befriend me," he cried.

Here their conference was interrupted by the entrance of a servant, who came to inform Sir Norman that luncheon was served.

The young baronet immediately arose, and with a significant look at Mrs. Austin, proceeded to the dining-room, where he found Eva and her aunt.

CHAPTER VII.

MRS. DAVENTRY'S ADVICE TO HER NIECE.

WHILE Sir Norman was occupied with the old house-keeper, as described in the foregoing chapter, Mrs. Daventry was sounding his praises to her niece.

"I was not prepared to find him so agreeable as he turns out," remarked the elder lady. "As I looked at him just now, when he joined us in the avenue, and thought of his gallant conduct in your behalf, I could not help wondering how you could possibly have refused so very handsome a man."

"I refused him simply because I did not like him well enough to accept him, aunt. I admit that he is very hand-some, remarkably well bred, spirited, agreeable—even clever —but I can never think of him as a husband."

"Well, my dear, I can only express my surprise. But perhaps you may now change your mind. Unless I am very much mistaken, he still cherishes a regard for you."

"If I thought so, aunt, I would not see him again, but leave you to entertain him at luncheon. There is no like-lihood whatever that my sentiments towards him will undergo a change, and that he perfectly understands."

"But it is impossible you can dislike him, my love."

"I don't say that I dislike him, aunt. I am simply indifferent to him. But please don't tease me any more about him, or I shall positively carry out my threat, and not appear at luncheon."

"You will never do so rude a thing as that, my dear. If Sir Norman has not been able entirely to conquer his passion for you, as I think is pretty evident, you ought to feel pity for him, not anger."

"He has no business to come here at all," said Eva, affecting a displeasure which she really did not feel. "He has done so contrary to his promise made at the Beau-Rivage, when he distinctly said that he wouldn't come near the house while we occupied it, unless invited. He knew very well that he would never be invited."

"He came to inquire after Mr. Pomfret, my love, and for no other reason, as he expressly stated. I am convinced there was no design of intrusion on his part. The tell-tale blood mounted to his cheek and proclaimed the state of his heart when he first spoke to you, but I am sure he did not utter a word of which you can justly complain. Really, he is such a charming man, that I wish I could prevail upon you to look upon him more kindly."

"My dear aunt, you are more pertinacious than Mr. Pomfret, who pleaded Sir Norman's cause so warmly."

"Did Mr. Pomfret plead his cause?" inquired Mrs. Daventry, rather surprised.

"To be sure. I thought you understood that. Mr. Pomfret was most anxious to make up the match. He gave me no peace during the whole time we were at the Beau-Rivage, but was perpetually dinning Sir Norman's praises into my ear."

"And why didn't you listen to what your guardian said, my love? He gave you excellent advice. Any one having your welfare really at heart would have given you similar counsel. Now that I have seen Sir Norman, I think it a thousand pities you should have rejected him. But it is not too late to retrieve the error. Very little encouragement on your part will bring him round again."

Eva shook her head, as much as to say she couldn't do it. "Can you find any fault with him?" pursued Mrs. Daventry. "Is he not young, spirited, handsome, distinguished-looking? Is he not of a good old family? Has he not a title? Is he not owner of the very mansion in which you are residing, and which you like so much? Do not the noble domains which we view from these windows belong to him? In a word, has he not a hundred recommendations, and not a single drawback, that I can perceive?"

"All this is very true, aunt. Sir Norman is unexceptionable. But I don't care for him."

"But you *will* care for him. Give him a chance of winning your affections. But if you behave coldly to him now, you will chill him effectually, and he may retire altogether."

"I hope he has retired, aunt."

"Now be a good girl, and do as I tell you. You may have had reasons for your former refusal of him, which don't exist now."

"What do you mean, aunt?" cried Eva, turning crimson.

"Nay, I really meant nothing particular, my dear. I want you to consider well before you entirely throw away this charming young baronet. I should dearly like to see you Lady Hylton."

CHAPTER VIII.

T was quite evident, from the young baronet's manner during luncheon, that the fire which had been smouldering in his bosom was called into fresh activity. Without loss of time, and to the great delight of Mrs. Daventry, who proved a most useful auxiliary, he began to lay siege to Eva. Though twice repulsed before and with serious loss, he thought—now that the most important obstacle was removed—that he should succeed in storming the citadel. It was impossible, however, as he soon discovered, to take it by a coup de main.

Whether Eva was really influenced by her aunt's counsel while feigning not to heed it, or whether Sir Norman had at last seized a more favourable moment than had hitherto been presented to him, he certainly did not meet with a decided rebuff. The young lady listened to him with more interest than she had ever previously manifested, and whenever a word could be advantageously thrown in, Mrs. Daventry supplied it. The enamoured young baronet took care to make the idol of his affections understand that she had been the cause of bringing him back to England.

"When you left the Beau-Rivage," he said, "the place appeared so dull that I could not remain there. So, as soon as I was able to travel, I moved off to Paris. There I found lots of acquaintances, and all sorts of distraction, and tried desperately hard to conquer the ennui that had taken possesion of me, but in vain. I got tired of the boulevards, tired of the Bois, tired of the cafés, tired of the theatres, tired of my friends, tired of myself."

"You must have been in a desperate plight, Sir Norman," remarked Mrs. Daventry. "I wonder you are here to tell the tale."

"Yes, it is a marvel that I was not found in the Morgue. I had serious thoughts of throwing myself into the Seine. Finding Paris do me no good—indeed it made me worse, for such noisy gaiety was intolerable in my then frame of mind—I considered where I should go next: to Vienna, St. Petersburg, Madrid, or Seville? Unable to decide, in a fit of despair I hurried off to London."

"A change for the better, I hope?" remarked Mrs. Daventry.

"I didn't find it so, and was just on the point of starting for Scotland, when I got a letter from Huntercombe, asking me to come down to his place for a week's shooting. For certain reasons, this suited me better than Scotland, and I accepted the invitation. I found the house full of company. Huntercombe's preserves are famously stocked, he is a delightful host, and Lady Huntercombe—who, by-the-bye, is a near relative of my own—is a charming person, lively, spiritual, witty. You ought to know her, Miss Bracebridge. She would be enchanted to make your acquaintance. Well, with good shooting, with an agreeable host and hostess, with so many pleasant people about me, so many pretty girls to flirt with, if I wanted to flirt, I ought to have regained my spirits, but I didn't. Just as melancholy as ever. Nothing amused me. Huntercombe noticed my gloom, and rallied me unmercifully upon it, and her ladyship said I must be suffering from a heart complaint. I had unmistakable symptoms, she declared, of a very severe attack."

"Well, if her ladyship's opinion of the case is correct, and I suppose it must be," remarked Mrs. Daventry, "it is to be hoped that the malady won't terminate fatally."

"Little fear of that, aunt," observed Eva. "Sir Norman gives a very deplorable account of himself, but his looks scarcely bear out his statement."

"I mustn't be judged by my present appearance," he said. "Had you seen me at breakfast, you would have commiserated me. I had no end of sympathy from the young ladies present, expressed in the most flattering terms."

"I can scarcely add my sympathy to theirs," rejoined Eva. "You seem to have recovered very quickly."

"No wonder. I have at last found a specific for my malady."

Mrs. Daventry smiled, but Eva affected not to understand him.

"I see you don't believe that I have been so wretched as I have stated," he continued. "On my honour for the last six weeks—ever since you quitted the Beau-Rivage, in fact —life has been a burden to me. As I have told you, I could not amuse myself either in Paris or London. Nothing interested me or excited me. Till I came here to-day I was a prey to despair. I am better now; and shall get quite well, if I don't have a relapse."

"I trust you are in no danger of that, Sir Norman," remarked Mrs. Daventry, with a smile. "Since this visit to Hylton Castle has been of service to you, I hope you will ride over frequently while you are in the neighbourhood. We shall always be delighted to see you."

"May I come?" said Sir Norman, with a supplicating look at Eva.

"Certainly, if it will do you good," she replied. "My aunt will always be glad to see you, and I hope poor Mr. Pomfret will be back in a few days."

"Then you still think my illness imaginary? I would rather have had poor Pomfret's accident than suffer as I have done. How fortunate he was to find so excellent a nurse! Pray, who is Mrs. Montfort, who has devoted herself so much to him?"

Perceptibly embarrassed by the question, Eva merely replied,—

"A very amiable lady, who is residing with Mrs. Carew."

"Very interesting—young, and extremely pretty," added Mrs. Daventry.

"A young widow, I suppose?" inquired Sir Norman.

"I cannot say," replied Mrs. Daventry. "I have only just

seen her when we have called on Mrs. Carew. But I was greatly struck by her appearance."

"Mrs. Montfort has had many misfortunes," said Eva. "She is in a position of most painful perplexity, and it seems as if ill luck constantly attended her. Mr. Pomfret rode over one morning to offer her aid and advice, and met with this dreadful accident."

"That is strange indeed," remarked Sir Norman, gravely. "From what you say, a fatality seems to attend the poor lady. It is evident that you take a strong interest in her. Can I be of any service to her?"

Eva shook her head.

"She had found a home with Mrs. Carew," she said; "but I fear she will be obliged to leave it."

"How so?" inquired Sir Norman. But he checked himself, and added, "Excuse me. Don't answer the question, unless you like."

"You may be quite sure that Mrs. Montfort has good reasons for leaving so kind a friend as Mrs. Carew," said Eva. "But though I know her motives for the step, I cannot explain them."

There was a slight pause. In order to change the subject, Sir Norman said :—

"Does Pomfret still adhere to his design of returning to Madras?"

"I cannot say. He has postponed his departure from time to time. And now, perhaps, he may postpone it altogether."

"Well, you will be glad of that?"

"I shall be very sorry, of course, to lose him; still, I think he ought to go. He has important affairs to attend to there."

"Aha! here's a change indeed!" thought Sir Norman. "Mrs. Austin was quite right.—Do you still wish to go back with him?" he asked.

"No. I have changed my mind. I no longer desire to revisit India. Mr. Pomfret dissuaded me from accompanying him, and now I wouldn't go if he would let me."

"Well, I think you are quite right. But may I venture to ask what has caused this change of opinion?"

"I don't know what has caused it. But I certainly shall not return to Madras with Mr. Pomfret."

"Come!" thought Sir Norman. "That's decisive. Well, I hope he won't start for a month or so," he added, aloud. "I have some arrangements to make with him."

"About this house?" she inquired.

"Partly," he rejoined, with a certain significance that did not escape Mrs. Daventry. "But let me say at once," he hastened to add, "if you have the slightest desire to prolong your stay beyond Christmas, the place shall be at your disposal."

"You are excessively kind. But I may be keeping you out of the house. What will you do?"

"Oh! never mind me," he rejoined. "You must let me come and see the place occasionally—that's all."

Mrs. Daventry smiled, and her countenance wore an expression that implied a good deal, though she made no remark.

"I shall hear what Mr. Pomfret has to say when he comes back," observed Eva. "I must be guided by him."

"If you desire to stay," said Sir Norman, looking fixedly at her, "I don't think there will be any difficulty on your guardian's part, and certainly none on mine."

Eva cast down her eyes, and made no reply to this remarkably gallant speech.

Matters seemed to be going on so well, that Mrs. Daventry thought it best not to interfere.

CHAPTER IX.

THE LEGEND OF DAME ALMERIA.

"YOU have not told me one thing, Miss Brace-bridge," remarked Sir Norman, after a pause. "Have you seen the ghost?"

"The ghost!" exclaimed Mrs. Daventry. "You don't mean to say the house is haunted?"

"Don't be alarmed, aunt," remarked Eva, smiling. "I sleep in the haunted chamber, and have never been disturbed. Sir Norman pretends that he has seen the ghost more than once, but I can't believe him. I suppose there is some story connected with your castle spectre?" she added, glancing at him.

"A story that forms the darkest page in our family annals," he replied. "You shall hear it. My ancestor, Sir Digby Hylton, who flourished in the time of James I., and enjoyed the favour of that monarch, had a remarkably beautiful wife, of whom he had the misfortune to be jealous. It cannot be denied that] Dame Almeria gave him cause for jealousy, for he intercepted a billet to her from the Earl of Southampton, which appeared to confirm his worst sus-picions. But this cannot extenuate his conduct, though it may explain it. Much against her will, and sorely to the

annoyance of her numerous admirers, and of the enamoured Earl of Southampton in particular, the lovely
Almeria was removed from court, brought down to this
castle, confined to her chamber, and rigorously watched
by her lord."

"Served her quite right, I think," remarked Mrs.
Daventry.

"Yes, if that had been all, Sir Digby's conduct might
perhaps be excusable," returned Sir Norman, "but he went
a little too far. Not unnaturally, Dame Almeria tried to
escape from her thraldom, but she could not elude Sir
Digby's vigilance, and he threatened, if she made another
attempt, to shut her up in a dungeon, which still exists in
the lower part of the castle."

"I have seen the dungeon," said Eva, with a shudder,
"and a dreadful place it is. Surely Sir Digby could never
have had the barbarity to carry out his threat?"

"You shall hear," replied Sir Norman. "Failing in her
attempts to escape, Dame Almeria was indiscreet enough to
write a letter to the Earl of Southampton, detailing her
sufferings, and imploring him to liberate her from her tyrant
lord. The letter fell into the hands of Sir Digby, and so
incensed him, that, with the aid of a devoted groom, he tied
a sheet round her face in order to stifle her cries, and then
dragged her down a secret staircase to the dungeon. There
he left her alone, as he said, to commune with herself and
repent. I won't harrow your feelings by attempting to paint
the frightful anguish which she must have endured. Enough
to state the result. When Sir Digby visited her next day, a
terrible spectacle was presented to him. The unfortunate
lady had attempted to lay violent hands upon herself, but
she still lived. Her senses, however, were gone, and her
raven locks had become white. Filled with remorse, Sir
Digby instantly conveyed her to her own room, and would
have tended her in person, but his presence inspired her
with such horror that he did not dare to come near her.
To make an end of this tragical story, I must state that the
ill-starred dame never recovered. After lingering for a few
months, bereft alike of reason and of her personal charms,
death released her."

"A tragical story indeed," said Eva. "But what happened to Sir Digby? I hope he was properly punished for his cruelty."

"He was killed at the battle of Naseby. His compunction, however, does not appear to have been lasting. He married again, but took care to choose a wife whose personal attractions should not cause him disquietude. But I now come to the supernatural part of my story. Shall I proceed?"

"By all means," cried both ladies. "Pray go on."

"After Dame Almeria's death, Sir Digby caused the apartment in which the sad occurrence took place to be shut up. A report soon spread among the household that the chamber was haunted. Strange noises were heard within it at dead of night, and those who were bold enough to watch declared that they had seen the door, which they knew to be locked, fly open, and a female figure, draped in a white garment that looked like a winding-sheet, glide forth, and pass down the secret staircase. Following the phantom, they saw it reach the door of the dungeon, and then disappear. Such is the legend. The secret staircase, I may say, has been long walled up, so that Dame Almeria has had no opportunity of late years of continuing her midnight rambles in that direction. But a fruitless attempt was made to lay the ghost with the other restless sprites in the Red Sea. The spirit could not be exorcised. Not one, I believe, of Sir Digby's male descendants, myself included, who has slept in the haunted chamber, but has seen Dame Almeria. I have seen her twice. On both occasions I beheld—or fancied I beheld, for of course I might have been dreaming—a female figure swathed from head to foot in a winding-sheet."

"How dreadful!" exclaimed Mrs. Daventry. "I declare I wouldn't sleep in the room for the world."

"I am not the least afraid," observed Eva. "While professing to have seen his ancestress, Sir Norman admits that he might have been dreaming at the time."

"You want to spoil my ghost story," he rejoined, laughing. "But I can assure you it is a veritable family legend."

16—2

"I suppose my maid Susan has heard of Dame Almeria, though I charged Mrs. Austin not to tell her about the ghost," said Eva. "She positively refuses to sleep in the dressing-room."

CHAPTER X.

LMOST immediately afterwards they quitted the dining-room, and walked out upon the yew-tree terrace.

By a lucky accident, Sir Norman was left alone with Eva for a few minutes, Mrs. Daventry being obliged to re-enter the house for some trifling matter that she required. Of course the opportunity was not neglected by the young baronet.

"Do not be angry with me, Miss Bracebridge," he said, "if I once again entreat you to listen to me. In what I have just said there was not the slightest exaggeration. I have found it utterly impossible to conquer my passion for you. I love you as devotedly as ever,—nay, do not check me, I entreat. Do not cast me off without a word. Do not condemn me to hopeless misery. Give me a chance of winning your affections."

"Were I to grant your request you would gain nothing by it," she rejoined. "Best forget me. You have suffered, no doubt. But the worst is over. Unrequited love may be conquered. Of that I am quite sure."

"You speak as if from conviction," said Sir Norman,

unable to repress a pang. " My own experience proves the contrary. Love, deeply rooted, cannot be torn from the heart. I have made the attempt, and failed. Forgive me if I venture to allude to what you have just said. I trust I shall not give you pain or displeasure if I say that I guess the import of your speech. Love like mine is quick-sighted. When you rejected me, I felt certain you nourished a secret passion. I told your guardian so."

" You told him ! " she cried, turning crimson.

" I did not know as much then as I know now, or I should not have been so indiscreet. But since you confess that your heart is free, let me have the chance of winning it."

She shook her head.

" I will not allow my affections to be again fettered, if I can help it. I am much happier as I am, and mean to continue so."

" Remember that the love you felt was unrequited. That makes all the difference. I ask only to become your suitor. At any time you can dismiss me."

" But will you take a dismissal ? " she cried, laughingly. " It would seem not."

" I will retire at the slightest word. But I am sanguine enough to believe that you will never utter that word."

" One stipulation I make before assenting, and I expect rigorous adherence to it. You are not to talk to me of love."

" Rather a hard condition that. But I agree."

" Another stipulation. You are not to speak to my guardian on the subject—without my express permission."

" Why not ? "

" Don't ask me for a reason. Do you agree ? "

" Oh, certainly. I will agree to anything you impose."

" Since you agree generally to obey my behests, I need not make any further conditions. But understand. I hold out no hopes, and if you are disappointed—as very likely you may be, notwithstanding your sanguine expectations of success—you will have no right to complain."

" That is perfectly understood. If I fail now, I won't complain."

At this moment Mrs. Daventry was seen descending the steps leading to the terrace. They went to meet her.

"The groom has just returned from Mrs. Carew's," she said. "Mr. Pomfret is going on most favourably. We shall soon have him back."

Naturally, this satisfactory report gladdened the hearers. The party then took a few turns upon the terrace. The conversation that occurred is scarcely worth repeating, but the young baronet's animated manner and joyous expression convinced Mrs. Daventry that he had not been repulsed. At last the ladies re-entered the house, and then Sir Norman felt that he must tear himself away.

Mrs. Austin had a word to say to him on his departure, and was enchanted to learn that he was coming over again next day. With a lightened heart he rode back through the avenue.

"Well, my dear," said Mrs. Daventry to her niece, as soon he was gone, "I am now quite sure that it will be your own fault if you are not Lady Hylton. Shall I tell you what passed through my mind when I watched you and the handsome young baronet as you were walking on the terrace just now?"

"No, don't, aunt. I won't listen to it. I am sure it's some silly nonsense."

CHAPTER XI.

OW Eva spent the rest of the day, and how she got through the evening, it boots not to inquire. She retired to her room early. She had made light of the grim legend of Dame Almeria, but it now recurred to her, and caused a sensation of something approaching to terror.

Susan, having performed her duties, had withdrawn and left her mistress alone. The chamber looked unusually gloomy, and as Eva gazed around it, superstitious fears, such as she had never before experienced, began to assail her. She was only deterred by very shame from recalling her maid.

All at once a slight sound caught her ear, and she almost ceased to breathe while listening to it. The door of the dressing-room, which had been recently occupied by Susan, was locked, and as she had every reason to believe, no one was there. But she now distinctly heard a slight noise within the room, as if some one was trying to open the door.

She was dreadfully frightened. Her superstitious fears

had given place to well-founded alarm. Some one must be concealed in the chamber. Still, she felt safe, for the door was locked, and the key was on her side. She could see it as she held up her taper.

As she listened, there was a tapping against the door. After a while it ceased. She was then about to quit the chamber, when the tapping recommenced, and she fancied she could distinguish a voice.

She paused, and again listened.

The tapping became louder and more importunate, and she felt certain that she heard her own name pronounced by a female voice.

Instantly her courage was restored. Stepping towards the door, she called out in firm accents, "Who is it?"

"'Tis I!" rejoined the voice. "Pray open the door."

Eva recognised the voice, and, though surprised beyond measure, did not hesitate a moment.

She unlocked the door, and there stood Sophy.

The poor lady was in walking attire, and her looks showed that she was in great distress.

"Is it really Mrs. Montfort?" cried Eva.

"Yes, it is really your unhappy friend," replied Sophy. "You will think it strange that I should appear before you in this manner, but, for reasons which I will proceed to explain, I wished my visit to the castle to be secret. I came here this evening, saw Mrs. Austin, and was conducted by her privily to the room from which you have just liberated me. She left me there, promising to return, but I suppose she has been prevented."

"I have seen nothing of her," replied Eva. "But I retired much earlier than usual. Possibly she may yet come. But now let me know the motive of this secret visit. Has anything happened? Can I help you? Put my friendship to the proof. You shall not find me wanting. If you require another asylum, you shall have it here."

"Your kindness quite overcomes me," said Sophy, in accents of profound emotion. "It is more than I deserve."

"How can I do otherwise than pity you, now that I know your history?" cried Eva—"now that I know the full extent of the wrong you have endured—of the perfidy of which you have been the victim? How can I do otherwise than feel for you, when I know whose wife you have been—whose wife you are!"

"You may imagine the effort it cost me to detail to you the whole of my miserable story," replied Sophy. "But after Julian's accident I felt it was absolutely necessary you should know the entire truth, and then you could act as you might see fit. I think I was justified in revealing his secret to you, even without his consent being first obtained, because without such knowledge you might have continued in a declusion. After the confidence you had unwittingly reposed in me, I could not allow you to remain in ignorance of the truth."

"I thank you a thousand times," cried Eva. "You have enabled me most effectually to crush a foolish passion, in which you were aware I had indulged. Poor Mr. Pomfret —I dare not call him Julian—I pity him from the bottom of my heart—but I love him no longer."

"Would he could be released from the ties that still unhappily bind him to me!" ejaculated Sophy. "His freedom would be cheaply purchased by so miserable a life as mine. But Heaven will not listen to my prayers, and take me hence!"

"Do not talk thus," cried Eva. "But tell me why you have come here."

"Dear Mrs. Carew's house is no longer a secure asylum for me, and I am compelled to fly from it. You are aware that Captain Musgrave has discovered my retreat, and has stripped me of all my resources?"

"Yes. What more?"

"He promised me solemnly, when I gave him all I possessed, that he would never molest me again. But what is a promise to him? He has written to say that he must see me, and that if I decline to receive him secretly, as before, he will force himself into my presence. After this, what was left me but flight? Were I to remain with Mrs. Carew, I should never be free from his persecution. I took counsel with her. I told her all. I showed her Musgrave's last letter, and she agreed with me that there

was no other alternative but flight. But she advised me to
see you before putting my plan into execution, and it is at
her suggestion that I have come here to-night. I came
here secretly, so that my movements may not be traced ;
but I have been obliged to make a confidante of Mrs.
Austin. Indeed, I found that she was already acquainted
with my unhappy story."

"I have related it to her," replied Eva. "She is
perfectly trustworthy. Mrs. Carew was quite right in
advising you to come to me. Here you can have a safe
asylum. No one but Mrs. Austin need know that you are
in the house. If you can reconcile yourself to such an
arrangement for a time, you can easily be concealed in
some out-of-the-way room. There are plenty to spare.
Indeed, more than half the house is unoccupied. No one
visits these deserted rooms but Mrs. Austin, so that, I
repeat, you will be perfectly safe."

" Nothing can suit me better than such an arrangement,"
replied Sophy.

At this moment the door opened and Mrs. Austin
entered the room.

"You have released the prisoner, I see, Miss," observed
the old housekeeper. " I should have been here long ago,
but I have been preparing a little room in the untenanted
wing of the house, and I couldn't get it ready sooner. I've
not been able to fit it up properly, but it may serve for to-
night, and I'll make it more comfortable to-morrow, if Mrs.
Montfort stays with us."

" She will stay," replied Eva. " But no one but yourself
must know that she is an inmate of the castle."

" Oh, I'll take care of that," said Mrs. Austin. " No
danger whatever of discovery, if proper precautions are
taken. No one can enter that wing of the house without
coming to me for the keys. Mrs. Montfort, I'll engage, will
be quite safe there. But, if she were to pass the night in
your dressing-room, Susan would be sure to find it out, and
then the story would be all over the house directly."

" No doubt," said Sophy.

" We will do the best we can to alleviate your confinement," observed Eva. " I will spend as much time with

you as possible, and bring you books and newspapers, and everything I can think of, calculated to cheer your solitude."

"The thought that I am free from the persecution to which I have been subjected, will make me feel quite happy," said Sophy. "I shall not heed the confinement. It will afford me plenty of time for meditation."

"Somewhat too much, I fear," remarked Eva.

"No, not too much," she rejoined. "I have renounced the world, and therefore solitude suits me. I shall look upon myself as a recluse."

"Let us go to the room at once," cried Eva. "I am impatient to see it."

"With your permission, Miss, I'll just put together a few things which Mrs. Montfort may require for the night," observed Mrs. Austin.

"Take whatever you think proper," cried Eva. "My wardrobe is entirely at her service."

Mrs. Austin, having made all preparations she thought needful, and put together a tolerably large bundle of things, went out to reconnoitre, but returned almost instantly to say that nobody was stirring, and that Mrs. Montfort might proceed to her room with perfect safety.

The old housekeeper did not carry a light, nor would she allow either of the ladies to take one, lest it might betray them, so they had to move along in total darkness.

To Eva this did not much signify, since she was familiar with the place; but Sophy was glad to take the hand extended to her by her companion.

After proceeding to some distance slowly and cautiously along the corridor, they turned into a passage on the left, leading, as Eva was aware, to the deserted wing.

Unlocking a door at the end of the passage, the old housekeeper admitted them into a vast but totally dismantled room. The windows being without curtains or blinds, the prudence of Mrs. Austin's injunction became apparent, as, if they had carried a light, their movements might have been discerned from without.

Hastily traversing a suite of unfurnished rooms, they entered another passage, mounted a short spiral staircase, and then reached the little chamber destined for Sophy's occupation.

The walls were panelled with black lustrous oak, and reflected the radiance of a cheerful fire that burnt in the grate. The chief furniture consisted of a small table, a couple of chairs, and a sofa, on which a bed had been extemporised. In other respects the room was sufficiently furnished for the purpose to which it was put.

"This was Sir Norman's room when he was a boy," remarked Mrs. Austin, "and I sleep in it occasionally myself. I can reach it without going through the dismantled rooms we have just traversed, but I thought it safer to take that course to-night. You needn't be afraid of damp linen, Ma'am," she added to Sophy. "The sheets are perfectly well aired, and the blankets are from my own bed. To-morrow I will make you more comfortable. You will find wine and biscuits in that basket, and I will come betimes in the morning to prepare your breakfast."

The old housekeeper then busied herself in arranging and spreading out the various things which she had brought from Eva's room, and while she was thus employed, the two ladies, who had sat down near the fire, conversed together in a low tone.

At last Mrs. Austin's task being completed, Eva thought it time to depart. Affectionately embracing Sophy, she bade her good-night, promising to come and see her in the morning. While taking her departure, the old housekeeper pointed out that the door could be bolted inside.

Sophy was then left alone, and making fast the door, knelt down beside her couch to pray.

CHAPTER XII.

OMFRET was now so much better that the surgeon told him, one morning, that he might return to Hylton Castle when he pleased. On receiving this permission, the wounded man made immediate preparations for his departure, and had just completed them, when Old Nathan informed him that his mistress would like to see him. He at once obeyed the summons, and accompanied by the butler, proceeded to the drawing-room, where he found Mrs. Carew alone. His changed appearance and extreme debility could not fail to excite the kind old lady's compassion. His attire hung loosely upon him, and the ghastly pallor of his visage was heightened by the black silk skull-cap which covered his head.

Mrs. Carew rose to meet him as he entered the room, and, after assisting the old butler to place him in an easy-chair, sat down beside him. This arrangement made, Nathan quitted the room.

After expressing in a very earnest manner his deep obligations to the old lady, Pomfret said, " I hoped to have found Mrs. Montfort with you, Madam, but as I may not see her before my departure, I must beg you to express my gratitude to her, and in the strongest terms."

"You owe a far deeper debt of gratitude to her than to me, Mr. Pomfret," said Mrs. Carew, gravely. "Under Heaven, she has been the means of saving your life."

"I am quite aware of it," he replied, deeply moved.

After a short pause, he added :—

"May I venture to ask, Madam, whether Mrs. Montfort has made any communication to you?"

"She has told me all," replied the old lady, regarding him steadfastly.

Unable to bear her searching looks, Pomfret averted his gaze.

"She has fully explained her cruel situation to me," pursued Mrs. Carew. "Need I tell you that I pity her from the bottom of my heart? Before that explanation, I took a wholly different view of the matter. I had learnt enough from Sophy's wild expressions, when she thought you mortally hurt, to be sure that you were her husband, and I hoped that the differences which I fancied might exist between you would be reconciled. It was a vain hope. I now know the whole truth, and am aware that reunion is impossible."

A deep groan broke from Pomfret.

"It is a sad business indeed," pursued the old lady; "but you must forgive me if I say that you are to blame. The miserable position in which poor Sophy is placed is attributable entirely to your conduct."

"You judge me severely, Madam," said Pomfret.

"Not too severely," she replied. "I love Sophy as dearly as a daughter, and my language is such as a mother would employ. You are the main cause, I repeat, of her misery. You put her to a trial to which no woman ought to be subjected. You led her to believe that you had destroyed yourself—nay, more, she was persuaded that you had committed the fatal act before her own eyes. It is wonderful to me that she survived the shock. For years you allowed her to mourn you as dead. Was such conduct consistent with good feeling or affection? Was it justifiable on any ground? What might have been the consequences?

True, Sophy performed the part of a devoted wife, and really remained faithful to your memory, but you had no right to count upon such fidelity. How many years of needless and profitless anxiety would a few words have saved her? Yet they were never uttered. You allowed her to consume her young life in unavailing grief."

"Spare me, Madam—in pity, spare me!" cried Pomfret.

"Your excuse is, that you were engaged in making a fortune for the wife whom you had thus abandoned," pursued the unrelenting old lady. "I can perfectly understand the peculiar feelings by which you were actuated, but I consider your conduct as in the highest degree reprehensible. Morally, you are responsible for all the sad consequences that have ensued. When you first wrote to her from Madras you ought to have avowed the truth ; but, instead of doing so, you resorted to further mystification, and created the very difficulties in which she became involved. To you the consequences are calamitous enough, but to poor Sophy they are fatal. She is placed in the power of a villain, from whom there is no escape. Great as is her wrong, she is without hope of redress."

"The wrong cannot be redressed, but she can be protected from further annoyance," said Pomfret. "And this must be done effectually. You say you love her as a daughter. Will you allow her to remain with you?"

"This house is no longer a secure asylum for her," rejoined Mrs. Carew.

"She is safer here than elsewhere," cried Pomfret. "Let me see her. I can easily convince her of that."

"I will not keep you longer in suspense," rejoined the old lady. "She is gone."

"Gone!" exclaimed Pomfret, as if a violent blow had been dealt him. "Gone! without consulting me. But no! I cannot believe it. She would not leave you—her best friend."

"The step is taken, and by my advice," rejoined Mrs. Carew. "She has left this house. I would not allow her to consult you, lest her resolution might be shaken."

"You did wrong, Madam," cried Pomfret, sternly. "You blame me, and justly, for what has already occurred, but if any fresh misfortunes arise, you will be responsible for them. Whither is she gone?"

"You must excuse my answering that question," rejoined the old lady.

"But she has no funds!" cried Pomfret. "She has been plundered by Musgrave of all her resources."

"You need have no anxiety on that score, Sir," said Mrs. Carew. "She is not without funds. If I had thought she could remain here safely, I should not have parted with her."

"Has anything happened to cause her further uneasiness?" asked Pomfret, anxiously.

"Yes. She has received a letter from Captain Musgrave. You shall see it. She left it with me."

With this she took a letter from a drawer, and gave it to Pomfret. Not without repugnance he opened the letter, and read as follows:—

"'I must have another interview with you. I am going abroad. You may expect me on the third night after the date of this letter. I shall appear at the same hour and in the same way as before. I must, and will see you. There are other ways of entering the house than by the window, and if you thwart my plan, I shall present myself at the door.

"'SCROPE MUSGRAVE.'

"Is she never to be free from this persecution?" groaned Pomfret.

"That letter decided me," said Mrs. Carew. "I would no longer allow Sophy to remain here. This is the appointed night. If Captain Musgrave comes, he will find me in Sophy's room."

"No, Madam," said Pomfret, sternly. "He must not find you, but *me*. I will be there."

"No meeting between you can take place in my house," cried Mrs. Carew, alarmed.

"I promise you there shall be no violence; but see him I must," said Pomfret. "No provocation shall force me to assail him; and, indeed, I have not strength for a personal encounter with him. But it is important to Sophy's future

17

peace that I should see him. He has some object in seeking this interview, which he will not disclose to you, but which I may be able to extort."

"Since you promise me there shall be no violence, I assent to the plan. Under these circumstances, I presume you will postpone your departure till to-morrow."

"I must needs do so," rejoined Pomfret. "I must trespass a little more upon your kindness."

"I will go at once and countermand the carriage which has been ordered for you," said Mrs. Carew, rising. "And as this sudden change in your plans might surprise Nathan, I will tell him that I have prevailed upon you to remain till to-morrow. That will quite satisfy him. But it will be best that you should return to your own room. When the servants have retired to rest, I will conduct you to Sophy's chamber."

CHAPTER X II

MUSGRAVE KEEPS HIS APPOINTMENT.

NIGHT came. Midnight. Pomfret was alone in the chamber recently occupied by Sophy.

His preparations had been made. The window was left partly open, and a light placed upon the table. But he himself was concealed behind the curtains of the bed.

All the servants had long since retired to rest, and no one was astir in the house but Mrs. Carew, who had brought him privily to the room. Her windows commanded the drawbridge, and she now and then looked cautiously forth, but the night being dark, and a dense mist brooding over the moat, she could not distinguish any object.

Pomfret did not quit his position for a moment, but patiently awaited Musgrave's arrival. Listening intently for any sound that might announce the coming of that hateful personage, he at last distinctly heard footsteps on the drawbridge. His heart beat quick at the thought that his foe was at hand. A rustling among the leaves of the ivy next warned him that Musgrave was climbing up to the window.

In another moment the visitor sprang boldly into the room, and glanced around it in search of Sophy. He did not detect Pomfret in his hiding-place.

"Where the devil is she?" he exclaimed, in tones bespeaking anger and uneasiness. "She evidently expects me, since she has left the window open and a candle burning. But why is she not here?"

Then stepping towards the door, he tried it, but found it fastened.

"Locked!" he exclaimed, with a fierce oath. "Is this some trick? No, she would not dare to play me false. She will be back presently."

He then turned, and to his astonishment and dismay found Pomfret standing between him and the window. So ghastly were the looks of the latter, that Musgrave for a moment doubted whether a living man confronted him. However, he speedily recovered his composure.

"A devilish clever manœuvre, upon my soul!" he cried, with a jeering laugh. "But it won't answer with me, I can promise you. I beg to observe, that I have come here on a peaceful errand, and merely to see my wife, who expects me. In order to avoid a serious disturbance—for serious it assuredly will be, if you attempt to molest me—I request that you will be good enough to send her to me without delay. Understand that I wish to see her alone. For obvious reasons I must decline any conference with you. We can have no business to settle together."

"Pardon, me, Sir," rejoined Pomfret, sternly. "We have a very important business to settle, and till it *is* settled, satisfactorily to me, you do not quit this room."

"Judging by your haggard looks, you are scarcely in a condition to oppose my departure," rejoined Musgrave. "But I have no intention of going till I have seen my wife; and I must again beg that you will do me the favour to send her to me."

"You cannot see her," rejoined Pomfret, peremptorily.

"I rather fancy you are mistaken, Sir," sneered Musgrave, "and I would recommend you, for *her* sake, and indeed for your own, not to force me to extremities. The right, as you will find, if you provoke me too far, is on my side, and not on yours. I shall be glad to be informed why you are here; and on what pretence you meddle in an affair in whch you are noway concerned? Your presence and conduct are alike damaging to the reputation of the lady whose cause you affect to espouse. How is it, I repeat, that I find you here, in her chamber, at this hour? As the guardian of my wife's honour, I am entitled, I think, to ask that question."

"Since you desire to know why I am here, I will tell you," rejoined Pomfret, his pallid features flushing, and his eyes blazing. "I am here to protect your unhappy victim. Do not imagine I am unacquainted with your errand. Not content with your previous robbery—for I will use no milder term—you have come again to attempt further extortion. But I am here to tell you on the part of the lady whom you have so foully wronged, that she will hold no further communication whatever with you, but if you persist in your infamous attempts, she will seek legal redress."

"I laugh at such idle threats," rejoined Musgrave, scornfully. "No one knows better than yourself that she dares not resort to legal redress."

"Do not presume too much on her forbearance," said Pomfret. "There are limits to her patience which you have already passed."

"I shall be better able to judge of that when I see her; and see her I will—even if I stay here till morning. If you want to get rid of me, you will acquaint her with my determination. I am unwilling to make a disturbance in the house, or I would go in search of her myself."

To prove that he was in earnest, he coolly seated himself, and proceeded to light a cigarette which he took from a case.

So indignant was Pomfret, that if he had had sufficient strength, he would have thrown him through the window; but he contented himself with saying, "I did not suppose that any one, with the slightest pretensions to the character of a gentleman, could act thus."

"Ah, indeed. A person who goes about under a

feigned name is not likely to have very correct notions as to what constitutes a gentleman. At all events, the opinion of such a one does not weigh much with me."

"Dastard !" cried Pomfret, trembling with rage. "You know that you can safely provoke me."

"Since you are unwell, I would advise you, for your own sake, to terminate this interview," rejoined Musgrave. "Let me see my wife."

"I have already told you that you cannot see her. She has left this house."

"Are you speaking truth?" demanded Musgrave, looking hard at him.

"She is gone, I tell you. Your intolerable persecution has driven her hence."

"She was a fool to go," cried Musgrave, "as even you would admit, if I cared to enter into explanation with you. If she and her advisers would only act with a little common sense, a great deal of unpleasantness might be spared. However, she must take her own course. I shan't trouble myself further about her. Some one, I make no doubt," he added, significantly, "will take good care of her."

"I repel your infamous insinuation with scorn," said Pomfret. "I know not whither she has fled."

"I daresay I should find her at Hylton Castle," rejoined Musgrave. "But whether or not you have constituted yourself my wife's protector is a matter of utter indifference to me, provided, as I have just said, that I am no more troubled."

"Be sure she will not trouble you if you will leave her alone," rejoined Pomfret. "But what faith can she have in you? On the promise that you would never again molest her, she gave you all she possessed, and now you threaten her with fresh extortion."

"It is false !" cried Musgrave, fiercely. "My letter to her has been entirely misinterpreted. I came here for no such base purpose as you impute to me."

"If not for that, for what purpose did you come?" demanded Pomfret.

"I owe it to myself to offer an explanation, or be sure I would render you none, Sir," answered Musgrave. "My object in coming here was to repay the money borrowed

from her for a temporary purpose. I told her I was goin
abroad."

"You cannot be surprised if I refuse credence to th
statement?" remarked Pomfret, sceptically. "It is scarcel
consistent with your previous conduct."

"Will this convince you?" cried Musgrave, taking fror
his breast-pocket a rouleau of bank-notes, and tossing i
towards him. "There is the precise sum she lent me
Give it to her. You will easily find an opportunity of doin
so, I make no doubt."

"This is more than I expected from you," said Pomfret
surprised.

"Spare me further remarks, Sir," rejoined Musgrave. "
desire to go away quietly."

"Go, then," replied Pomfret, stepping aside.

Hereupon, Musgrave strode deliberately to the window.

Before passing through it, however, he looked out, anc
after a moment's scrutiny, came back.

"I fancy there is a man on the drawbridge," he said
"Is he set there to waylay me?"

"Dismiss the notion at once," rejoined Pomfret. "Nc
one is on the drawbridge."

"Well, I may have been deceived by the fog. Since
you assure me that a guet-à-pens is not intended, I wil
go."

And he passed through the window.

But he had only partly accomplished his descent, when a
rough voice called out to him.

The person who called was the gardener. Thinking
there were robbers on the premises, the stout old fellow
had armed himself with a fowling-piece, and taken up a
position on the drawbridge, with the design of cutting off
their retreat.

Receiving no answer to the challenge, he repeated it more
lustily, with an emphatic warning which, being disregarded,
he let fly at the supposed robber.

The shot rattled amongst the ivy-leaves, but whether
much damage was done to Musgrave, Pomfret, who rushed
to the window, was unable to determine. If hit, Musgrave
was clearly not disabled, for, on reaching the ground, he at
once made for the drawbridge.

Here a struggle took place between him and the gardener, but the old man released him on hearing Pomfret's vociferations, coupled with those of Mrs. Carew, who threw up her window on hearing the shot; and Musgrave, with a furious oath, hurried away.

End of the Fifth Book.

BOOK VI.

BELFIELD.

———◆———

CHAPTER I.

BOOTLE RECEIVES A LETTER FROM HIS MOTHER, AND A
TELEGRAPHIC MESSAGE FROM HIS FATHER.

R. AND MRS. BOOTLE SHELMERDINE, whom we conducted as far as Folkstone on their wedding-day, spent their honeymoon, and another month besides, at Paris. They were quartered at the Grand Hôtel.

The pretty little Englishwoman, who dressed so charmingly, and who had such fine eyes, which she knew so well how to use, soon became an object of attraction in the Bois. The incense offered her by the cavaliers whom she daily encountered in her drives near the lakes, was far from displeasing to her. The young Parisian élégants stared very hard at her, but did not abash her. Neither did she return their audacious looks with the disdain they deserved. Bootle, who always accompanied his wife in her drives, was flattered by the admiration she excited, persuading himself that the

possession of such a treasure made him an object of envy
to all who beheld her.

Bootle was really very fond of his pretty little wife, and
very proud of her.   He liked to see her well dressed, and
he liked her to be admired.   This may seem odd in one
who was constitutionally jealous, like our friend ; but there
are unaccountable contradictions in human nature, and
Bootle's· was by no means a consistent character.   No
doubt there was something very piquant in his wife's
coquettish manner, for she always contrived to surround
herself with admirers; and where many a far handsomer
woman of a quieter turn would have been passed by with
very little notice, she succeeded in attracting attention.
Love of admiration was Mrs. Bootle's ruling passion.   She
had long desired to attach a number of captives to her car,
and she was now gratified.   With her the aim and end of
wedded life was not quiet domestic bliss.   Of that she
never dreamed for a moment.   Quietude and domesticity
would have been no bliss to her.   She never would have
given her hand to Bootle if she had imagined she would be
condemned to live in seclusion with him.   Her notions of
married life, founded upon many examples that had come
under her own observation, and fortified by the precepts
enunciated in her favourite French novels, were that, as á
married woman, she would only have her own inclinations
to consult, and she felt quite sure that Mrs. Bootle
Shelmerdine would be far more admired, far more sought
after, than Miss Flaxyard.   The result proved she was
right.

During their stay at Paris the newly-married couple made
many acquaintances, both French and English; and so
much attention was paid to Bootle by his new friends, that
he began to think there was considerable advantage in being
a married man.   Sometimes he felt a little jealous, but his
wife soon laughed him out of such ridiculous notions.

After a couple of months spent very pleasantly in the
French capital, they were still undecided in their plans.
Bootle, who was rather surfeited with gaiety, wished to
return to England, and if matters could have been made
comfortable with his mother, he would have liked to pass
the winter at Belfield.   Mrs. Bootle had no sort of objection

to this plan. Bury would be a change, and she had a natural curiosity to see a house of which she expected one day to be mistress.

Mrs. Bootle had written several times to her mother-in-law, but had failed to propitiate her. The letters were handed over to Mr. Shelmerdine and answered by him.

At last Bootle nerved himself to the task, and wrote to his mother, saying that he and his wife were returning to England, and proposed to come at once to Belfield. A prompt reply was sent, couched in the following terms:

" MY DEAR BOOTLE,—I think you had better defer your proposed visit to Belfield until the spring, when I trust I may in some degree have recovered from the mortification and disappointment which you have inflicted upon me by your marriage. At present, a meeting between me and your wife could not be agreeable to either of us. Deeply hurt as I have been, I feel I could not put a constraint upon my feelings, and my daughter-in-law might have reason to complain of her welcome. I will not invite her till I can receive her properly.

" I am bound to state that your father is ill pleased with me for taking this course, but I must bear his displeasure, knowing that I am right.

" You tell me that your wife is greatly admired in Paris, and that whenever she drives in the Bois de Boulogne, or is seen in the Champs Elysées, or on the boulevards, her personal charms and elegant toilette attract general attention.

" I can only say in reply, that I sincerely hope all this admiration won't turn her head. In my opinion, you ought not to expose her to it; but knowing advice to be useless, I shall not offer it. Men's notions in regard to beauty seem to have vastly changed since my time. What appears to be admired now, would not have been so then. Mere charms of person, unaccompanied by breeding, refinement, and grace, would not have been admired in former days, except by a certain class of men, whose admiration was considered a very poor compliment.

" You say that if you do not come to Belfield you will spend the winter in Rome. You will find plenty of society there, and I daresay your wife will be quite as much admired in Rome as in Paris. I am not so sure that she would produce the same effect here, as we are rather old-fashioned folks in this part of Lancashire.

"Say whatever you think right from me to Mrs. Bootle. That you may not repent your choice, is the heartfelt wish of

"Your affectionate mother,
                    "ELIZABETH SHELMERDINE."

"By Jove, Tiff! here's a stinger!" cried Bootle, handing her the letter.

"What a dreadful old termagant!" cried Mrs. Bootle, after she had scanned it. "But never mind, dearest boy, We'll go to Belfield in spite of her."

"There'll be a jolly row if we do," he rejoined, laughing. "But I don't like this sort of thing. I don't approve of the tone of her letter. You shan't be affronted in this way."

"Who cares for what she says?" cried his wife, snapping her fingers. "I don't. To Belfield we will go, dear boy!—to Belfield we will go. We're safe of the governor's support."

"That's not much," observed Bootle. "It won't do to count upon him. In a dispute with the old lady he invariably shows the white feather. He's not master of Belfield, I can tell you."

"High time he should be, dearest boy," remarked Mrs. Bootle. "It's important to us to establish ourselves there. We must do so without delay."

"If I felt quite sure of the governor I shouldn't hesitate," rejoined Bootle. "But you see he daren't write."

Just then a garçon entered the room.

"Une depèche télégraphique, pour Monsieur," he said, giving him a letter. "Arrivée à l'instant."

"From the governor, I'll bet a hundred!" cried Bootle. "Now we shall know how to act. Here, read it," he added, handing it to his wife.

Mrs. Bootle tore open the envelope, and with a scream of delight read the following message:—

"'Never mind what your mother says. Bring your wife to Belfield. The sooner the better.'

" There ! what do you say to that, darling boy ? Wasn't I right ? "

" Of course, my love. You're always right. I fancy the old lady will meet her match in you, Tiff."

"I flatter myself she will, darling boy," responded Mrs. Bootle, confidently. " As you say, it's a great point to have the governor with us. The old lady has had her own way far too long. A little opposition will do her good, and she shall have it from me, I can promise her, as soon as we're fairly settled in the house. She has set her face against my family, but I'll have them all at Belfield before I'm many weeks older."

CHAPTER II.

A FEW days after this determination had been come to, Mr. and Mrs. Bootle Shelmerdine quitted Paris, and proceeded to London.

Everything was prepared for them at the Acacias, and it is almost superfluous to say that they were warmly welcomed. Both Flaxyard and his wife had missed their daughter sadly, and though anxious to get her married, as we have shown, they felt quite lonely when she was gone. The Acacias seemed quite changed without the lively Tiffany, and was given up in a great measure to Hornby and his friends. The delight of the worthy couple at having her back again may therefore be imagined.

Mrs. Bootle Shelmerdine was now a very important member of the family indeed, and treated with proportionate respect. Hornby thought his sister wonderfully improved, though he couldn't exactly tell how, and he was greatly amused by finding that she had got what he called, "the upper hand of her caro sposo." Bootle, however, seemed perfectly contented and happy, and if his wife "could turn him round her little finger," as Hornby insinuated, the process did not appear to be disagreeable. It must be owned that Tiffany ruled her husband in a very agreeable way. If she occasionally took him to task, and exacted implicit obedience to her will, she was, on the whole, very good-natured, petted him, amused him by her drollery, allowed him to smoke any number of cigars, and never reproved him for drinking too much claret.

But the thing that astonished Hornby most of all in his brother-in-law was, that Bootle had entirely got rid of his jealousy. When young Flaxyard had heard of the admiration excited by his pretty sister at Paris, he had pictured to himself all sorts of stormy scenes between her and her husband. He now learnt that Bootle had been enchanted by the homage paid his wife, and what was still more surprising, that Bootle did not object to the presence of any of her former admirers. On making this discovery, Hornby of course invited Rufus Trotter and all his bachelor friends, who had been tabooed before the marriage, and many a jolly dinner-party they had.

Cheered by these dinners, Bootle passed a very pleasant week at the Acacias, and would willingly have prolonged his stay under his father-in-law's hospitable roof, but his wife was eager to commence her projected campaign. Bootle had written to announce his return, conveying a cordial invitation from old Flaxyard, and hoping his father would run up to town; but John excused himself on the plea of business.

Naturally, Mrs. Bootle had confided her scheme to her family. Old Flaxyard had many misgivings about it. He thought the plan very hazardous, and calculated to make matters worse. At all events, he said, a little conciliatory correspondence ought to take place first.

Mrs. Flaxyard was quite of a different opinion, and in favour of a bolder policy. She had perfect faith in her daughter's management. Had she not succeeded with Bootle? Could she fail now?

Flaxyard argued that Mrs. Shelmerdine and her son were two very different persons, and required very different management; but he admitted that his daughter had spirit and cleverness for anything, and he would not, therefore, dissuade her from the attempt.

Acting upon her papa's suggestion, Mrs. Bootle resolved to try the effect of a preliminary letter, so she sat down and penned the following :—

" The Acacias, Clapham, Nov. 20, 186—.

" MY DEAREST MAMMA,—We have just returned from our delightful Continental trip, and are spending a few days here with papa and mamma before proceeding to Lancashire. You may expect us very shortly. I shall not feel at all like a stranger in my new home, for darling Bootle has talked to me so much about Belfield, that I seem familiar with every room in the house.

" I should think that the large room with the French furniture, and the dressing-room attached to it, would suit us best. If we don't like it, we can easily make a change.

" I am looking forward with the greatest pleasure to a few months' residence in Lancashire. Darling Bootle tells me that you have many very agreeable neighbours noted for their hospitality, and that in Manchester they have excellent concerts and assemblies. I have no doubt I shall contrive to get through the winter very well.

" I must now tell you, dearest mamma, what Bootle and I have decided upon. We must have a grand ball to celebrate our arrival at Belfield. That will set everybody going. Darling Bootle says there can be no difficulty in getting dancing men, since there is a cavalry regiment in Manchester. Cards, I think, ought to be sent out at once. I fear our proposed ball may put you to a little inconvenience, but you won't mind that, once in a way. Perhaps it might be well to have a dinner-party, followed by a musical soirée, a few days before the ball. If you approve of this suggestion, ask the nicest people you know to the dinner, including the colonel of the regiment and three or four of the officers, with lots of refreshers for the evening. As we mean to be very gay this winter, a dinner and ball will ensure us plenty of invitations.

" And now, dearest mamma, a word in conclusion. If I understand myself at all, I am of a very amiable disposition, and remarkably forgiving. In referring for a moment to the little misunderstanding which occurred before my marriage, I do so merely to say that I desire to think no more about it. It must be satisfactory to you to hear that darling Bootle and I get on together famously. He adores me—at least, he tells me so, and I am bound to believe him. When you know me better, I am quite sure you will like me, or you will be an exception to the general rule, for everybody does like me. Mrs. Malaprop, as you know, says it is well to begin with a little aversion, and, as you disliked me at first, so I feel certain you will end by becoming excessively fond of me.

"With our united best love to dearest papa and yourself, '

"Believe me,

"Your very affectionate daughter,

"THEOPHANIA SHELMERDINE."

Before despatching this letter, which she considered a masterpiece, Mrs. Bootle read it to her husband and her mother. Bootle was greatly amused by it, but Mrs. Flaxyard, though equally amused, expressed her disapprobation.

"You mustn't send such a letter as that, my love," she said. "If you do, you'll never enter Belfield."

"We shall see," replied Mrs. Bootle, confidently. "I must take the high hand with the old lady. If I were to write in a humble strain, she would think nothing of me—probably decline to receive me. This letter will bring her to her senses. She will perceive that I won't stand any nonsense—that I mean to be treated properly—as her daughter-in-law should be treated —and she will give way."

"I sincerely hope she may. But I own I feel rather nervous about it."

"You are always nervous, mamma. I have no misgiving. What will you say if I ask you and papa and Hornby to the ball?"

"I shall say that you have worked wonders. But I shan't believe it till we get the invitation."

18

"She'll do it if she sets about it," remarked Bootle. "The little woman is equal to anything. I hope you will all come to Belfield. We shall have a jolly time of it if you do."

"Little chance of it, I fear," rejoined Mrs. Flaxyard.

"Every chance, mamma," said Mrs. Bootle. "This is the first step towards it. See this letter posted, darling boy," she added, giving it to her husband.

CHAPTER III.

HE letter was sent, and reached its destination next morning.

Mr. and Mrs. Shelmerdine were at breakfast in the spacious and well-furnished dining-room at Belfield when it was delivered. Glancing at the direction, Mrs. Shelmerdine laid it down, but curiosity getting the better of her disgust, she opened it.

A perfect explosion of rage succeeded the perusal.

"What's the matter, my dear?" inquired John, who had some suspicion of the truth.

"Read that, and you will learn," rejoined his wife, tossing the letter to him. "This is of a piece with her previous conduct, though I must say that it goes beyond any notions I had formed of her."

After scanning the letter, John laughed very heartily.

"So she wants to give a dinner and ball on her arrival," he remarked. "Not a bad idea, eh!"

"Before she gives a dinner and a ball at Belfield she must first get into the house," rejoined the lady, haughtily. "This is not a laughable matter, Mr. Shelmerdine. It is

18—2

very serious,—at least, to *me.* If you were not a party to the scheme, you would be shocked, and not laugh. All things considered, there never was a more impudent proceeding. After I had positively declined to receive her, she coolly writes to say she is coming, selects her own room, and enjoins me to issue invitations for a dinner and a ball to announce her arrival to the neighbourhood. Can impudence go beyond that?"

"Take a more good-natured view of the matter, my dear, and comply with her request. This letter I believe to be written at Bootle's suggestion."

"Maybe so," she rejoined, sharply. "But that does not alter my opinion of it. If Bootle had married a lady, I should have been delighted to have his wife with me as long as she chose to make this house her home. But here is a vulgar creature, who tries to force herself upon me whether I will or not, who dictates to me what I am to do, and almost intimates that she means to take the reins out of my hand."

"No such thing is meant, my dear," said John, in a deprecatory tone. "However disagreeable it may be, you cannot refuse to receive Bootle and his wife, and to give them a home in this house as long as they choose to stay with us. Indeed, it is my express wish that you should do so. And I think you will do wisely, as well as kindly, to carry out their suggestions. Before Bootle's marriage, opposition might have answered some purpose, but now that the step has been taken, you must reconcile yourself to it."

"Since it is your express wish, Mr. Shelmerdine, that I should receive her, I will do so," replied his wife, after a little reflection, which she aided by a cup of tea. "I should very much prefer waiting till the spring, to see how she goes on ; but if you desire to have them here now I will obey, however repugnant compliance may be to my own feelings."

"Kindly and sensibly resolved, my dear," said John, "and just what I expected from you. I am sure you will like our daughter-in-law."

"To like her is an impossibility," she rejoined, in a scornful voice. "But I will strive to tolerate her. Belfield will be no longer Belfield when she sets foot in it."

"Nonsense, my dear; the house will be a great deal livelier, that will be the only difference. We want a little stirring up. .I am of opinion that you will find Mrs. Bootle an exceedingly agreeable companion. Everybody seems to like her. Bootle, as you know, says she has been greatly admired on the Continent, and I feel convinced she will be very popular here."

"Amongst men, perhaps. But to me her manner is detestable. I wish I could correct it."

"Pray don't make the attempt, my dear. And since you have so kindly consented to waive your objections, let me entreat you to go a little further, and make up your mind not to meddle with our daughter-in-law. This is quite necessary for Bootle's sake. Interference with married people always makes mischief. However, I need say no more. Your own good sense and feeling will prompt the right course to be taken. Will you answer her letter, or shall I?"

"I could not trust myself to answer it—at least in the spirit you desire."

"Then I will," cried John. "Shall I say anything about the dinner and the ball?"

"Just as you please," she rejoined, heaving a deep sigh. "I may as well resign myself at once. If anything goes wrong, the responsibility will rest on your shoulders."

"They are quite wide enough to bear it," he rejoined, cheerfully.

So he wrote a letter to his daughter-in-law, which caused her the most extravagant delight.

"You see what I have accomplished," she cried, triumphantly, after reading it to her mother and Bootle. "All difficulties have vanished before the stroke of my magical pen. Mrs. Shelmerdine has eaten humble pie. We shall be made heartily welcome at Belfield, and are to have the dinner and the ball. So far well. But my triumph will be incomplete," she added to her mother, "unless you are all present at the ball. I will have you there."

Mrs. Flaxyard lifted up her hands.

"And she'll do it, too, since she says so," remarked Bootle, who was lost in admiration of his wife's generalship. "Never was such a wonderful little woman!"

When old Flaxyard and Hornby came home from the City, and the good news was imparted to them, they could scarcely credit it.

That night there was great rejoicing at the Acacias, and an immense deal of Lafitte was imbibed by the young men.

CHAPTER IV.

THE ARRIVAL AT BELFIELD.

ELFIELD—whither we now propose to conduct the reader—is pleasantly situated on the slope of a hill, about a couple of miles to the north of Bury, on the road to Haslingden. It is a large white mansion, of formal, but imposing appearance, and overlooks a country agreeably diversified with hill and valley, with brown bleak moors, and a bolder and higher range of hills in the distance. The view from the terrace, comprehending the adjacent town of Bury, with Bolton on the one hand, and Rochdale on the other, would be very striking, but for the evidences afforded to the beholder that he is in the midst of a populous manufacturing district. Cotton-mills—the ugliest structures ever devised by man—offend the gaze on all sides, and darken the air with the smoke .from their tall chimneys. The fields are converted into bleaching-grounds, and the once clear rivulets, coursing through the once charming valleys, are polluted by dye-works, and empty themselves into the Irwell, which flows past the grounds of Belfield on its way to Manchester.

Our worthy friend Mr. Shelmerdine, we are quite aware,

differs from us most materially in regard to the charm of the prospect commanded by his residence. In his eyes the picture has no blemish. He does not dislike cotton factories —not he!—neither does he object to print-works nor to bleach-works. The dingy colour of the Irwell does not offend him, and he rather likes to look upon the cloud of smoke hanging like a pall over distant Manchester. His earliest associations being connected with this district, it still retains a strong hold upon his affections. Nothing to his mind can be more beautiful than the neighbourhood of Bury, and he would not change his large formal mansion, with its uniform ranges of windows, its stately Ionic columns, its rustic stone basement, and broad double flight of steps, leading to the principal entrance, for the oldest and most picturesquely situated hall in Cheshire.

From the stately terrace of Belfield our worthy friend can distinguish a miserable row of cottages—such cottages as are only to be seen in a manufacturing district. In one of the poorest of those hovels dwelt his mother—he never knew a father's care—and she has long since been released from toil and misery. John's eye often wanders in the direction of that lowly hut, and he thinks of his early struggles and aspirations. His ambition was to become a mill-owner, and by prudence and indomitable perseverance he has realised the dream.

While making his way to wealth, Mr. Shelmerdine often said that when he had sufficient means he would build the handsomest mansion in the neighbourhood of Bury. He kept his word, and built Belfield, which he flatters himself *is* the handsomest and best-situated house in the neighbourhood.

Mrs. Shelmerdine, whose associations are different from those of her husband, and who likes old mansions and well-timbered parks, and abominates factories and dye-works, would fain have had him purchase a place in Cheshire. But John would not listen to the suggestion. Having built Belfield, he resolved to stay there.

We must not find fault with Belfield, or we shall forfeit our friend's good opinion; but we confess that, like Mrs. Shelmerdine, we should prefer a place in Cheshire. However, that is mere matter of taste. Beyond dispute, Belfield is a very fine mansion, and possesses a vast number of spacious apartments. The magnificent entrance-hall is adorned with busts ,statues, and groups of marble, executed by modern Italian sculptors. The dining-room, which will accommodate no end of guests, has a coved ceiling, supported at one end by pillars, and its walls are covered by the best specimens of modern art. Then there is a vast saloon, gorgeously fitted up in the style of Louis XV. Another and somewhat smaller morning-room has a conservatory attached to it. Besides these, there are several other apartments on the same floor—namely, a library, a billiard-room, and a smoking-room. A splendid staircase conducts from the entrance-hall to the upper story. Here many of the rooms are spacious, and all lofty and well furnished. Owing to the number of windows and the width of the passages, the house has a remarkably light and cheerful air.

The grounds of Belfield, though not very extensive, are nicely laid out. The shrubberies, which of course were planted by our friend, are getting on tolerably well, but unquestionably the place looks too new. It wants timber; and something, perhaps, besides timber. The tallest trees among the plantations are poplars, and these add to the formal character of the edifice. A large lawn, smooth and soft as velvet, is spread out in front of the mansion, and in summer the parterres and borders are embellished by the choicest flowers. There is also an excellent walled-in garden, with hothouses and greenhouses. The slopes on the further side of the hill are skirted by the Irwell, which bounds our friend's property in this quarter; but the river, owing to its Stygian hue, does not enhance the beauty of the scene.

About half-past nine, on a fine frosty day towards the end of November, Mr. and Mrs. Bootle Shelmerdine left the Euston station for Bury. The young couple were accompanied by two French servants, whom they had brought with them from Paris—namely, Monsieur Émile Pochet, a very fine gentleman, who condescended to serve Bootle in the capacity of valet, and Mam'selle Léontine Latrompette, Mrs. Bootle's pretty and extremely coquettish femme de chambre.

Mam'selle Léontine, a lively brunette, whose chief personal attractions consisted in a pair of remarkably fine black eyes, capable of any expression, and two ranges of small pearly teeth, which she took frequent occasion to display, and Monsieur Emile, whose jet black hair was cropped close to the head, and whose sallow cheeks were so carefully shaven that they looked perfectly blue—these two personages, we say, who knew nothing more of England than had come under their observation between Dover and London, were tolerably well pleased with the country through which they travelled till they reached Stockport. Then the forest of tall chimneys that burst upon them as they crossed the viaduct that carries the railway over the town, the smoke-begrimed buildings, and the reeky atmosphere filled them with intense disgust.

"Mon Dieu! what a frightful town!" exclaimed Léontine. "A thousand times worse than Lille."

Monsieur Emile never had had the misfortune to see Lille, but he felt sure it could not possibly be so bad as Stockport.

Manchester, which seemed almost to begin when they got out of Stockport, heightened their disgust, and they gazed almost with horror at the huge, black, many-windowed piles that rose before them on all sides.

"What a city! what buildings! what a populace!" exclaimed Emile, piteously. "Till now, I had no idea what perfidious Albion was like. Execrable country! We must go back to Paris, Mam'selle. I cannot exist in an infernal region like this."

Léontine quite concurred with him in opinion, and they continued to abuse everything they beheld till they arrived at Bury, when the necessity of attending to their master and mistress turned their thoughts in another direction.

Mrs. Bootle had shared the sentiments of her suivante. Stockport and Manchester, as seen through the windows of the coupé occupied by herself and darling Bootle, had positively appalled her. Never having been in this part of the country before, she had but a very imperfect notion of what a large manufacturing town is like. Nothing so ugly as those clusters of factories, with the surrounding dingy habitations, had entered into her ideas. With a sickening heart she turned to her husband, and said,—

"I hope Bury is not like this, dearest boy."

"Ten times worse," replied Bootle, who was tranquilly enjoying a cigar. "At Bury there are twice as many cotton-mills, five times as many chimneys, and the air is so full of smoke that you can't swallow it."

"I can't swallow your description, dear boy," she rejoined. "But if it really is worse than this, I shall soon bid adieu to Belfield.".

"Well, you'll see what it's like presently."

The aspect of the country improved as they went on, and by the time they reached their destination Mrs. Bootle had quite recovered her spirits. Attired ih a most becoming toilette de voyage, of which a blue velvet mantle trimmed with sable formed the most conspicuous feature, and wearing the prettiest little chapeau rond that ever came from the Rue Vivienne, she looked charming in the eyes of Papa Shelmerdine, who was waiting her arrival on the platform. Kissing her very heartily as he helped her out, he at once conducted her to a well-appointed barouche which was drawn up close by, and while doing so attempted some apologies for the absence of his wife. Mrs. Bootle, however, quickly relieved his embarrassment by saying that she didn't in the least expect to see her.

Having bestowed his daughter-in-law safely in the barouche, John then returned to Bootle, who, with the aid of his own valet and his father's footman, Broadbent, was getting sundry cloaks, wraps, and other articles out of the coupé. Mam'selle Léontine was standing by, and perceiving that she could be of little use, John good-naturedly took her to the barouche, and placed her opposite her mistress. A discussion next took place between father and son in regard to the enormous quantity of boxes which Mrs. Bootle had brought from town; the result being that Broadbent, "a very intelligent chap," according to John, was left in charge of a van-load of milliners' boxes and trunks. This important matter settled, Mr. Shelmerdine and Bootle got into the barouche, the old gentleman seating himself beside his pretty daughter-in-law, of whom he felt not a little proud, and Bootle taking the only vacant place, which of course was next to Léontine, while the gentleman-like Emile mounted to the seat erstwhile occupied by Broad-

bent. In this manner they drove off, exciting the admiration of a number of persons on the platform, who had
lingered to witness their departure.

Whether it was that she was gratified by her reception, or
determined to see everything *en beau*, Mrs. Bootle appeared
delighted with Bury. John pointed out his mill to her, and
though it exactly resembled one of the large factories she
had seen at Manchester, boasted as tall a chimney, numbered
as many windows, smoked just as much, and made just as
great a din with its machinery and engines, she professed to
be wonder-struck by it, and told her dearest papa that he
must take her over it one of these days, which he readily
promised to do. Even Léontine was in ecstasies at the
sight of the grand bâtiment. Bootle smoked his cigar
quietly and said nothing, but a twinkle in his eye betrayed
his thoughts.

A splendid pair of horses being attached to the barouche,
and Pollard, the coachman, putting them along as soon as
he got out of the town, which was crowded with waggons,
the party soon reached the rather ostentatious lodge that
guarded the entrance to Belfield. The gate was thrown
wide open, and the good dame who occupied the lodge
with her daughter—the latter being a fair specimen of a
Lancashire lass—curtseyed respectfully to Mrs. Bootle, and
said something which that young lady did not understand,
though she guessed its import. The mansion, now coming
full in view, elicited a genuine burst of admiration from
Mrs. Bootle, and sundry exclamations of rapture from the
irrepressible Léontine.

"Ah! quelle jolie campagne! c'est délicieuse—superbe!"
exclaimed the soubrette. "Madame doit être bien heureuse
ici—et moi aussi."

Mr. Shelmerdine did not talk much French. In fact, he
didn't speak the language at all, but Léontine's looks and
gestures were so expressive that he could not fail to understand her. Her enthusiasm gratified him. Whether
Léontine's raptures were feigned or not, we won't pretend to
say, but Mrs. Bootle really was struck by the appearance of
the mansion. It was a much finer place than she expected,
and she told Mr. Shelmerdine so with a frankness that
charmed him. Not being called upon to express any opinion,

Bootle never took his cigar from his lips, but laughed to himself at what was said. The drive to the house was skirted by a plantation, and fenced off from the meadows by iron hurdles, and, the gentle ascent being at length surmounted, the carriage drew up at the foot of the nearest flight of steps. Mr. Knowles, the portly butler, and two footmen in the Shelmerdine livery, were on the steps, but no Mrs. Shelmerdine could be seen.

John alighted first, and conducted his daughter-in-law into the house—the swing-doors being thrown wide open by the bowing servants. He detained her for a short time in the entrance-hall, under pretence of pointing out the various objects to her, and hoping his wife would appear; but being disappointed in the expectation, he took his daughter-in-law to the drawing-room.

The only person who went with them. was Bootle, Mr. Knowles no doubt comprehending that his presence at the meeting might not be desirable.

Mrs. Shelmerdine was seated in a fauteuil near the fire at the farther end of the spacious saloon, and was too much engrossed, we may suppose, by the newspaper she was reading to notice their entrance. At all events, she did not look round, or change her posture in any way, till admonished by her husband, who called out rather loudly, "My dear!—Bootle and his wife?"

She then arose, deliberately laid down the newspaper, and advanced with a slow and dignified step to greet her daughter-in-law. Bootle watched the proceedings through his eye-glass, prepared to support his wife if occasion should require it.

Nothing daunted by her mother-in-law's cold and repelling looks, and feeling that something must be done, Mrs. Bootle sprang forward, and flinging her arms round the proud lady's neck, kissed her affectionately. The embrace, we may be sure, was not returned, and as soon as Mrs. Shelmerdine could release herself, without offering a word of welcome, she prayed her daughter-in-law to be seated, and addressed herself to Bootle, probably intending to favour him with a maternal salute, but the irate young gentleman drew back.

"No, thank you, Ma'am!" he cried. " Much obliged to

you all the same. If you won't kiss my wife, you shan't kiss me. I didn't bring her to my father's house to be treated in this style, I can tell you. Let us have no more of it, if you please."

Never before having been addressed in such language by her son, Mrs. Shelmerdine was quite taken aback.

"How silly you are, dearest boy!" cried Mrs. Bootle. "What would you have dear mamma do? She has given me a most cordial reception."

"Has she!" cried Bootle. "Then I don't know what a cordial reception is."

"I'm sure I'm delighted to see *you*, my dear," observed his mother.

"Bother!" cried Bootle. "Behave properly to my wife. Say you're glad to see her, and I shall be satisfied."

Mrs. Shelmerdine did not say this, but seated herself in a stately manner beside her daughter-in-law, expressing a hope that she had had a pleasant journey from town—expressing a further hope that she had left Mr. and Mrs. Flaxyard and Mr. Hornby quite well.

"All quite well. Nothing could be pleasanter than the journey. Darling Bootle and herself had occupied a coupé, and he smoked all the way."

"Very agreeable," remarked Mrs. Shelmerdine; dryly.

"Yes, I don't mind the odour of a cigar in the least. I never interfere with my darling boy's enjoyments. I'm afraid you will think I spoil him sadly, for I let him do just what he likes. The old people are in capital preservation, and desire all sorts of kind messages to you. They are longing to see Belfield."

"I hope they will soon run down, and have a look at us," remarked John.

"Of course they will," said Bootle, greatly to his mother's horror.

But her dismay was increased when Mrs. Bootle added,—

"If quite agreeable to you, dear mamma, I should like to ask them and Hornby to the ball."

"We'll talk about that by-and-by," rejoined Mrs. Shelmerdine, evasively.

"Well, to tell you the truth, dearest mamma, I have

already invited them," said Mrs. Bootle. "I thought I might venture to do so."

"Invited them!—without my sanction!" cried Mrs. Shelmerdine. "You have taken an unheard-of liberty. I shall put off the ball."

"No, no, my dear. The ball cannot be put off," said John, gravely and firmly. "It is quite proper that our new relations should he invited, and as I have just said, I shall be very glad to see them. In the presence of my daughter-in-law, whom I am proud and happy to welcome here, I declare that I like her family, and am better pleased that my son has connected himself with them than if he married a duchess. Mr. Flaxyard cannot object to me on the score of my humble origin, neither can I object to him for a like reason. We have both made our own way in the world. The match, therefore, between our children, is perfectly suitable. Don't let family pride stick in your throat, my dear, but gulp it down as you would a bitter draught, and have done with it."

The draught was too bitter for Mrs. Shelmerdine. She made a wry face, but could not swallow it.

"I must stand up for papa and mamma, at the hazard of giving you offence, Ma'am," said Mrs. Bootle. "They are very nice people—though perhaps I ought not to say so—very much liked in their own society ——"

"And not in the least vulgar," supplied Mrs. Shelmerdine.

"Not half so vulgar as many other people who are proud of their musty ancestors," retorted Mrs. Bootle. "If not well born, they are well bred, and always show proper consideration for the feelings of other people. If I am to remain in this house, papa," she added to him, "they must not be excluded from it."

"They shall not be excluded," said John, emphatically. "They shall come to the ball."

"Oh! thank you, dearest papa! thank you!" cried his daughter-in-law.

"Mr. Shelmerdine, you are master here, and can do as you please," said his wife; "but I beg that the invitation may not be sent in my name."

"It has already been given in mine," observed Bootle. "I knew the governor wouldn't object."

"You judged him quite right, my boy," said John. "Your wife shall ask anybody she pleases—anybody." "Oh! you are the dearest and best papa in the world!" cried Mrs. Bootle, with effusion. "But I shall always consult dear mamma—if she will let me."

"Consult *me!* That is quite unnecessary, after what Mr. Shelmerdine has said. I am no longer to have a voice in my own house, it appears."

"Nonsense, my dear," said John. "No interference whatever with you is intended. But I wish my daughter-in-law to feel perfectly at home here, and to do exactly what she likes."

"Then she is mistress, and not I, and I may as well resign my authority at once."

"Papa does not mean anything of the sort, dear mamma," cried Mrs. Bootle. "Be sure that I have no intention of usurping your authority. Perhaps I resented your remarks upon the elderly parties at home rather too strongly, but I trust you will forgive me, on reflection."

"You were quite right to stick up for them, Tiff," said Bootle. "I won't allow them to be run down."

"You are a degenerate boy, Bootle, and have no proper pride," rejoined his mother.

"Yes I have," he retorted. "I am proud of my little wife, and I fancy before long you will become proud of her too."

"Never was such infatuation," muttered Mrs. Shelmerdine.

"Infatuated or not, I'm perfectly happy, and that's the main point," said Bootle.

"Come, there must be an end of this," interposed John. "We must contrive to live together in peace and harmony. You must concede certain points, my dear," he added to his wife, "in order to make your daughter-in-law comfortable. And you, my love," he continued to Mrs. Bootle, "must study your mother-in-law, and take all she says in good part. These things attended to, we shall go on very smoothly."

"I'm quite agreeable," said the younger lady, readily.

"You don't answer, my dear," observed Mr. Shelmerdine to his spouse.

" Before answering, I should like to know what concessions I am expected to make," she rejoined.

" Only such as your own good feelings will prompt," said John. "Mrs. Bootle is to be quite at home here—to do what she likes, without the slightest interference from either of us—and may ask whomsoever she pleases."

To prevent any further rejoinder, he then proposed to show his daughter-in-law over the house, and hurried her out of the room, rejoicing that the dreaded meeting had been got over so well.

CHAPTER V.

RS. BOOTLE'S impressions of Belfield will, we think, be best conveyed by a letter which she addressed to her mamma about a week after her arrival.

Belfield, Bury, Dec. —, 186—.

"I sent you a hurried letter, dearest mamma, to announce our arrival here ; but I have purposely delayed writing again till I could tell you exactly what I think of the place. I am delighted with Belfield, and with all belonging to it—with one important exception.

"Darling Bootle is not half so attentive to me as his papa, who makes the greatest possible fuss of me, and never likes me to be out of his sight. With madame la mère I am now on tolerably good terms. We hate each other just as heartily as ever, but have agreed to keep the peace, and though we have now and then a little sparring, in which I am sure to get the best of it, being the lighter and quicker of the two, we never come to actual fisticuffs. What we may do one of these days I won't say, for my angelic temper is often ruffled ; but, if there should be a fight, it will be a good one, I can promise you.

"Immediately after our arrival we had a slight set-to, in which both Bootle and the governor backed me up, and, as you may suppose, with so many against her, the old lady was obliged to give in. This acted as a caution. However, I am never alone with her if I can help it, and I always make Bootle accompany us in our drives. The darling boy displayed as much spirit as Mr. Moor of Moor Hall in our first encounter with this terrible old dragon of Wantley.

"Our preliminary breeze had one effect, not exactly anticipated by the old lady. It completely established my position in the house. I am to do just what I please—to invite whom I please—and am not to be interfered with in any way whatever. Such was the governor's emphatic declaration in the presence of his spouse. Oh! he is such a dear good old fellow, and I am so very, very fond of him.

"My first invitation is to you. You must all come down to the dinner on the 5th and stay over the ball, which will take place on the 10th. Both will be very grand affairs, I can tell you, and I think you will like Belfield. It will also, I fancy, gratify you to see your daughter at the head—no, not quite, but nearly at the head of such a splendid establishment. It is astonishing how well things are done here. The cuisine is first-rate, as it ought to be, for Marcellin, our chef, is a veritable cordon bleu. Emile, Bootle's valet, declares he has never seen such dinners out of Paris. Hornby, who likes French cookery, will be enchanted.

"The establishment is immense—at least, it appears immense to me—but it is remarkably well ordered, and goes as smoothly as the spinning-jennies in the governor's cotton-mill, but without their noise. Unwilling as I am to admit it, I really think the old lady deserves some credit for her management. She makes an admirable housekeeper, and on no account would I deprive her of the place. Léontine attends to me, and Emile to Bootle. Bring Charlotte with you, if you like, but don't let Hornby bring his valet.

"Though I delight in Belfield, I can't say that I like the neighbourhood, it is so different from anything I have been accustomed to, but I daresay I shall get reconciled to it in time ; but whatever you may think, be careful to admire the view, for the one point on which Mr. Shelmerdine is sensitive

19—2

is the situation of his house.   Give papa and Hornby a hint
on this subject.

"You will be glad to hear that I have the most delicious
little boudoir imaginable, where I am writing this letter, and
where I can converse freely with Léontine, who is really
indispensable to me.   You know how indulgent I am to
darling Bootle, but I won't allow him to smoke in my
boudoir, so he rarely troubles me, and his mother never
troubles me at all   Tell Hornby we have a famous billiard-
room, and a regular smoking divan.   He can hunt four or
five times a week with the Cheshire fox-hounds, if he is so
inclined.

"Since our arrival has been made known in the neighbourhood, we have had lots of morning visitors.   Everybody,
who is anybody, I believe, has called upon us.   As we have
had to return all these calls, our time has been fully
occupied, and we have naturally seen a great many houses
and a great many people.   I like best the Huncoats of
Coldcoats, and I expect Hornby to fall in love with Milicent
Huncoat, the youngest daughter, who is uncommonly pretty
and lively.   The Booth Bacopes of Hawbrook Hall, the
Oswaldtwistles of Chaidley, the Accringtons, the Briercliffes,
and the Walmsleys, are also nice people.   But you will soon
see them, and judge for yourself.   All our friends are
wealthy, have got large houses, and live in very good style.
We have dined with the Huncoats. and Oswaldtwistles, and
have had very sumptuous entertainments.   Almost every
day we have a little dinner-party at home.   Mr. Shelmerdine,
I believe, is rarely without company.

"I flatter myself that I have caused a sensation.   Nothing
like my toilettes, I am sure, have been seen in these parts,
and I can make myself agreeable, if I like, to men.   Women
are so jealous of each other, that they won't admire you if
you are at all out of the common run.   Some antiquated
dames, and a few not quite so antiquated, I can see, think
me too fast, but their better halves and sons don't share the
opinion.   Milicent Huncoat, who is the prettiest girl I have
seen here, has taken to me amazingly.

"And now, dearest mamma, I am about to astonish you.
Yesterday we all drove over to Manchester in the barouche.
Mrs. Shelmerdine had some shopping to do in St. Ann's

Square, so we drove there at once and set her down. Bootle and I were left in the carriage, amusing ourselves by quizzing the natives, when who should come up but Captain Musgrave. There! are you not astonished? Yes, it was Musgrave himself, and looking particularly handsome. Wasn't it droll? He was sauntering along listlessly, but the moment he beheld your pretty little daughter in her French chapeau and redingote, he sprang towards the carriage. Recollecting the scene that had occurred at the Acacias, I felt rather uneasy, not knowing how Bootle might take it, but the darling boy behaved charmingly, as you shall hear.

"'Ah, Captain Musgrave, is it really you?' I cried, as he came up and shook hands, bowing at the same time to Bootle. 'Who would have thought of seeing you in Manchester!"

"'It is an unlikely place to see me at,' he rejoined, laughing. 'But I have some friends in the 40th Dragoons, who are quartered here, and I have been spending a day or two with them. I should have been equally surprised to see you, had I not heard that you are at Belfield. I intended to do myself the pleasure of calling on you to offer my felicitations. Pray accept them now.'

" He then addressed Bootle, whose placid looks showed him it was all right, and said :—

"'For the last fortnight I have been staying at Peovor Hall, in Cheshire, with your uncle, Mr. Egerton Bootle, and an awfully jolly time I have had of it—good hunting, good shooting, good society, good living, good everything.'

"'Bravo!' exclaimed Bootle. 'Peovor is a capital house to stay at. Madam has not yet made her uncle's acquaintance. That's a pleasure to come—eh, Tiff?'

"'Does he resemble his sister?' I whispered.

"'Rather,' replied my husband.

" Captain Musgrave guessed what I had said, even if he didn't overhear the remark, for he immediately gave me a very amusing picture of the old gentleman, which made us both laugh immoderately. We were in the very midst of our merriment, when Mrs. Shelmerdine, whom I had quite forgotten, came out of the shop. Captain Musgrave must be a striking-looking person, for she immediately recognised him, though she had only seen him once before for a few

minutes, as you know, at the Acacias. Never shall I forget
her look of surprise. It was truly comical. Not in the
least abashed, Musgrave made her a most respectful bow,
and Bootle hastened to inform her that the captain had been
staying with her brother at Peovor. This altered matters in
a moment. Musgrave, you may be quite sure, saw the right
line to take, and his praises of Mr. Egerton Bootle, and
enumeration of the county people whom he had met at
Peovor, acted like the softest of sawder. Mrs. Shelmerdine
thawed at once. Didn't raise the slightest objection when
Bootle asked the captain to come and spend a few days at
Belfield, but graciously added, as he assisted her into the
carriage, that she should be very glad to see him. So it was
settled that he should come next day; and come he did.
Indeed, he is here now.

"But I have not quite done with Manchester. Just as
we were about to drive off, and Musgrave was bidding us
adieu, two of the officers of the 40th came up. These were
Major Fullarton and Captain Frère, both beaux garçons, as
you will own, for you will see them at the dinner and ball;
and Musgrave's particular friends. The carriage was
instantly stopped. Presentations and a vast deal of
babillage took place, in the course of which many pretty
things were said to me by the officers; the result being that
Bootle was invited by Major Fullarton to dine that day at
the barracks at Hulme, or some such place. The major
apologised for taking my husband away, but I said I could
spare him, and the dear boy accepted the invitation. This
is the first time he has dined out alone; but I am not sorry
that I let him go; for though, by his own account, he got
rather screwed, he became better acquainted with Musgrave,
who, of course, formed one of the party. He slept at the
Queen's Hotel in Manchester that night, and came over
next morning with the captain.

"You won't wonder that Musgrave has made his way
rapidly at Belfield, when I tell you that he pays the most
deferential attention to the old lady, and has quite
succeeded in gaining her good graces. Mr. Shelmerdine
was rather surprised when he learnt that Bootle had invited
the captain to the house; but he made no objection, though
I heard him mutter that his son was a fool. I daresay

Musgrave would like to flirt with me, if I would allow him, but I won't. Quite right, I know you will say. Darling Bootle and the captain are the best friends possible.

"As I naturally feel some curiosity about poor Mrs. Musgrave, I have questioned the captain about her, but can learn very little from him. Whatever her faults may have been, and I fear she must have had great faults, she is much to be pitied. How beautiful we used to think her! There is something very strange in their sudden separation that I never can make out, and Musgrave declines to enlighten me on the subject. To say the least, the poor lady must have been excessively foolish. The worst feature in the case, it appears to me, and the circumstance that tells most against her, is that she has not returned to her family, but is living somewhere in absolute retirement. I am sure papa knows the whole truth of the story, if he would only tell it. But he is so very close. Can't you get it out of him? I don't know why I take so much interest in the matter, except that I should like to know positively whether she was to blame, or Musgrave. This, at least, you can ascertain for me. You will naturally ask, what does this signify to me? Not much; but I am curious.

"Having full permission to ask whom I please to Belfield, I have exercised my privilege in favour of Eva Bracebridge, and have invited her to stay with me. I think she will come, though she has only accepted the invitation conditionally. I like her, though we differ on so many points, and I want her to see how well I am married. I am sure she will be impressed by Belfield. She is still residing at Hylton Park —Sir Norman Hylton's place—and, as she could not reside there alone, her aunt, Mrs. Daventry, performs the part of gouvernante, and takes care of her. She said she didn't like leaving her aunt, so I have begged her to bring the duenna with her. It will be good fun if they come. Her time will pay for all. She cannot do better, for he is exceedingly handsome, gentleman-like, and agreeable. He is a great friend of Major Fullarton, who, as well as Captain Frere, dined with us yesterday, and the major talked to me a great deal about him. He says that Sir Norman was quite au désespoir when Eva left the Beau-Rivage, but his hopes were unexpectedly revived during a morning call which he made, contrary to his convention with mademoiselle, at Hylton Park. Eva permitted him to become her suitor, but would not give any promise of ultimate acceptance—took him on trial, in fact.

ı " Major Fullarton was staying at Lord Huntercombe's, where Sir Norman was a guest at the time, and heard all about it. Things still remain precisely in the same state. Eva won't be hurried into a decision, and Sir Norman dares not be too urgent, for fear of dismissal. The major hears frequently from his friend, who has taken up his quarters at a small place in the neighbourhood of his own castle. I have such a strong sympathy for a despairing lover, that if Eva decides upon coming to me, I shall get Bootle to invite Sir Norman at the same time.

" There is one little obstacle in the way of this, and that is Captain Musgrave. But perhaps he may be gone before the others arrive.

" What a long letter I have written. I am afraid you will never have patience to read it. But I have entered into these details to make you au fait with everything before your arrival here.

" I don't know what papa will say about Captain Musgrave being here, but you must keep him quiet. Hornby, I know, will be delighted. Tell·him he will be able to get up a rubber, but the governor won't stand lans-quenet or écarté. Musgrave and Bootle spend half the day in the billiard-room. They are there now.

" But I must bring this interminable letter to a close.

"With dearest love to papa, Hornby, and yourself,—
"Believe me,
" Your very affectionate daughter,
" THEOPHANIA SHELMERDINE.

"P.S.—Darling Bootle and Musgrave have just entered

my boudoir, but their habiliments exhaled such a powerful odour of tubac, that I turned them out, after sprinkling them liberally with eau-de-Cologne. Musgrave descried my voluminous despatch to you, and wanted to read it. Of course I wouldn't let him. Dearest B. desires to be remembered to you all."

In acknowledging her daughter's letter, which she did very promptly, Mrs. Flaxyard expressed the great gratification it would afford them all to visit her at her new home, where they were rejoiced to learn she was so happy, and to take part in the proposed festivities. She also expressed her satisfaction at the good understanding that subsisted between her daughter and Mrs. Shelmerdine, to whom she begged the united kind regards of herself and her family.

But she made no allusion to Captain Musgrave, and concluded a rather brief letter—singularly brief and guarded, in comparison with the letter she had received—by saying that she had already begun to make preparations for the anticipated pleasurable visit.

CHÁPTER VI.

OOTLE and Musgrave had been playing billiards all morning, as was their wont; Emile, who could play a first-rate game himself if he had the chance, acting as marker, when Bootle, who had won two games running, and who was, consequently, in excellent spirits, declared that he must go and have a look at his wife, and throwing his cigar into the fire, left Musgrave alone with the valet.

For a few minutes after his departure, Musgrave continued knocking the balls about for his own amusement, making some wonderful strokes, and showing Emile, who was looking on in admiration, what he could do.

"Monsieur le Capitaine plays superbly," observed the valet. "He can do what he likes with the balls."

"Your master plays better than I do, Emile," rejoined Musgrave, with a peculiar smile. "He has beaten me twice this morning. In fact, as you know, he generally beats me."

"There may be a reason for that," said Emile. "But if I am not mistaken, M. le Capitaine could give him thirty, and still win."

"You think so, Emile?"

"If I were in a position to do so, I should like to make a bet upon it, provided monsieur would engage not to give away the game."

"You are a sharp fellow, Emile," cried Musgrave, laughing, and going on with his play.

"Billiards is not the only game at which M. le Capitaine is habile; but he cannot hide his play from me. I am quicksighted, but other people are quick-sighted too, and I would recommend extreme caution. Monsieur will excuse me. It is in his interest that I venture to offer this advice. There are people capable of opening my master's eyes."

"But you are not one of them, I am sure, Emile," said Musgrave, leaning upon his cue, and regarding him steadfastly.

"Moi! M. le Capitaine!—I despise such cowardly infamy. I would never betray a gentleman who inadvertently placed himself in my power, but trust entirely to his generosity. I might make more perhaps by a contrary line of conduct, but that would not suit me. Je puis me rendre très utile, Monsieur."

"Ou bien dangereux, n'est ce pas, mon ami?" remarked Musgrave.

"Monsieur has said it," rejoined Emile, bowing.

"Well, then, you may count upon my generosity, Emile."

"Monsieur has adopted the wisest course, and may perfectly rely upon my zeal and fidelity," said Emile, placing his hand on his heart. "I am not to be bought at any price. But it will be necessary to secure Léontine, whose suspicions are already awakened. A French femme de chambre is endowed with wonderful acuteness, and can detect an affair of this sort in a moment. But if acute, Léontine is also loyal, and would scorn to betray her mistress. The very first day that M. le Capitaine arrived at Belfield, she observed to me, 'Je vois bien que ce beau monsieur est l'amant de madame.'"

"Votre Léontine a joliment menti," rejoined Musgrave.

"No doubt she was too free with her tongue; but as she only made the remark to me, it did not much signify. I will answer for her, if ——"

mouth must be stopped, Emile. Here is wherewithal to do it," he added, taking out his purse, and giving him all the gold it contained.

Emile quickly pocketed the shiners.

"Henceforth Léontine and myself are entirely devoted to Monsieur. A little message or a billet can be securely delivered at any time. Ah! voici monsieur et madame."

Flying to open the folding-door, he 'admitted Bootle and his wife, and withdrew.

Mrs. Bootle, who was fresh from the hands of Léontine, and charmingly dressed as usual, looked in such good spirits that Musgrave could not help asking the cause.

"I'll tell you what it is," said Bootle. "She has just had a letter from her dearest mamma, to say they will all be here to-day."

"Isn't that delightful?" cried the young lady.

Musgrave didn't think it delightful, but he tried to look pleased, and said what was proper to the occasion.

"Who else do you think is coming?" said Mrs. Bootle.

"Haveu't the least idea."

"Guess. No, you'll never guess, so I'll tell you. Eva Bracebridge."

"Eva Bracebridge!" exclaimed Musgrave, in astonishment. "May I inquire when you expect her?"

"On the 9th—the day before the ball. She is bringing her aunt, Mrs. Daventry, with her. I suppose you know that Sir Norman Hylton is renewing his suit?"

"Yes, I heard so from Fullarton, who corresponds with him. I hope he will be refused for the third time."

"What a shocking wish! You ought to conquer your dislike to him. I must make you friends."

"I don't think that very probable, after our meeting at Evian."

"That's the very reason why you ought to be friends. I must bring it about. Bootle is going to invite him here at the same time as Eva. I hope to have them both at the ball."

Musgrave's brow darkened.

"I am afraid I shall not have the pleasure of appearing at the ball," he said.

"Nonsense!" she cried. "I won't hear of your departure." Then, turning to Bootle, she added. "Do go and write the invitation to Sir Norman, dearest boy, and I'll enclose it in my letter to Eva."

"I wish you wouldn't send the invitation," remarked Musgrave. "Sir Norman won't like to find me here. It will be a bore to both of us—but to me especially."

"Sorry for that, but I must adhere to my arrangement."

"Don't you see, she has got some scheme in her head," observed Bootle. "When that's the case, the little woman always will have her own way."

"Never mind my scheme, but go and write the note—there's a dear boy."

So Bootle left the room.

"You look displeased," she said to Musgrave, as soon as they were alone.

"I may well look so," he rejoined, moodily. "You seem to have taken every step to make my stay here impossible. To-day your family arrive, and I feel almost certain Mr. Flaxyard will object to my presence. This perhaps was unavoidable, though I wish their visit could have been postponed; but you have gone out of the way to invite Eva and Sir Norman, and I shall be compelled to leave the house before they come."

"No. I won't allow you to go," she rejoined. "I see no difficulty whatever in the matter."

"Well, I will remain if you desire it—coûte que coûte. You have now such absolute power over me, that I must obey all your behests. I begin to wish that I had never come here at all."

"Why so?" she cried. "You told me yesterday you had never been so happy as now."

"I told you the truth. But to-day I am wretched. All my dreams are dispersed—all my hopes crushed by what you have just told me."

"You ought not to indulge any such hopes, and I am very glad they are crushed."

"You are a heartless coquette. You give me encouragement for the mere pleasure of disappointing me."

"Call me what names you please, but I forbid you positively to make love to me any more. You see how fond darling Bootle is of me."

"He does not love you half so well as I do!" cried Musgrave, passionately.

"I know better. I don't mind a little innocent flirtation, but I cannot allow any serious love-making."

And she prepared to leave the room.

"You cannot be insensible to a passion like mine," cried Musgrave, detaining her. "You must listen to me."

"Release me instantly," she cried. "I won't listen to a word more."

Musgrave still retained her hand, when the door opened, and Emile entered. The discreet valet, however, appeared to see nothing.

"Monsieur would like to speak to Madame for a moment in the library," said Emile, without raising his eyes.

"Say I will come to him instantly," she replied.

And the valet departed.

"You have compromised me with that man," she said, in a reproachful voice. "What must he think of me?"

"Heed not what he thinks," replied Musgrave. "He is perfectly safe. Forgive me if I have offended you."

"Only on the assurance that you never presume to address me in this strain again," she rejoined.

"You are without pity," he cried.

"Entirely so," she rejoined. "You will find it in vain to move me, so I would recommend you not to make any further attempt."

Musgrave uttered an ejaculation of despair. But he laughed aloud as the door closed upon her.

"I shall win the game yet," he mentally exclaimed, as he took up a cue and returned to the billiard-table.

CHAPTER VII.

MRS. BOOTLE'S BOUDOIR.

N the afternoon of the same day the Flaxyards arrived at Bury, and were met at the station by the young people. Mrs. Bootle took charge of papa and mamma and the lady's-maid; Bootle conveyed Hornby in his brougham; and the luggage was sent up to Belfield in the van.

It would be useless to describe the raptures of the elderly folk as they approached the mansion. Mr. Shelmerdine was waiting for them on the terrace with Captain Musgrave, and greeted them most cordially. A disagreeable ordeal had to be gone through within doors, but it was got over better than might have been expected, and without any of the unpleasantness that attended Mrs. Bootle's entrance into the mansion.

Luncheon was ready for the new comers, but they declined it. Contenting themselves with a glass of sherry, which was pressed upon them by their host, the two gentlemen went out to take a survey of the premises, and visited the gardens, the hot-houses, and the stables. Old Flaxyard thought everything perfect. Hornby, who was not a bad judge, declared that he never saw finer horses than those exhibited to him. Both father and son took care to praise the view, though they could not see it very distinctly, but the factories, being already lighted up, produced rather a brilliant effect.

While the gentlemen were thus employed, Mrs. Bootle showed her mamma over a portion of the house, with which the elderly lady was enchanted, and then took her to the boudoir, that they might have a quiet chat together.

"Well, mamma!" cried the younger lady, laughing, "who was right—you or I? Here you all are at Belfield. Own that you have got a very clever little daughter."

"Yes, I do own it," said Mrs. Flaxyard, kissing her affectionately. "I am delighted to see you in this charming mansion. My only anxiety is that you should maintain your position."

"Maintain it, mamma! No fear of that. You will soon find out what a favourite I am with Mr. Shelmerdine. Besides, I have managed to put down all opposition."

"Not quite, I fear. I did not trust myself to write on the subject—especially as we were to meet so soon—but I was excessively sorry to find Captain Musgrave installed in the house. He is very agreeable, I own—very fascinating— but I know something of his character, and he is not the sort of person who ought to be here. On no account, my dear child, must you get talked about; and talked about you will be, depend upon it, if he remains here long."

"You alarm yourself very unnecessarily, dearest mamma. As far as I am concerned, I have no desire that Captain Musgrave should remain an hour longer; but I can't exactly turn him out. As I explained to you in my letter, he was invited by Bootle, not by me."

"Excuse a mother's uneasiness, my love. You are so delightfully circumstanced, and have obtained such an enviable position, that I wouldn't for the world you should forfeit it by an indiscretion. Not that I fear anything wrong —don't misunderstand me for a moment—but the world is very censorious. Captain Musgrave is notoriously a mauvais sujet—you are very pretty and very lively—and his attentions to you are certain to be commented on."

"But, dearest mamma, he pays me no attention—as you will find."

"That only convinces me he has a dangerous design. His attentions to Mrs. Shelmerdine—his attentions to Bootle—are part of a fixed plan. However he may seek to disguise it, you are his real mark. Belfield would have very little attraction for Captain Musgrave without you, my dear."

"I don't at all agree with you, mamma; but if you think it necessary, I can easily give him a hint to go. But please let him stay over the ball. I hope you admire my boudoir," she added, in order to change the subject. "Isn't it pretty? There is such a delightful look-out into the garden."

"So I see," replied Mrs. Flaxyard, rising, and advancing to the window.

Just at this moment, Léontine entered. Not perceiving Mrs. Flaxyard, who was concealed from her by the window-curtains, she exclaimed :—

"Un billet pour Madame de la part de M. le Capitaine."

"From whom?" cried Mrs. Flaxyard, coming back quickly. "From the captain, did you say, Léontine?"

"I said so, Madame," rejoined the soubrette, made aware of her indiscretion, and eager to repair it, "but I know nothing about it. The billet was given me by Emile. Most likely he was mistaken. He is very stupid."

"The note is not for me, but for Mrs. Shelmerdine," said Mrs. Bootle, with perfect composure. "Most likely an answer to an invitation. Take it to her at once, Léontine. I hope Emile will make no more such mistakes."

Mrs. Flaxyard was on the point of asking to see the note, but the soubrette darted off instantly.

"This is a matter of frequent occurrence," pursued Mrs. Bootle. "Mrs. Shelmerdine's letters are constantly brought to me. But it is strange the mistake should occur just at the time we were speaking of Captain Musgrave."

"Almost too strange to be credible," rejoined Mrs. Flaxyard, who looked by no means satisfied. "You are sure you are not deceiving your mother, darling?"

"Why these unjust suspicions, dearest mamma? Have I ever deceived you?"

"I hope not. But I am more than ever anxious about you now, because I know that the slightest error would be irretrievable. The explanation you have given seems perfectly natural, but Léontine's manner was extremely suspicious. I am sorry you brought those French servants with you. I don't like either of them."

"Why mamma, you are a great deal more nonsensical than Mrs. Shelmerdine. You seem to forget that I am married. If you take me to task in this way, I shall never let you into my boudoir again. Nobody is allowed to scold me here."

"I wish you would never let Léontine enter your boudoir, my love," rejoined Mrs. Flaxyard. "But I hear your papa's voice outside. I must go to him."

"Not a word about Captain Musgrave, please, mamma,"

"Don't be afraid," rejoined Mrs. Flaxyard, as she went out.

CHAPTER VIII.

THE DINNER.

THE grand dinner took place next day.
A little before eight, which was the hour
appointed, the guests began to arrive, and were
received in the drawing-room by Mrs. Shelmerdine; and Mrs. Bootle, who was exquisitely dressed, and
looked remarkably well, was stationed a little behind her.
Presentations next took place to the Flaxyard family.
The party was large—above thirty. There were Colonel
Lancefield of the 40th Dragoons, Major Fullarton, and
two other officers; several wealthy manufacturers, Mr.
and Mrs. Booth Bacope, Mr. Thornley Bacope, and the
Misses Bacope; Mr. and Mrs. Oswaldtwistle; Mr. and
Mrs. Huncoat, Miss Huncoat and Miss Milicent Huncoat; the Rev. Mr. Rasbotham and Mrs. Rasbotham;
Dr. and Mrs. Molyneux of Bury; the Accringtons, the
Orrells, the Briercliffes, and several others. Some of the
persons we have enumerated occupied large houses in the
neighbourhood, and others came from a distance. Colonel
Lancefield and the officers drove over from Manchester,
as did the Orrells. For the most part, the younger

ladies were extremely pretty, and very well dressed, though their toilettes could not vie with Mrs. Bootle's.

All the guests having arrived with commendable punctuality, the gong sounded, and Mr. Knowles announced the important and agreeable fact that dinner was served; whereupon Mr. Shelmerdine offered his arm to Mrs. Flaxyard, and led her through the hall, which was lined with servants, to the dining-room. They were followed by the company, Mrs. Shelmerdine being brought in by Colonel Lancefield, and Mrs. Bootle by Major Fullarton. Mr. Flaxyard had to take charge of Mrs. Bacope, and Bootle escorted Mrs. Oswaldtwistle. As a matter of course, the fair Milicent was assigned to Hornby, his sister having specially introduced him to her friend.

The repast was served à la Russe, the table being ornamented with corbeilles of the choicest fruits and flowers, all of which came from Mr. Shelmerdine's hot-houses and conservatories.

The dinner was admirable, and impressed all who partook of it—all, at least, who understood what a good French dinner ought to be—with the skill of Mr. Shelmerdine's chef. Colonel Lancefield, who was something of a gourmand, told Mrs. Shelmerdine that he had never eaten so good a dinner—even at St. Petersburg.

Having seen the menu, we are able to state that there was a tortue claire à l'Anglaise as well as a potage à l'Impératrice, a superb turbot, sauce Hollandaise, rougets grillés, lamproies de Bordeaux, a dinde truffée from Strasbourg, a jambon de Montanches glacé, a quartier de chevreuil, sauce poivrade, a gigot de mouton braisée, a pâté chaud à l'Allemande, a timballe à la Toulonnaise, becasses, bardées, bavaroises, soufflets, compotes, gelées, glaces, and a hundred other good things. The wines were rœderer and clicquot in the way of champagne, rudesheimer and cabinet johannisberg, Xerez au retour de l'Inde, incomparable serchial madeira, with bordeaux for those who preferred it. After quaffing a few glasses of the cabinet johannisberg, which suited him exactly, Mr. Flaxyard felt supremely happy, and regarded his pretty daughter with an air of great contentment.

Some people assert that less wine is drunk now-a-days

than formerly. No doubt very little, comparatively speaking, is drunk after dinner, but during the repast, if the wine be as excellent as our friend Mr. Shelmerdine's, a good deal, we venture to say, will be drunk.

On the present occasion there was a tolerable consumption of hock and champagne, to say nothing of sherry and madeira, and ·Mr. Knowles, the best and most intelligent of butlers, kept the glasses constantly filled. The effect of these agreeable wines was soon manifested by the increased animation of the company, and a great deal of lively conversation ensued.

But neither clicquot nor johannisberg seemed to have much effect upon Musgrave, for though he drank freely enough, his spirits did not rise in proportion, and he sadly neglected Miss Bacope, next whom he sat.

Could he be jealous of the smiles bestowed by Mrs. Bootle upon the handsome Major Fullarton?

Hornby, as his sister anticipated, was charmed by the bright eyes and blooming cheeks of Milicent Huncoat, and began to debate with himself whether it would not be advisable to take a wife out of Lancashire, and he resolved to make some inquiries of his sister as to the fair girl's expectations. Meantime, he gave her several amorous mottoes, culled from bonbons.

A large dinner, such as we have described, takes some time to get through, and before the ladies had retired, the guests invited to the musical soirée had begun to arrive, and consequently the gentlemen were not allowed to sit long over their wine. The spacious saloon, being now brilliantly lighted up and filled with company, presented a very gay appearance. Several of the girls played and sang remarkably well, so that the musical part of the entertainment was a decided success. Mrs. Bootle, of course, took a prominent part at the piano, and was much admired. After the concert there was a little dancing. Mrs. Bootle valsed with Major Fullarton and Captain Frere, but she would not dance with Musgrave. By this time Hornby's head was completely turned by Millicent Huncoat, who valsed delightfully, and he was on the very verge of proposing. Before committing the rash act, he resolved to consult Bootle, but he found him engaged in a rubber with

Musgrave, Mr. Oswaldtwistle, and Mr. Huncoat. Precisely at midnight supper was served, and a great deal more champagne was drunk. This concluded the entertainment. There was no more dancing, and immediately after supper the guests prepared to depart—prepared, we say, for they did not get away quite so soon as they expected.

Mr. Knowles brewed the strongest ale in the neighbourhood—a fact well known to the butler's intimates. This being a particular occasion, all the footmen were regaled in the servants'-hall, and many a foaming glass of bright October was drained to the health of the young couple. Nor did Mr. Knowles forget his friends outside, but sent a liberal supply to the coachmen—far too liberal, indeed, for the potent ale got into their heads. Before the hour of departure arrived, there was scarcely one among the set, footman or coachman, who was not powerfully refreshed. The first carriage called up was Mr. Booth Bacope's; but Mr. Oswaldtwistle's coachman being nearest the steps, refused to move on, whereupon Bacope, without the slightest hesitation, drove right across the lawn, with the intention of taking up at the farther flight of steps. But his design was frustrated by the surly Oswaldtwistle, who, just touching his horses, blocked up this entrance, and all the long line of carriages in the rear moved on, in the midst of a tremendous roar of laughter from the various half-intoxicated footmen gathered round the steps. All laughed except one, and this was Mr. Bacope's footman, who immediately endeavoured to remove the obnoxious Oswaldtwistle. While he was engaged in this attempt, the whip descended upon his head and shoulders, and the porch, in which stood Mr. Booth Bacope with his wife and daughters and three or four young men, resounded with furious imprecations. Twenty footmen at least, all shouting and swearing, rushed to the scene of action, and a battle-royal seemed imminent. But though menaced on all sides, and though his horses kicked and plunged, the dogged Oswaldtwistle would not move on.

While this took place outside, the entrance-hall was filled with young ladies, with their mammas, all enveloped in very pretty hooded mantles and cloaks, prepared for their departure. With them were Major Fullarton, Captain

Frere, Musgrave, Hornby, and others, talking and laughing, when the noise reaching their ears, most of these young fellows rushed out to ascertain the cause of the row, and being amused by the disturbance among the flunkies, encouraged it by their laughter. Presently, Mr. Oswald-twistle, having been summoned by Knowles, ordered his coachman authoritatively to move on; but even thus en-joined, the obstinate fellow refused. His master then directed the footman to take his place, but on hearing this command, the coachman lashed his horses, and scattering the flunkies on either side, drove furiously across the lawn, calling out, with an oath, that his master might get home how he could. However, he was eventually stopped at the lodge gates, and compelled to come back.

A fresh scene of confusion followed this contumacious act. Other coachmen at once started out of the line, and tearing across the lawn, which seemed destined to be cut to pieces that night, strove to get into his place, while the others, shouting and swearing, filled up just as quickly behind. Collisions took place in consequence, and lamps were smashed. Half-a-dozen coachmen were discharged by their masters on the spot, but, like the first mutineer, they refused to give up the reins, and the ladies, naturally much alarmed, hesitated to enter their carriages. For a few minutes the storm raged with unabated fury—the coachmen continuing to swear and cut at each other with their whips ; but eventually, by the combined efforts of Mr. Shelmerdine and Knowles, three or four carriages were got off, and then the rest went away more quietly.

CHAPTER IX.

LD FLAXYARD and his son enjoyed their visit to Belfield immensely. Almost every day there was a dinner-party on a grand scale at some large house in the neighbourhood. What with hunting with the Cheshire fox-hounds, and flirting with Milicent Huncoat, whom he met at every house where he dined, Hornby passed his time very agreeably. Not less happy was old Flaxyard. He liked good dinners, and never had his tastes been more thoroughly gratified than they now were. What struck the jolly old boy with astonishment was, that everybody seemed to have an extraordinarily fine cellar of port. Having made this remarkable discovery, he drank a good deal, and the wine must certainly have been very good, since he seemed none the worse for it. John always took charge of him in the morning, and the old gentleman was quite content to sit down in the counting-house, or to take part in any conversation on business. Occasionally they went over by train to Manchester, and passed an hour or two on 'Change, and then had luncheon at the club of which Mr. Shelmerdine was a member. Brought thus closely together, and having abundant opportunities of exchanging their ideas, the two old gentlemen, who had always entertained a strong regard for each other, became fast friends. There were many points of resemblance between them, both being shrewd, sensible, warm-hearted men. On all occasions John spoke with the greatest affection of his daughter-in-law, who, it was evident, had quite won his heart. He had not a single fault to find with her, and his commendations brought tears into old Flaxyard's eyes.

The anxiety which Mrs. Flaxyard felt about her daughter somewhat damped the pleasure of her visit. Feeling how much was at stake, she exercised the utmost vigilance over Mrs. Bootle, and took care that she should never be alone with Musgrave. That cautious personage paid Mrs. Bootle very little attention, but the vigilant mother was not to be duped by this mode of proceeding. When they sat apart, she had often surprised a glance of intelligence between them, and she could not be blind to the jealousy exhibited by the captain at the encouragement given to the handsome Major Fullarton. Though Mrs. Flaxyard had never succeeded in detecting anything further, she felt almost certain that communications passed between her daughter and Musgrave through the medium of Leontine. Had she dared to do so, she would have insisted upon the immediate dismissal of the artful soubrette ; but she feared that some *esclandre* might ensue. Bootle was the most unconcerned of the whole party. Not a suspicion seemed to enter his head.

But the ball was at hand, and fresh guests were expected. Eva and her aunt were certainly coming; but no answer had as yet been received from Sir Norman.

One morning, Mrs. Bootle and her mamma were again closeted together in the boudoir, when Bootle burst in upon them with a letter in his hand. He had likewise a cigar in his mouth, but it was immediately taken out and tossed into the fire by his wife's orders.

" Here's a letter from Sir Norman !" he cried. " He's coming. I thought he would."

" I'm very glad of it," responded madame. " Have you told Captain Musgrave about it ? "

" I showed him the letter. He means to leave us to-day. He won't meet Sir Norman. I'm deuced sorry that he should be driven away. Perhaps you can persuade him

"I have tried, darling boy, but without success," she re-joined. "I think he'll come back to us when Sir Norman leaves."

"I wish you hadn't made me invite that young baronet. He will be a confounded bore."

"Sir Norman is exceedingly gentleman-like and agree-able, and will give éclat to the ball," remarked Mrs. Flax-yard. "Pray when does Captain Musgrave leave?"

"Not till after dinner," replied Bootle. "He means to remain for a few days in Manchester."

"In Manchester!" exclaimed Mrs. Flaxyard. "Why not go back to town at once?"

"I'm sure I can't say. You had better put that question to him yourself, Ma'am."

"I think I shall," said Mrs. Flaxyard.

"Why on earth should you interfere with Captain Mus-grave's movements?" cried Bootle. "What can it possibly matter to you if he does stay in Manchester?"

Mrs. Flaxyard was about to make an angry reply, but she checked herself.

"Well, I must go back to him," said Bootle. "I left him with Hornby in the billiard-room. We shall drive out after luncheon."

No sooner did the door close on him than Mrs. Flaxyard said to her daughter, in a serious tone,—

"My dear, Captain Musgrave must *not* remain in Man-chester, and I am really surprised he should think of doing so. People will wonder why he has left so suddenly—why he is not at the ball—and why he is staying in the neighbourhood. All the officers are coming from Man-chester. Some sort of explanation must be given them."

"Major Fullarton will give all the explanation that may be requisite to his brother-officers, mamma."

"Well, I am rejoiced that Captain Musgrave is going. But we must get rid of him effectually. Either you or I must give him clearly to understand that he can never enter this house again, and that it will be useless, therefore, to remain in the neighbourhood. The last thing I desire to do is to warn Bootle—but I *will* warn him, if necessary."

Mrs. Bootle at first looked angry, but she now became excessively pale.

" I will do exactly what you tell me," she said, with a quivering lip. " He shall never return—never ! "

" You are a dear good child ! "

" You have judged me shamefully, mamma—shamefully ! —but I shall not attempt to defend myself."

" My darling, I don't judge you at all. I am merely trying to protect you from the designs of a roué. Your papa will be as much rejoiced as I am that you have done with Musgrave for ever, for he has been a source of great anxiety to both of us."

" Don't say any more," cried her daughter, pushing her from her. " I will do as you wish. Leave me to myself."

Mrs. Flaxyard quitted the boudoir, and went to her own room, which was not far off. She left the door ajar, and remained on the watch.

Shortly afterwards a bell rang, and Léontine was seen tripping towards the boudoir.

CHAPTER X.

IN THE CONSERVATORY.

THE soubrette did not remain long with her mistress, but, on coming out of the boudoir, hurried away. Feeling convinced that she was charged with a message to Captain Musgrave, Mrs. Flaxyard waited the result. Léontine, however, did not reappear, but after the lapse of a few more minutes, during which the anxious mother did not quit her post of observation, Mrs. Bootle issued from the boudoir, and went down-stairs. Presently Mrs. Flaxyard followed her. On reaching the entrance-hall she encountered Knowles, and asked him if her daughter was in the drawing-room. The butler replied that his young mistress had gone to the conservatory; whereupon Mrs. Flaxyard hastened in that direction.

We will precede her.

The conservatory, which was full of the choicest plants, opened out from the morning-room, and of course had an entrance from the garden. As Mrs. Bootle went in, Captain Musgrave, who was walking by himself outside, caught sight of her though the glass, and immediately joined her. Her looks showed that she was agitated and uneasy.

"Emile has just delivered the message which you sent

me through Léontine," he said. "You want to speak to
me. What is the matter? Nothing wrong, I hope?"

"I have just gone through a very painful scene with
mamma."

"About me, I suppose? Well, I am going away.
Won't that content her?"

"She insists that you shall not return. You must not
remain in the neighbourhood. I promised her that I would
give you an absolute dismissal."

"Quite right," rejoined Musgrave, laughing. "Make
any promise she may require. As to keeping it—that's
another question."

"I shall keep my promise. I don't mean to see you any
more—neither will I receive any more messages from you,
nor any more billets. When you leave this house to-day,
we part for ever, and must henceforward be strangers.
Mamma has convinced me that my reputation is in danger.
I have been very silly and thoughtless, but you have presumed a great deal too much on my amiability. You don't
believe that I love my husband——"

"I can't believe it," he interrupted. "I think it utterly
impossible that any woman, constituted like yourself, can
love such a person. He is incapable of inspiring a great
passion in a breast like yours. But I cannot obey your
injunctions. I cannot—will not be thus dismissed. I will
consent to anything you propose, but not to utter dismissal.
As well condemn me to death at once—better, indeed. I
will wait patiently till your family have left—till Sir Norman
and Eva Bracebridge are gone—but then you must recal me."

"I dare not recal you, even if I would. Mamma
declares that if you ever enter this house again she will
warn Bootle."

"An idle threat. Not worth thinking about. She is far
too fond of you to do anything of the sort. Don't be in
the least afraid of her."

"I am not afraid. I don't think she would execute her
threat. But she has completely opened my eyes to the
danger to which I have exposed myself. You have built
hopes on an entirely baseless foundation."

"Then you have been merely trifling with me all this
time?" he cried, bitterly. "I said you were a heartless

coquette. But I will not be cast off thus. You have gone too far to retreat. You have more reason to be afraid of me than of your mother."

"Ah, you threaten! Now I see what a fearful risk I have run. But don't fancy for a moment that I am in your power."

"You forget that you have sent me notes that might be misconstrued. But forgive me. I know not what I say. I would not injure you for the world. You are dearer to me than life itself." Then, perceiving by her looks that his passionate language had made a certain impression upon her, he added, "I know you are not happy here. Fly with me. My existence shall be devoted to you."

"You have said this to a dozen others. No persuasion shall induce me to leave my husband."

At this moment voices and laughter were heard outside in the garden.

"Ah!" she exclaimed. "Bootle is coming here with my brother."

"They must not find me," cried Musgrave.

And he flew to the door communicating with the morning-room. But his exit was stayed by Mrs. Flaxyard.

"You here, Madam!" he cried, drawing back in confusion.

"Yes, I have been here all the time that you have been in the conservatory," she returned. "I have heard all that has passed between you and my daughter, and I rejoice that she has behaved so well. For her sake, I will screen you from the indignation of the husband whose friendship and hospitality you have abused; but no consideration shall deter me from exposing you, if you ever seek to renew your infamous addresses. When you leave this house, all further intercourse between you and my daughter—between you and the friend you have sought to wrong—must cease. You are warned."

Musgrave attempted no reply, and, indeed, had no time to make a reply, for at this juncture Bootle and Hornby entered the conservatory by the garden door.

"Holloa! what are you all doing here?" cried the foremost young man. "I thought you were gone to pack up your traps, Musgrave?"

"I have stopped Captain Musgrave," interposed Mrs. Flaxyard. "I want him to execute a commission for me in town to-morrow."

"In town!" exclaimed Bootle. "Is he going up on purpose?"

"Of course I am," replied Musgrave. "I would do anything to oblige Mrs. Flaxyard. She has engaged me on a confidential mission."

"What the deuce is it?" cried Hornby, astounded.

"Don't ask, Sir," interposed his sister. "Don't you hear that it is a confidential matter?"

"Well, you are a wonderfully good-natured fellow, I must say," observed Bootle. "Catch me undertaking such an errand for my mother-in-law, or for any one else. When are you coming back?"

"Upon my soul, I don't know," rejoined Musgrave. "My return will depend upon circumstances."

"Over which you have no control," laughed Hornby.

"Exactly," rejoined Musgrave. "But, as I shall travel by the night-train, I must go and put up my things."

And he quitted the conservatory.

"There is some mystification in this," cried Hornby, as soon as he was gone. "Why has he changed his plans so suddenly? As to the commission, that's all bosh."

"Don't you be so inquisitive, Sir," said Mrs. Bootle. "Captain Musgrave is obliged to go to town."

"Obliged, eh? It's my opinion he has had a telegraphic message from his wife."

"That would send him in the opposite direction," laughed Bootle. "More likely he wants to get out of the way of Sir Norman. But let us go and look after luncheon."

CHAPTER XI.

THE PLAN IS ARRANGED.

N entering his own room, Musgrave found Emile there arranging his things.

Scarcely noticing the valet, he flung himself into an easy-chair near the fire. Emile waited for a minute or two before addressing him.

"Monsieur le Capitaine is really going away to-day?" he inquired.

"Going away for good," rejoined Musgrave, without looking up.

"I do not quite understand," observed the valet. "Monsieur will not return—is that it?"

"That's it. Monsieur can't return. His plan has been thwarted by Mrs. Flaxyard. She has thought it necessary to interfere."

"Diable! that's unlucky. Léontine told me that the old lady's suspicions were awakened. I hope she has not made mischief."

"She has succeeded in frightening her daughter; that's bad enough."

"Oh! if it's no more than that, monsieur need not be uneasy. The alarm will speedily pass. Léontine will easily reassure her mistress. After all, there is no real danger from Madame Flaxyard. But there *is* danger—great danger—from another person."

"You don't mean Mrs. Shelmerdine? She likes me."

"Monsieur thinks so. Perhaps she does. But if she likes monsieur, she hates her daughter-in-law, and would not scruple to destroy her. Since monsieur has done me the honour to employ me, I have studied the affair; looked at it carefully on all sides. The real danger is from Madame Shelmerdine. I have watched her; and Léontine, so far as she could, has watched her. In fact, to tell you the plain truth, Monsieur, she would willingly have employed Léontine as a spy upon her mistress; but, as I have already observed to you, the girl is honest."

"This is indeed a danger which I did not foresee," said Musgrave. "But a number of little circumstances convince me that you are right, Emile. The old lady has completely taken me in. I thought myself quite safe in that quarter."

"You did well to employ me, Monsieur. I can serve you effectually. Madame Shelmerdine meditates a vilain tour towards her daughter-in-law. Sooner or later, if you had remained here, she would have made some discovery, and then ——"

"There would have been the devil to pay!" cried Musgrave, with a forced laugh. "I am glad you have told me of this, Emile. It reconciles me to my departure."

"Will monsieur permit me to inquire his present plans? Surely he does not mean to abandon the game?"

"There is no help for it, Emile. All the chances are against me. It would be sheer madness now to think of returning to this house."

"Monsieur need not return. I do not for a moment advise it. But he has friends who can serve him in his absence."

"The game's up, I tell you, Emile. I made a desperate attempt this morning, but failed. I proposed flight to madame, but she indignantly rejected the proposition."

"You were too precipitate, Monsieur. You need not despair. Madame is a great prize—such a prize as does not often turn up in the lottery of life, and pains must be taken to win her. If I am rightly informed—and it is the common talk among the servants here, who ought to know the truth—she has a large fortune settled upon herself?"

" She has thirty thousand pounds which cannot be taken from her, do what she will. Madame is very pretty, and very captivating; but I will own to you, Emile, that her money is the grand attraction with me. An elopement with her has been always my idea, but as I have told you, she derides the proposition."

" If I enable you to carry her off, what will you give?"

" Whatever you choose to ask," cried Musgrave, eagerly. " Thirty per cent. on the thirty thousand. I will make your fortune. But though you are a deuced clever fellow, Emile, I have no great faith in your achieving an enterprise like this."

" Monsieur has yet to learn what I can do. But I shall work through the agency of Léontine, who must likewise be considered. In fact, the success of the scheme will mainly depend upon her."

" She shall have a handsome *dot*. You shall have enough between you to set up business together in the Boulevart des Capucines. You should have something on account, but I am not in funds just now."

" Monsieur's word will suffice. We do not desire to be paid beforehand. Monsieur can send his full instructions to me, and they shall be attended to. All his letters shall be safely delivered to madame, and her answers forwarded as he may direct."

" You quite raise my spirits, Emile. I fancied the game was up, but now I begin to think I shall still win."

" Monsieur has everything in his favour. Madame is certainly in love—that is the main point. Léontine will take care to sharpen her regrets at his absence, and to keep his image constantly before her. Next will come his letters—ardent, of course. More persuasion from Léontine. At last, at the right moment, the plan will be proposed; the decision made; and the elopement will take place."

Musgrave laughed. After some further discussion of their infamous project, he directed the valet to pack up his portmanteau, and prepared to go down-stairs.

"Mind one thing, Emile," he said. "Before I leave I shall say something to your master that will make him jealous—furiously jealous—of Sir Norman."

"I will attend to the hint, Monsieur."

Luncheon being over, Musgrave proceeded to the drawing-room, where he found the whole party. Mrs. Shelmerdine, who had only just heard of his intended departure, expressed her great regret, and tried hard to induce him to stay over the ball. Failing in this, she expressed a hope that he would soon pay them another visit, and the invitation was warmly seconded by her son.

"Mrs. Bootle will be quite disconsolate at your departure," remarked the old lady. "Out of consideration for her feelings you ought to come back soon."

"You will make Captain Musgrave a great deal too vain, mamma," said the younger lady. "I shall be sorry to lose him, of course, but I don't think I shall quite break my heart if he doesn't come back."

Captain Musgrave felt greatly flattered by the observations of both ladies, but feared it would be utterly impossible that he could return.

Mrs. Shelmerdine's unmistakable disappointment and ill-concealed annoyance convinced him of the correctness of the information he had just received from Emile.

The two old gentlemen did not make their appearance till dinner-time, and whatever they might assert, we don't think that either was particularly sorry to lose the captain. The only person among the men who really regretted Musgrave's departure, was the one who had most reason to rejoice at it.

What Mrs. Bootle felt on the occasion we shall not inquire, but Mrs. Shelmerdine, who watched her carefully, could detect no emotion, neither could she intercept a significant glance, when the captain took leave. The pair were perfectly on their guard.

Musgrave's last words to Emile were, "I have done Sir Norman's business with your master."

So Musgrave quitted Belfield, and travelled up to town that night. He fixed his quarters, as he had told Emile he would, at the Charing Cross Hotel.

CHAPTER XII.

THE BALL AT BELFIELD.

EXT day the expected guests arrived at Belfield. The carriage, of course, met them at the Bury station, and brought them to the mansion. A general introduction took place in the entrance hall, where Mr. and Mrs. Bootle and John, surrounded by a grand array of servants, received them. Even Mrs. Shelmerdine was present on the occasion, though she had declined to pay such a compliment to her daughter-in-law.

Mr. and Mrs. Flaxyard did not assist at the ceremony, thinking they were better away, and Hornby could not, having gone out that morning with the Cheshire fox-hounds. The manner in which Mrs. Bootle greeted Eva was a thing to see. She flew towards her as she entered, embraced her, and told her how enchanted she was to see her. Having introduced her darling boy and her darling boy's papa, she then led Eva to the stately Mrs. Shelmerdine, who, being very favourably impressed by the young lady's personal charms and refined manner, received her most graciously—as she subsequently did Sir Norman, for pretty much the same reasons. Even Mrs. Daventry had no cause to complain of the cordiality of her reception, for Mrs. Shelmerdine was unusually affable. Indeed, she was very well pleased with the party, offering, as they seemed to do in her eyes, a marked contrast to the vulgar Flaxyards.

"Oh, if Bootle had married a girl like this, how happy I should have been!" she mentally ejaculated, while regarding Eva. "She has the air and manner of a lady."

John, who did not stand upon much ceremony, had already shaken hands heartily with Sir Norman and welcomed him to Belfield, and Bootle followed suit, though in a far less cordial manner—Musgrave as we know, having contrived to prejudice him against the handsome young baronet.

A great many obliging things having been said, which it would be tedious to repeat, Mrs. Bootle took the two ladies up-stairs and showed them their rooms, with which they could not fail to be pleased. Nothing, indeed, could be more striking than the contrast offered by the gaily furnished and cheerful-looking rooms of Belfield to the sombre apartments of Hylton Castle, and Mrs. Daventry did not hesitate to say that she greatly preferred the modern mansion. If her niece could not agree with her, she at least admitted that Belfield was a most delightful place.

Mrs. Daventry's opinion was shared by Susan, who shortly afterwards made her appearance, and declared with an air of the most perfect sincerity, that these were the sort of rooms she liked, and that she shouldn't be at all afraid of sleeping in that pretty little French bed in the nice dressing-room.

Sir Norman had the room assigned him lately vacated by Musgrave, and Bootle, who introduced him to it, told him that his own valet, Emile, should attend to him, and with this assurance left him. Presently Emile tapped at the door, and the young baronet, having confided the keys of his malles to him, went down-stairs.

Finding that his host and Mr. Flaxyard were in the garden, he joined them, and passed an hour or so in inspecting the hot-houses, the stables, and the grounds. By this time Sir Norman had seen enough of the place to satisfy himself that he was in excellent quarters, and he was further satisfied that Mr. Shelmerdine was a very good sort of fellow. Bootle did not please him so much, and he felt it would be rather difficult to get on with that young gentleman. On returning to the house, they found Bootle by himself in the billiard-room. Sir Norman played a game with him, and did not exalt himself in Bootle's opinion by the ease with which he beat him. They had just finished the game when Hornby came in, and taking Bootle's place, proved a much better match for the young baronet.

There was a very agreeable dinner that day. In addition to the party staying in the house, there were the Huncoats, with Major Fullarton and Captain Frere, the major having been specially invited to meet his friend, Sir Norman. Mrs. Shelmerdine's impressions in regard to both Sir Norman and Miss Bracebridge were confirmed by further acquaintance with them. Eva's beauty was of a kind that compelled admiration, and she entirely eclipsed both Mrs. Bootle and Milicent Huncoat. But it was her manner more than her beauty that delighted Mrs. Shelmerdine, and the old lady again sighed internally as she thought that so charming a person had not fallen to Bootle's lot.

Eva's accomplishments, as we have heretofore had occasion to remark, were of a very high order. She played and sang delightfully, and Mrs. Shelmerdine declared emphatically that she had never before heard so good a private performer—never enjoyed so great a musical treat.

Sir Norman, who possessed the art of pleasing in an eminent degree, made himself extremely agreeable to everybody, except Bootle, who regarded him with growing dislike. Strange to say, our young friend was quite indifferent to the attentions paid to his wife by Major Fullarton and Captain Frere ; put when Sir Norman laughed and chatted with her, which he did as a matter of course, the silly fellow looked angry and jealous.

Not a word was said about Captain Musgrave either to Sir Norman or Eva. He might never have been in the house. The young baronet would not have been aware of his visit if Major Fullarton had not alluded to it as they were talking together. Greatly surprised by the information, Sir Norman took his friend aside, and put several questions to him. While they were thus conversing, the young baronet's brow darkened and his eye wandered towards Mrs. Bootle, who was chatting in a very lively manner at the time with Captain Frere.

" You really think he had a design in that quarter ? " observed Sir Norman.

" I'm sure of it," replied the major. " Luckily, he's gone; and, for her sake, I hope he won't come back. He's a deuced dangerous fellow, as you know."

Nothing more passed between them, for Bootle at the moment conducted Eva to the piano, and they both moved in that direction.

The party broke up early, as there was the ball on the morrow—at least the Huncoats went away betimes, for all the others were staying in the house.

When the ladies had retired, Bootle and the other young men adjourned to the billiard-room, where they had seltzer water and cognac, and smoked and played to a late hour. Emile, as usual, officiated as marker, and attended to their requirements. The wily valet, who had his eyes about him, remarked Bootle's sullen manner towards the young baronet, and felt sure that Musgrave's insinuations had taken effect. He also caught a few words that passed between Sir Norman and the major. These set him thinking, and gave rise to a subsequent consultation with Léontine, the result of which will be shown anon.

On the next night, as the reader is aware, the ball was to take place, and as it was to be on a grand scale, considerable preparations had to be made for it. These had been going on, as far as practicable with a house full of company, for a week beforehand.

The large and well-ordered establishment at Belfield, though equal to most emergencies, was totally inadequate to the demands upon it on the present occasion. Waiters had to be hired by the dozen, as well as other assistants. Throughout the day the house was a scene of great con-

allotted to the dancers. The substantial part of the supper was prepared by Marcellin, but the glaces and some other things were furnished by a renowned Manchester confiseur. The band, which was an admirable one, came from the same city.

By dint of almost superhuman exertion on the part of Mr. Knowles and his assistants, among whom the most active and most intelligent was Emile, all was got ready in time, and when the guests began to arrive about ten o'clock, they found the magnificent entrance-hall filled with hot-house plants and flowers, and the spacious saloon into which they were first ushered, and where they were received by Mrs. Shelmerdine and Mrs. Bootle, lighted up by a thousand tapers. The guests arrived so quickly, that very shortly afterwards a general move was made to the salon de danse, which was likewise very brilliantly illuminated, the band being placed in the conservatory, which, as we know, opens out of that room. The ball commenced by a quadrille, in which the home party chiefly figured, Sir Norman having the honour of dancing with Mrs. Bootle, with Eva and Bootle vis-à-vis. Hornby of course had secured Millicent Huncoat. Opposite them were Major Fullarton and Miss Bacope.

Four prettier persons are not often beheld than those who took part in that quadrille, but the palm was unquestionably borne off by the belle demoiselle whom Bootle was lucky enough to obtain for a partner. He did not, however, sufficiently appreciate his happiness, but looked so moody, that his wife whispered, as she took his hand:—

"What's the matter with you, darling boy?"

To this question he made no response.

Mrs. Bootle was lively enough, exquisitely dressed—indeed, there was no toilette in the room at all comparable to hers—and if she thought at all of the absent, it was not apparently with regret. Her features were radiant with pride and delight. This fête, at which all her family were present, and of which she was queen, was the completion of her triumph. The exultant look that she gave her mother as she stood up with Sir Norman, conveyed a great deal. Influenced by her vanity, caring very little what people might think, caring just as little for Eva's feelings, she wished to produce an impression that Sir Norman admired her, and talking to him in a very sprightly manner, forced him to adopt the same tone. This it was that darkened Bootle's brow, and ravaged his heart. Eva likewise was annoyed, and for the first time began to understand that she really liked Sir Norman.

"My dear little husband is quite jealous of you, I can see, Sir Norman," laughed Mrs. Bootle. "If I can only make Eva jealous, your business will be done in that quarter. Ask me to valse with you. I can give you number four. Will that do?"

Sir Norman replied very gallantly that she had only just anticipated him; declaring that he had meant to ask her for that very valse, and adding, rather mysteriously, as she thought, that he had a word for her private ear.

"What could it be?" she thought to herself. Could she have captivated *him*. That were indeed a triumph.

Sir Norman had previously engaged Eva for the first valse, and of course they danced it together, but it was evident that she was piqued, and some of her observations were so pointed, that Sir Norman became piqued in his turn, and a slight—very slight—disagreement ensued.

Eva's annoyance was increased when she saw her suitor, who seemed to her to be completely enthralled, lead the syren out for a valse. Bootle did not dance after the first quadrille—his rôle being to provide people with partners and furnish them with programmes—and he, too, was highly incensed at the proceeding, though he did not make himself ridiculous by noticing it.

Mrs. Bootle greatly enjoyed the valse with Sir Norman, but declared, when it was finished, that she must have a little repose. So she threw over Major Fullarton, who came to claim her for the Lancers, promising him another dance later on, and, still retaining the young baronet's arm, took him to the library, which, like all the rooms, except the dining-room, where supper was to be served, was thrown open.

There were a few couples in the library when they entered it—amongst others, Hornby and Milicent Huncoat —but these soon disappeared, and, by the time they had seated themselves on a sofa, they were left alone,

Mrs. Bootle laughed as she looked round the large empty room, and said,—

"People will think we are going to have a desperate flirtation—but never mind! I am dying with curiosity to learn what you have to tell me, Sir Norman."

"I hope I sha'n't offend you by what I have to say," he rejoined, looking very serious, "but I must run the risk."

"Oh no! I'm not easily offended," she cried. "Speak! I am ready to listen."

"I am about to undertake a part which I have no right to assume," he said. "I am going to put you on your guard against the designs of a villain. I will not breathe his name, but, for Heaven's sake, beware of him!"

"I won't for a moment affect to misunderstand you, Sir Norman," she returned, with a look of displeasure; "but I fancy I am able to take care of myself."

"Do not be angry with me," he said. "I feel so strongly the peril in which you are placed by this man, that I must point it out to you. To a certain extent you are aware of the misery he has caused, but I could tell you things of him that would make you abhor him."

"You are not quite unprejudiced, Sir Norman."

"I am well informed. What I say to you I would say to his face, and would have so said it, had I found him here. If you care to know aught of his deeply injured wife, ask Eva, who will give some particulars concerning her that cannot fail to excite your profound commiseration. You knew her, I think, when she was in Paris?"

"Yes, and was greatly charmed with her. Where is she now?"

"I am not at liberty to tell, but she has found a secure retreat. Poor lady! she is in a very precarious state of health, and I think her troubles will soon be over. This is a sad tale, and I would not have told it at such a moment, but I feel that you ought to know it. I cannot relate Mrs. Musgrave's history, nor is it needful. But the villain who now dares to raise his eyes towards you has behaved with the blackest perfidy towards her, and has for ever destroyed her happiness."

"You need not alarm yourself about him. He is not likely to return here,"

"That assurance might relieve my uneasiness did I not know him. But if he has once formed a design, he will not easily abandon it. Though banished, he may find means of secretly communicating with you. But do not answer his letters. Be sure his object is to ensnare you."

While he was addressing her thus earnestly, neither of them remarked that Bootle and Mrs. Shelmerdine had entered the library. Mother and son exchanged significant looks. They could not, of course, hear what Sir Norman was saying, but his manner almost warranted the construction they put upon it, and the way in which Mrs. Bootle agitated her fan showed that she was greatly excited. She was just about to answer the young baronet's last observations, when she caught sight of the intruders, and, mistress as she was of herself, could scarcely hide her confusion. Sir Norman himself appeared slightly embarrassed.

An explosion of jealousy on the part of Bootle would infallibly have taken place if a glance from his mother had not restrained him.

"Were you looking for me, darling boy?" inquired Mrs. Bootle, getting up, while Sir Norman arose at the same time.

"Yes, we have been looking for you everywhere," replied Bootle, sharply. "Emile told us you were in the library."

"I came here for a few minutes to rest myself after the valse, and have been listening to a deeply interesting story from Sir Norman."

"But you ought not to have run away with Sir Norman from the ball-room, my dear," remarked Mrs. Shelmerdine. "The young ladies won't forgive you."

"Well, I'll take him back at once, and make them happy," cried Mrs. Bootle. "They have only lost him for a single dance."

And taking Sir Norman's arm, she hastened with him to the ball-room. On their way they passed Emile, who was standing near the door of the library.

After resigning Mrs. Bootle to Major Fullarton, Sir Norman sought out Eva in order to make his peace with her, but was rather coldly received.

The spirit and gaiety of the ball were in no wise affected

by these incidents, which, indeed, were unnoticed. Bootle had to conceal his anger under a smiling exterior, but fresh fuel was added to his jealousy when Sir Norman took his wife to supper.

A splendid supper it was, with no end of champagne, and for two or three hours afterwards dancing was continued with unabated spirit.

Long before this, Eva had begun to feel a little weary; but as she was staying in the house, she could not very well retire till the ball was brought to a close.

To the guests generally the party afforded unmitigated satisfaction. All the young ladies had plenty of partners, and several of them made conquests. The elderly people certainly enjoyed the supper. Mr. and Mrs. Flaxyard, who were playing a rubber at the time when the little incident occurred in the library, and were entirely ignorant of it, thought the ball had gone off admirably. So did Mr. Shelmerdine, who heard nothing but praises of his daughter-in-law. So did Hornby, who had proposed to Milicent, who was accepted, with a reference, of course, to papa.

If Mrs. Bootle wore a mask, it was so pretty, so bright, so natural, that no one could have suspected what was beneath it. Throughout the evening she seemed full of spirit and enjoyment, and exhibited no symptoms of flagging even at the close. There must have been a certain witchery about her, since all her partners thought her enchanting.

The only malcontent was Bootle.

Late as it was, the young men who were staying in the house repaired to the smoking-room to talk over the events of the evening.

Hornby got a good deal chaffed, but didn't mind it.

CHAPTER XIII.

MACHINATIONS OF LEONTINE.

NEARLY a week had elapsed since the ball, and the whole party were still staying at Belfield. Mr. and Mrs. Flaxyard had begun to find themselves quite at home, and did not like to move. Besides, the old gentleman had now another matrimonial affair to arrange—Mr. Huncoat having given his consent to Hornby's union with Milicent. Eva Bracebridge and her aunt still remained, and of course Sir Norman tarried likewise.

As we have seen, there was a good deal of society in the neighbourhood, and what with a concert, and an assembly at Manchester, and three large dinner-parties, the week was almost filled up. The mornings were got through in various ways—riding, driving, lounging about, and billiards.

All this time Bootle's jealousy of Sir Norman was on the increase, and he had perpetual quarrels in private with his wife on the subject of the young baronet. His mother's remarks, too, had materially aggravated the feeling.

One morning Mrs. Shelmerdine was passing along the gallery towards her own room, when she saw Léontine come out of her mistress's boudoir, and being struck by the soubrette's expression, took her to her dressing-room.

"Shut the door, Léontine," she said. "You look as if you wished to speak to me?"

"I have been anxious to speak to you for some time, Madame, but have not had the courage," replied the artful soubrette. "Some things are very painful to relate—still more painful to hear. You will understand what I mean, Madame," she continued, with a remarkably expressive look and gesture.

"Yes, I fancy I do," replied Mrs. Shelmerdine. "But pray be explicit, Léontine. Don't mind giving me pain, if you have anything to tell that I ought to learn."

"You will remember, Madame, that you put some questions to me relative to Captain Musgrave. At that time I was able to relieve your anxiety—but now ——"

"Well!"

"I think there is a certain gentleman who is—how shall I say it?—épris de ma maîtresse. M. Bootle est très jaloux. Madame laughs at him, but he takes the matter seriously. I fear there may be a great quarrel between them. Monsieur est très violent."

Mrs. Shelmerdine did not seem at all pained by this narration.

"Do my son and his wife frequently quarrel, Léontine?" she asked.

"Sans cesse, Madame. They have quarrelled ever since the ball, when something occurred—I know not what—to excite M. Bootle's suspicions. Madame aime à faire la coquette, vous savez. No harm in that. All the same, these constant quarrels may have ill consequences. Madame Bootle has great spirit. She may resent such treatment."

"Does she complain to you, Léontine?"

"Mais oui, Madame—souvent. I fear she may do something rash. That is why I venture to speak to you. Can you not advise M. Bootle? He will assuredly listen to you —his mother. By his present conduct he may provoke his wife beyond endurance. He may bring about the very result he dreads. Ma foi! that is the way with men."

"You are quite in your mistress's confidence, I know, Léontine. I won't ask you to betray it. But ——"

"It is my zeal for my mistress that induces me to speak, Madame. She is so young, so pretty, so captivating, that she cannot fail to be admired. Madame must allow that M. Bootle's jealousy of Sir Norman is absurd—causeless."

"Humph!" ejaculated Mrs. Shelmerdine. "Not altogether causeless, Léontine. My son, I think, has grounds for jealousy. I cannot bid him shut his eyes, or hold his tongue. If your mistress would cease to flirt with Sir Norman, her husband would cease to be jealous."

"But I try to point out to you, Madame, that there is danger in the course pursued by M. Bootle; and if he persists in it, he will drive my mistress to extremities."

"No fear of that, Léontine. Your mistress is far too discreet."

"But perhaps a word might prevent mischief. Will not Madame utter it?"

"I cannot interfere in a matter so delicate, Léontine," replied Mrs. Shelmerdine, decidedly. "Nevertheless, I am greatly obliged to you for the information you have given me. You must allow me to make you a little present. If you have anything more to communicate, pray come to me."

So the soubrette departed, having accomplished her purpose, and leaving Mrs. Shelmerdine delighted at the prospect of a rupture between Bootle and his wife.

CHAPTER XIV.

MACHINATIONS OF EMILE.

ORE than once had it occurred to Bootle to put some questions to Emile in regard to Sir Norman, but he did not exactly know how to set about the matter. However, the wily valet, who seemed to divine his intentions, saved him the trouble by broaching the subject.

Thus he remarked one morning while assisting Bootle to dress,—

"Will Monsieur allow me to to ask him if Sir Norman is a prétendant to the hand of Mademoiselle Eva?"

"So I understand, Emile. But why the deuce do you ask? Do you think he pays more attention to some one else than to Miss Bracebridge—eh?"

"I dare not exactly tell Monsieur what I think," replied the valet, with a demure look.

"But I will have it out of you, Emile."

"Has not Monsieur some notion of what I mean?"

"Well, perhaps, I have. I have fancied—but never mind what I have fancied—I may be wrong."

"No, Monsieur, your conclusions are correct. You cannot disbelieve your own eyes. Impossible to mistake the scene in the library on the night of the ball. I sent Monsieur there on purpose. I do not like him to be duped."

"What do you mean by 'duped,' Emile?" cried Bootle, fiercely. "Explain yourself. Do you dare to insinuate that my honour has been outraged by this cursed baronet?"

"Oh no, Monsieur! I insinuate no such thing. But I am sure he pays court to madame. Besides things that have come under my own observation, the questions he asks me prove the interest he takes in her."

"Then he talks to you about her? ha!"

"His passion renders him indiscreet—but, after all, there is no harm in it. Madame merely amuses herself with him, and his vanity is flattered by the trifling encouragement she gives him. Voilà tout."

"No, it's not all. He's an infernally dangerous fellow. Captain Musgrave cautioned me in regard to him. I ought never to have let him into the house. But I cannot get rid of him just now without a disturbance. I tell you what it is, Emile. You must play the spy upon him."

"It is not a part I like, Monsieur, but I am ready to do anything you may desire. I think you could at once put a stop to the affair."

"In what way, Emile?"

"By telling madame decidedly—very decidedly—that you won't allow it."

"I have told her so, Emile, but she only laughs at me. She denies most emphatically that Sir Norman does make love to her."

"What does she say to the interview in the library?"

"She scarcely condescends to give any explanation at all —but she pretends that Sir Norman had some communication to make to her."

"That is what I meant by saying that monsieur is duped."

"But you are wrong, Emile. I am neither duped by my wife nor by Sir Norman. I see plainly what they are both about, and I constantly tell her so. It is that which so much provokes her. Last night she threatened to leave me, if I continued to annoy her."

22

" A silly menace. Monsieur need not mind it. He should be still more energetic—dreadfully energetic. That is the only way to put a stop to the affair."

" I'll follow your advice, Emile—put myself in a towering passion. I'll frighten her."

" That's it, Monsieur. Frighten her."

Later on in the same day, the valet and the femme de chambre met to compare notes. Evidently, their plan was to disgust Mrs. Bootle with her husband, and induce her to elope with Musgrave, three or four impassioned letters from whom had already been delivered to the infatuated lady by Léontine.

The plot was most unintentionally assisted from another quarter. Naturally, Mrs. Flaxyard was made the receptacle of her daughter's complaints of Bootle's absurd jealousy of Sir Norman, and as, in this instance, the good lady was convinced that her son-in-law's suspicions were groundless, she was highly indignant. From many things which she herself noticed, and from the artful representations of Léontine, she felt certain that Bootle was incited by his mother, and she therefore added her own opposition to what she believed to be an insidious attack on her daughter's happiness, and counselled vigorous resistance on the part of Mrs. Bootle.

Of course Mrs. Flaxyard was in complete ignorance of the real state of affairs, and had no idea of the web in which her daughter was entangled. She knew nothing whatever of the letters which Mrs. Bootle had received from Musgrave, and had not the slightest suspicion of the snares contrived by the French servants who were in his pay. She did not even comprehend Mrs. Shelmerdine's sinister designs, but merely fancied that the malignant old lady was endeavouring to foment a quarrel between the young couple. Deluded by this belief, Mrs. Flaxyard upheld her daughter in her disputes with Bootle.

The effect of these various circumstances, we regret to say, was highly prejudicial to Mrs. Bootle. Musgrave's letters quite unsettled her. As yet she had returned no answer to them ; but he was promptly informed by Emile of the effect they had produced, and wrote again and again, and with increasing ardour. Still, though shaken and wavering, the infatuated lady came to no decision.

How, during this struggle, she maintained her usual gay demeanour we can scarcely pretend to say, though we know that she was an accomplished actress.   But none of those around her—except, perhaps, Sir Norman—suspected the truth.

Little more than a puppet in the hands of the designing valet and of his vindictive mother, Bootle acted just as they chose to pull the strings.   His jealousy was constantly excited by the false statements of Emile, and his resentment kept alive by the remarks of his mother.   Never before had he made himself so disagreeable to his wife as by his present conduct.

Thus aided, the contrivers of the infamous plot felt certain of success.

Our worthy friends Mr. Shelmerdine and Mr. Flaxyard were entirely ignorant of what was going on, and never dreamed of the serious misunderstanding between the young couple.   They both, however, perceived that Bootle disliked Sir Norman; but this circumstance did not trouble them, and only made John more attentive to his guest.

We have intimated that Sir Norman had some suspicion of the truth.   But it was merely suspicion.   From his knowledge of Musgrave's character he felt almost certain that he would try to keep up a clandestine correspondence with Mrs. Bootle, and he discerned the means of doing so through the agency of the French servants.   But he knew not how to act.   Having ventured, one day, to make a few observations about Musgrave to Bootle, they were taken in extremely bad part, and produced the opposite effect from that intended.   Bootle became quite warm in the captain's defence.   On another occasion, when Sir Norman sought an opportunity of a little private conversation with Mrs. Bootle, they were interrupted in their *tête-à-tête* by the jealous husband; so no good result ensued.

Though he had thus surmised the truth, the young baronet failed to perceive that he himself was merely used as a tool to excite Bootle's jealousy.   Sir Norman, indeed, was rather awkwardly circumstanced.   Eva was as jealous of Mrs. Bootle—and as unreasonably so—as Bootle was jealous of him.   If he sat next the charming coquette at dinner, all his looks and words were sure to be misinter-

preted.   Mrs. Bootle, who had a little malice in her
composition, liked to tease her friend, and so made matters
worse ; but, on the whole, we are inclined to think she assisted Sir Norman's suit.   Eva could no longer affect to be
indifferent to the young baronet.   Still, her manner did not
encourage him to make a fresh proposal.

CHAPTER XV.

A LAST ADIEU.

EVA had made more than one attempt to terminate her visit, but she was prevailed upon by Mrs. Bootle to prolong her stay, and good-natured Mr. Shelmerdine would not allow Sir Norman to take his departure. During all this time, Eva had heard nothing from Hylton Park; but one morning she received a couple of letters, which she reserved for perusal in her own room.

The first she opened was from her guardian. It had been sent on by Mrs. Austin. Its contents greatly surprised and distressed her. She learned from it that Mr. Pomfret had been seriously ill. On reaching Suez, en route to India, he had been seized by fever, consequent, no doubt, on his recent severe accident, and had been utterly unable to proceed to Madras. After a long detention at Suez, he recovered sufficiently to move to Cairo, where he had a return of fever; but he was now better, and having abandoned his intended voyage to India for the present, meant to return immediately to England.

"I have heard nothing from you, or from any one since

I left," he wrote in conclusion, " but I have a strange presentiment of ill which I cannot shake off. Having experienced the same sort of feeling before, and found it justified, I cannot despise the warning. I have therefore postponed my voyage to Madras for a time, and shall return at once to England, where I trust to arrive very shortly after this letter.

" Heaven grant that I may find you all well, and that my foreboding of calamity may prove groundless! When I thought myself dying at Suez—and I was nearly at death's door—my chief desire was to see Sophy—to bid her an eternal adieu. And now I fear I shall never have that consolation, for something tells me she is no more.

" It will rejoice me to find that you have at last consented to bestow your hand upon Sir Norman. If this should be so, may you long enjoy the happiness which has been denied to

" YOUR UNFORTUNATE GUARDIAN."

The perusal of this letter, as we have said, occasioned Eva great distress, and she remained for some time reflecting upon the series of disasters that had befallen her guardian.

She then opened the other letter, which was far more bulky than the first. It was from Sophy, though the address was not in her handwriting, but in that of Mrs. Carew.

" I cannot tell you how much I have missed you, dearest Eva. When you were near me, you sent constant messages by Mrs. Austin, and never failed to visit me morning and evening, and sometimes more frequently—in my little cell, as you designate my chamber. I never then felt the solitude in the slightest degree irksome. When I used to wander with you over those vast dismantled apartments, and look out upon the park, I never wished to quit this retreat—never wished for other society than yours; but now that you have left me, dearest girl, I sometimes feel that I am quite alone.

" Yes, quite alone! I ought not to indulge the feeling, and blame myself for it, because I have kind, good Mrs.

Austin with me, and she is even more attentive tha n heretofore.   But I cannot talk to her, as I can to you.   I am
really a recluse now.   All my time is passed in meditation
and prayer.   I rarely quit my cell during the daytime; but
at night—for I sleep indifferently—I wander like a ghost
about the great deserted rooms.   How weird they look
when flooded by moonlight, and how well-suited to such a
thin, shadowy, phantom-like object as I have become!   It
will not be long, I think, ere I shall have entered the world
of spirits.

"Do not let anything I may say about myself, dearest
Eva, cause you the slightest uneasiness, or interrupt your
happiness for a moment.   To me withdrawal from this
world can only be a merciful release from trouble.   Therefore, if I am suddenly taken, you must not grieve, but
rather rejoice that I am at rest.   Come when it may I hope
to be prepared for the blow.   My repentance has been deep
and sincere.   Certain symptoms convince me that the end
is not far off.   I grow daily feebler, and am wasting so
rapidly, that I shall soon be fully qualified for the part of a
phantom.   Austin implores me to have medical advice; but
I steadily refuse.   What good can medicine do me?   What
surgeon can cure a broken heart?

"A thousand thanks for your amiable letter, conveyed to
me through Austin.   I am glad to learn that you are so much
pleased with Belfield, and trust you will continue to enjoy
the visit.   Little as I now care for society, your description
of the Shelmerdine family interested me and for the moment
diverted me.   You place them all before me.   I can see
the worthy and warm-hearted cotton-spinner, his stately wife,
and the silly young couple.   From your account of her,
Mrs. Bootle Shelmerdine does not seem to be much changed,
or at all improved by marriage.   Coquetry is too much part
of her nature to be ever eradicated.   Her conduct to her
husband—foolish as he is—appears to me inexcusable, I
hope she will go on well; but I have great fears, and you
will guess why, since you tell me that a certain person
whom I will not name, has been visiting in the house.   Ah!
if she only knew him as I know him!   If she could only
understand his falsehood and perfidy—if she could discern

the black heart that lurks beneath his breast—she would not be beguiled by him.

"One word on another matter with which that silly coquette is mixed up. Out of my love for you, out of my earnest desire for your happiness, dearest Eva, I must tell you that you are wrong to entertain even a momentary doubt of Sir Norman's fealty. From all you have told me of him, I am certain his nature is loyal and chivalrous. Do not mistrust him. That a coquette like Mrs. Bootle may try to captivate him does not surprise me; but her lures will be vain. She will never detach him from you, for I am certain that he loves you profoundly. You do not positively confess that you requite his passion, but the uneasiness you display in regard to this silly creature convinces me that you do love him. Forgive me if I say that you have trifled with him too long. Having tested his devotion, you ought now to reward it. He will make you happy! He will grace you with a title, and in return you will restore his fallen fortunes. I shall not live to see this ancient mansion restored, but I foresee that it will be so.

"You know that you have confided to me the secrets of your heart, and that I am aware you long indulged a hopeless passion. The obstacle to the realisation of that dream will soon be removed. But even when Julian is free, I do not think he will take another bride. None could be worthier of your love 'than he—no man, under certain circumstances, could have made you happier. But his heart is seared. He will never love again. Therefore, I rejoice to find that you have transferred your affections to a high-born honourable man who loves you devotedly, and who will be to you what your guardian never could be!

"As I offer this heartfelt aspiration for your happiness—for the most unhappy woman in the world may wish happiness to another—the thought crosses me that I shall never behold Julian again. He is far away, and cannot return before all is over. My lips will then be mute. But say to him, I implore you, dear girl, that which I would say with my last breath were he near me—that I have never ceased to regret the wrong I have done him. If penitence can expiate the offence, mine is expiated."

"I have a horrid event to relate, but it must be told. I have mentioned that I have lately been in the habit of wandering at night through the suite of disused rooms contiguous to my cell. I have never been alarmed during these nocturnal rambles, for I have no superstitious fears; but last night I was greatly terrified, as you shall hear.

"I had completed my walk, and was slowly retracing my steps through the long room, occasionally pausing to look out upon the park, which was beautifully lighted up by a full moon, when I distinctly heard a sound in the apartment I had just quitted.

"I listened intently, thinking I must be deceived. The next moment a figure appeared at the door. It was he—my eternal persecutor. I screamed, but no one could hear me, and fear rooted me to the spot. He was beside me instantly.

"'You cannot hide yourself from me, you see,' he cried. 'I am sure to find you out. You fancied yourself safe here, but I have managed to reach you. You wonder how I discovered your retreat, and how I obtained admittance. I don't mean to enlighten you on those points, but I will tell you thus much—I didn't make use of a window. My last experience in that line was not pleasant. That cursed Myddleton Pomfret caused me to be shot at by a fellow whom he had planted on the bridge. Luckily, the bungler missed his aim. I hope Pomfret gave you the money I left with him?'

"'You may be certain that he did,' I rejoined. 'Is it to satisfy yourself on the point that you have come hither? If so, you are answered, and may depart.'

"'Not just yet,' he replied. 'I am glad to learn that you got the money. You cannot have spent much of it, for you can be at no earthly expense here. You must lend it me again for a short time—a month at the outside.'

"'For what wicked purpose do you require the money?' I asked.

"'For no wicked purpose at all,' he replied. 'I have a chance, and don't want to throw it away.'

"Something prompted me what to say to him.

"'A chance of running away with some foolish woman—Mrs. Bootle Shelmerdine, perhaps—is that it?'

"He recoiled; proclaiming by his surprise and confusion that I had guessed the truth.

"'I will never assist your infamous schemes,' I continued. 'Begone!'

"'Not without the money,' he rejoined, recovering himself. 'You have it, I know. Fetch it at once!'

"On my firm refusal, he seized me by the arm, and strove to drag me along. I resisted; but the little strength I possess soon failed me, and I fell to the ground. He looked at me as I lay in an almost fainting state, but without a trace of compassion on his countenance; and then despairing, I suppose, of obtaining his object, quitted the room as he had entered it. How I regained my cell I scarcely know, but my first impulse was to make fast the door.

"When Austin came to me in the morning she was quite alarmed by my appearance, and declared that I looked so ill that I must have advice. My malady indeed has been greatly aggravated by the shock I have received. My sufferings have been severe, but I will not pain you by a description of them. They cannot endure much longer.

"Feeling certain of this, and that I ought not to remain here, I have again—and for the last time—appealed to dear Mrs. Carew's motherly affection, and entertain no doubt that she will come for me in the course of the day. You may therefore conclude that I have been removed to her house, and that I am lying in the little couch in which her daughter died.

"It has cost me a great effort to send you this narrative, but I wished you to know precisely what has happened, since I feel that the scene I have just gone through will hasten the inevitable catastrophe.

"In all probability, these lines are the last I shall ever address to you. Farewell, dearest Eva—farewell for ever! I embrace you in the spirit. Think tenderly of me. When you see Julian, console him, for my heart now tells me he will need consolation.

"A last adieu!

"SOPHY,"

CHAPTER XVI.

A BROKEN HEART.

ITH eyes well-nigh blinded with tears Eva concluded the foregoing letter.

But there was an enclosure from Mrs. Carew, and to this she anxiously turned, as soon as she could master her emotion.

MRS. CAREW'S LETTER.

"I have sad tidings to relate, my dear Miss Bracebridge, but I will write as firmly as I can.

"Poor dear Sophy entrusted the accompanying letter to me, giving me an injunction in regard to it with which I felt bound to comply.

"I brought her here two days ago—on the afternoon of the day mentioned in her letter—and as Austin came with us in the carriage, the removal was effected without much distress to the dear sufferer. At all events, she bore it without a murmur.

"As we passed the little church adjoining my residence, she looked towards it, and then, turning to me, whispered:

"'Lay me in that churchyard, near your daughter.'

"I pressed her hand gently, and she understood me, for her wan features were lighted with a smile. It consoles me to recal these slight circumstances now. She smiled again as we approached the house, and remarked :—

"'How pretty it looks. I feel as if I were coming home. I shall never cross this drawbridge again, except ——' And her voice failed her.

"The servants were all collected at the door, gazing at her wistfully. The gardener displayed most emotion, though I did not imagine the rugged old man could shed a tear. But the sternest heart might have been melted. We carried her up-stairs, poor dear, for she was far too feeble to walk, and those who bore her said she was light enough. She was conveyed to her own room, and when placed in her little bed by Austin, seemed easier than she had done before, and murmured :—

"'My prayer is granted. Here I wished to die !'

"You know the bereavement I have endured, dear Miss Bracebridge. At that moment Sophy looked so like my own lost child that I felt as if the sad scene were being re-enacted, and was obliged to rush out of the room to give vent to my distress.

"While I was away, Mr. Southwood saw her, and afterwards informed me that there was not a hope of recovery. She was in the last stage of a deep decline. The case must have been hopeless from the first, but the progress of the disease had been accelerated by the shock she had just undergone. The crisis could not be far off.

"'I can do little for her,' he said, 'except to ease her sufferings. She is perfectly aware of her condition, and, in all my professional experience, I have never seen any one more resigned, or apparently better prepared.'

"As soon as I had got my feelings under control—and this was no easy task—I went back to her, and the sight almost upset me again. Austin was sitting beside the bed, and rose to give me her place. Never shall I forget the angelic smile bestowed upon me by the sweet sufferer. How beautiful she looked ! but her beauty was no longer of earth. Her features were wasted, but the delicate outline was preserved, and the large eyes had even more than their former brilliancy.

"'You have heard what Mr. Southwood thinks of me?' she said. 'He tried to disguise his opinion from me, but I soon induced him to speak frankly.'

"I could not trust myself to make any direct reply, but she tried to cheer me by her looks, and becoming more composed, though my voice still faltered, I inquired whether she wished to have any of her relations summoned.

" She answered in the negative, alleging that the presence of her sister, for whom she felt the greatest affection, but whose character differed essentially from her own, might disturb the tranquil frame of mind she had arrived at, while her father's state of health was such that he could not support the meeting. She charged me to write to them, but not till all was over. She wished all her money to be given to her sister, and, indeed, everything she possessed, except a few trifles, about which she gave special directions. To my inquiries whether I should write to you, she simply replied :—

"'Not yet. I have told you when to send her my letter.'

" She spoke much of her dear Eva, and always with heartfelt gratitude and affection. Very fervent were her wishes for your happiness, and more than once she exclaimed :—

"'I hope she will marry Sir Norman.'

"Austin, who is greatly attached to her young master, assured her that she might rest easy on that score.

"With a tranquillity that was really surprising, though inexpressibly affecting, she spoke to me of a great many matters, and gave me particular directions, which of course I shall attend to. She has left a ring for you, given her by Julian, which she hopes you will wear for her sake, as well as for *his* sake.

"After she had been talking for some time she became silent, and her eyes being closed, I thought she slumbered. I noticed many changes in her countenance, and at last, fancying something pained her, I gently touched her, and she at once opened her eyes.

"'I have been thinking over my past life,' she said. 'I have known so little happiness during my brief career that I can bid the world farewell with scarcely a regret. Yes, I have one regret,' she added, with an irrepressible pang, which showed itself in her countenance. 'I should like to see Julian again—if only for a moment.'

"I did not dare to give her a hope, because I feared she would never again behold him on earth.

"That night Austin watched by her couch. The dear patient slept little, and appeared disturbed and feverish.

"Next day, Mr. Southwood again visited her, and, finding her very feeble, gave her some slight stimulant, which revived her ; but she was evidently rapidly sinking.

"An eager desire to see Julian had now taken possession of her, and she asked me if I thought he would come. But before I could reply, she exclaimed :—

"How unreasonable I am to put such a question, when I know he is in India.'

"Just then, Austin, who had left the room a short time previously, returned. I could see from her looks that she had something to communicate. As she came up she said, in a low voice, that I was wanted down-stairs.

Softly as she spoke, Sophy, whose sense of hearing was preternaturally quickened, caught the words, and fixing her eyes inquiringly on the old housekeeper, said :—

"'Is he come ?'

"I was terrified by the excitement she displayed, fearing it might prove fatal.

"'What is to be done, Austin?' I said. 'Try and calm her.'

"'Go down-stairs at once, Madam,' rejoined the house-keeper, in a low voice. 'I will prepare her.'

"Not a word was lost by Sophy, who exclaimed with a look of agonised impatience :—

"'Ah, he *is* come ! I knew it. Oh, let me see him ! Bring him instantly, or I shall die ! Go, I adjure you !'

"I needed no further exhortation, but hurried down-stairs.

"There indeed, was Julian.

"He had just returned—not from India, but from Egypt, where he had been detained by illness, and had arrived, almost providentially, before it was too late. He had been to Hylton Park, and, learning what had taken place, had come on at once to my house. He appeared fearfully changed, and his looks betokened the most intense anxiety. After exchanging a few hasty words with him, I led him up-stairs, beseeching him, as we went, to maintain his composure.

" I want words to describe the scene that followed as I opened the door. A cry, such as I never heard before, but that thrilled to my very heart, burst from Sophy as she caught sight of him. While I was absent, Austin had propped her up with pillows. On entering the room, Julian stood still for a moment as if transfixed. He then rushed forward, and threw himself on his knees by the bed, while she clasped her arms round his neck. In this attitude they remained for a short space, and nothing could be heard but half-stifled sobs.

" At last she raised herself, and said :—

" ' Look up, dear Julian—look up ! Let me gaze on your beloved features once more before my eyes grow dim.' And as he complied, she added, ' You look ill—very ill ! What ails you, dearest Julian ? '

" ' Waste not a thought on me,' he replied. ' Have you aught to tell me ? Is there aught I can do ? '

" ' You can make my last moments happy by a word,' she rejoined. ' Say you forgive me ! '

" ' I do forgive you, from the bottom of my heart, my ever dear Sophy,' he rejoined. ' I have never ceased to love you.'

" ' Oh ! this is too much bliss ! ' she cried. ' It suffocates me. Yet say it once more. Say you love me, Julian—and kiss me ! '

" He repeated the words, pressed his lips to hers, and received her last breath.

" He laid her gently on the pillow, and remained gazing in mute despair on her angelic countenance, which wore a smile even in death. Not a groan escaped him.

"We allowed him to remain thus for some little time, but at last I took his hand with the intent of leading him away.

" He offered no resistance ; but just as we reached the door, he turned round, and, with a fearful cry, rushed towards the body, and clasped it to his breast."

CHAPTER XVII.

IR NORMAN, with Bootle and Hornby, were out that day with the Cheshire foxhounds. They had some famous runs; killed three foxes—Sir Norman was in at the death of two of them—and only just got back in time to dress for dinner. They were all much surprised to learn that Eva and Mrs. Daventry had left Belfield that afternoon. The cause of their sudden departure was the receipt by Miss Bracebridge of very distressing intelligence, which completely unfitted her for society, and necessitated this abrupt termination of her visit.

Such was the explanation afforded by Knowles, while delivering to the young baronet a letter which Eva had left for him. Sir Norman hurried with this letter to his own room, and, fastening the door that he might not be disturbed, read as follows :—

EVA'S LETTER.

" I have just learnt from Mrs. Carew that poor Sophy's

sorrows are over. As I could neither indulge my grief un-restrained in this house, nor answer the questions that would naturally be put to me, I shall hurry away as soon as possible, and get my aunt to make my excuses and adieux. If I can help it, I shall not see Mrs. Bootle before my de-parture. There are circumstances connected with this sad event which would make any conversation with her, at this juncture, excessively painful to me.

"I have much to tell you—much that will surprise and afflict you, but I am so overwhelmed with grief that I can scarcely write. There are one or two things, however, that I must mention. Poor dear Sophy, as you know, when I left her—how could I leave her?—was in a most precarious state. But her death was accelerated by another nocturnal visit from the perfidious villain who betrayed her. He came to her, as before, for money, and when she refused him—for she guessed the base purpose for which he sought the loan—his violence killed her. I say killed her; for though she lingered for two days, she never recovered from the terrible shock. I look upon Musgrave as her murderer.

"I shall ever regret that I was not with her at the last. Yet she was most carefully tended by Mrs. Carew and Austin, and she had a consolation which my presence could not have afforded her. As if in answer to her supplications, some pitying angel brought Julian to her at the last moment. He had been detained by illness in Egypt, and was unable to prosecute his voyage to India. A warning voice seemed to call him back, and he obeyed the summons. It is well he did so. He arrived in time. A few moments later, and all would have been over. But she still lived, though the spirit was ready to take its flight. She saw him. She knew him. She heard his well-known voice. She received his forgiveness. They were re-united—in death !

"She is gone. Her errors, I doubt not, will be forgiven by her Supreme Judge, as they were forgiven by her un-happy husband.

"With this sad scene before me, and with poor Sophy's last injunctions fresh in my mind, I will no longer attempt to disguise the feelings I entertain for you, dear Sir Norman. You have won my heart. My hand shall be

23

yours whenever you choose to claim it, and my life shall prove the depth of my affection for you.

" I have written this because I shall not see you before I leave, but I should not have shrunk from the avowal. Though I ought not to think of myself at this moment, I feel that I ought to think of *you.*

" Having thus unburthened my heart, let me refer to another matter. I am very uneasy about a certain charming person of our acquaintance, whose thoughtlessness may cause her to fall into the snares which, I fear, are laid for her. I cannot help connecting that villain's secret visit to Hylton Castle with some dark design against her happiness. I may be wrong, but such is my distinct impression. Even if I should see her before I leave, I cannot warn her. But you may warn her—you may save her. Leave no means untried to foil the villain's schemes. Do not let another victim be added to his list.

" By your love for me, I charge you to do this. If plot there be, and you can detect it, thwart it at any hazard. But, for the sake of the infatuated lady, for the sake of all connected with her, do not let exposure take place. I tremble to think of her peril, but I trust you will rescue her from it. Do not abandon your post till this is accomplished. You will be doubly welcome at Hylton Castle when you can relieve my anxiety. Adieu !

" Eva."

Sir Norman was standing beside the fire thinking over this letter, which had filled him with so many opposite emotions—some sorrowful, some joyous, some wrathful— that he quite forgot that it was necessary to dress for dinner, when a tap was heard at the door. This roused him from his reverie, and he admitted Emile, who had come to help him to take off his hunting habiliments. While he was thus employed, the valet espied Eva's letter, which the young baronet had laid upon the table, and he contrived to push it out of the way, though he did not venture to abstract it.

Having hastily made his toilette, Sir Norman went down-stairs, and had just reached the drawing-room door, when suddenly recollecting that he had left Eva's letter on the table, he flew back to his own chamber to secure it. Emile was still there, as he burst suddenly into the room, and Sir Norman almost fancied that he saw the valet take the letter quickly from his breast-pocket and lay it down. But the manœuvre was so quickly executed that he could not feel quite sure, and, snatching up the letter without a word, he hurried down-stairs again.

Rather a dull dinner that day. The sudden departure of Eva and her aunt, or some other circumstance, had damped Mrs. Bootle's spirits. Tired with his day's work, Bootle looked sullen and stupid. Later on in the evening the young men adjourned to the billiard-room, and when preparing to play, Sir Norman took off his coat, and told Emile, who was there as usual, to hang it up. While doing so, the valet felt the pockets ; but perceiving that his movements were watched by Sir Norman, he did not venture to take out the letter, and shortly afterwards the young baronet, whose suspicions had been excited, put on the coat again.

On retiring to his own room, Sir Norman took out the letter with the intention of reading it before he sought his couch. To his great surprise, he found that he had obtained possession of a missive from Musgrave to Emile, which the valet, in his haste, had inadvertently substituted for Eva's letter. Hence the rascal's uneasiness.

Sir Norman had not the slightest scruple in reading the letter, which was in French, and to the following effect :—

"You tell me that Madame still continues undecided, but exhibits signs of yielding. Why will she not write? She appears awfully afraid of committing herself. Not a single line in answer to all my letters. Cannot L. induce her to send me a few words? Then there could be no retreat. Now she may throw me over at the last moment.

"But a truce to these misgivings. L. is so clever, and has such influence over her mistress, that we cannot fail. It makes me laugh to hear that Madame and her spouse quarrel so much. I felt sure I had sown the seeds of discord between them. How well Monsieur helps our plan. We could not have a better ally. Madame will not stand such treatment long. She has too much spirit. There must be no reconciliation. L. must take care of that.

" Now, for fear of mistake, I will recapitulate my instruc‑ tions. We will suppose that all goes well—that Madame consents. No step must be taken until three days after her family have left. Three days, mind. Precision is the soul of an enterprise like ours. You will inform me when the time of the departure of the Flaxyards is fixed, so that I may have all ready. On the third day, then, Madame will come up to town by the morning train. A pretext for the journey will easily be found—perhaps a short visit to mamma. But Madame will arrange this better than I can. You and L. will come with her. I will meet her at the Euston station. Then hey for Dover ! The next news of us shall be from Paris.

" There must be no change in this plan, or it may mis‑ carry. I will propose it in a letter to Madame. L.'s per‑ suasions, combined with other circumstances, will ensure its accomplishment. I count upon L. and you, because you have both as much interest in the success of the scheme as I have myself."

Chance seemed to have placed this letter in Sir Norman's hands, in order that the infamous scheme which it revealed might be defeated. Yet how could it be defeated, without fearful consequences to the lady against whom the machi‑ nations were directed? Not merely must she be saved, but her reputation must be screened. This might be done, Sir Norman thought, since he was in possession of the details of the scheme. But an apparently insuperable difficulty at once presented itself. Emile's uneasiness had shown that he was aware of the mistake he had made in regard to the letter. How deceive him? Determined to trust to chance, which had so far befriended him, Sir Norman left the letter in his coat pocket, certain that the valet would find it in the morning, and might suppose it had not been read. And it turned out exactly as he anticipated. Emile, who had passed a sleepless night, came as usual to attend to him in the morning. The valet was full of uneasiness, but was quickly reassured by Sir Norman's manner, and lost no time in carrying off the clothes. By-and-by he reappeared, and, while placing the carefully folded habiliments on a chair, he observed :—

"You left a letter with your cigar-case and handkerchief in your coat-pocket last night, Sir Norman. Shall I lay them on the table?"

"Yes," replied the young baronet. "I forgot to take out the things. I was tired last night, and went to bed immediately."

The careless and half-sleepy tone in which this was uttered disarmed the valet's suspicions, and he left the room quite easy. When Sir Norman got up shortly afterwards, he found Eva's letter on the table.

CHAPTER XVIII.

MRS. BOOTLE'S DECISION IS MADE.

IVA'S sudden departure seemed to be the signal for a general dispersion of the company at Belfield. The Flaxyards had intended to remain a little longer, but letters which came by that very morning's post informed the old gentleman and Hornby that their presence in town was required on matters of business; and as such a summons could not be neglected, it was settled that they should leave on the following day. Old Flaxyard would fain have started sooner, but there was a dinner, that day, at the Huncoats, which Hornby would not forego. How could he disappoint Milicent? Though very sorry to lose his friends, John allowed them to do as they pleased, and we may be sure Mrs. Shelmerdine made no attempt to detain them. Mrs. Bootle said she could not possibly part with dear mamma; but dear mamma, who, if truth must be told, was rather tired of her visit, and had had more than enough of Mrs. Shelmerdine, declared that she must go.

This discussion occurred during breakfast, and while listening to it, Sir Norman thought Mrs. Bootle rather over-acted her part. Notwithstanding her professions to the contrary, it was evident to him that she wanted to get rid of her family. Since everybody else was going, Sir Norman felt he had no excuse for remaining longer, and he therefore announced that he, too, should be obliged to leave on the following day. The intimation was received with ill-disguised satisfaction by Bootle.

After breakfast, Sir Norman tried to obtain a few words in private with Mrs. Bootle. But she was never alone. At last, he contrived to whisper that he had an important communication to make to her, and she told him to come to her boudoir in an hour. Unluckily her reply, though uttered in a low voice, was overheard by Mrs. Shelmerdine, and immediately reported to her son.

At the appointed time Sir Norman proceeded to the boudoir. Mrs. Bootle was there, but her mother was with her. Mrs. Flaxyard, however, immediately arose.

" I understand, Sir Norman, from my daughter, that you have something to say to her about Eva," she remarked. " Nothing, I hope, has occurred ——"

"Nothing adverse to my happiness," he interrupted. "I have the great satisfaction to inform you that I am accepted. The young lady's decision was made yesterday, and was conveyed in a letter which she left for me on her departure."

" I am truly rejoiced to hear it," cried Mrs. Flaxyard. " Pray accept my sincere congratulations. You have indeed won a prize. I can quite understand now what you have to say to my daughter.

And she quitted the boudoir."

" I felt sure this would come to pass, Sir Norman," said Mrs. Bootle, as soon as they were alone. " I flatter myself that I have assisted your suit, though whether I have acted a friendly part towards you in doing so time alone can show. But I really think you have a good chance of happiness with Eva, if married people ever are happy, which, from my own experience, I almost begin to doubt."

"I am sorry to hear you speak thus bitterly of married life," he rejoined ; "but I trust you are merely jesting with me."

"I speak in sad earnest," she replied, "I will not say

that I am wretched—but I am far from happy. I look gay enough in society; but when alone, and the mask is taken off, I am what you see me now."

"How is it possible—situated as you are!—that you can be unhappy?"

"Because—but I will not complain. Perhaps the fault is mine—no doubt it is. Everybody, at least, would say so —would blame me. Apparently, I have everything to make me happy. I ought to be happy. Yet you see how wretched I am!"

And she burst into tears.

"Command yourself, I entreat," cried Sir Norman, "and listen to what I have to say! I am at no loss to understand by what perfidious arts you have been brought to your present unhappy state. I see, only too clearly, the mischief that has been wrought. But be counselled by me. Do not let your fancied grievances—for fancied they are—induce you to take a false step which will plunge you into real misery."

"A false step! What mean you, Sir Norman?"

"All is known to me. I have discovered the villain's deep-laid design, and would aid you to defeat it. Struggle resolutely against the evil that environs you. Rouse all the good within you. You will then be strong enough to resist him. Yield, and you are lost for ever!"

She hung down her head, and attempted no reply. Amid the silence that prevailed, the door softly opened, and Bootle and his mother entered the boudoir.

"You will not betray me!" murmured the unhappy lady on perceiving them.

"Fear nothing," he replied in a whisper. "You are safe with me."

"Ha! how's this?" cried Bootle, stepping towards his wife. "In tears! What's the matter?"

"I'll tell you some other time," she replied. "I'm not in the mood to give you any explanation now."

"But I insist upon an explanation," he cried. "That is, if you have any to offer. I ask you again how it is that I find you in tears? No use in denying the fact. Your eyes are quite red. What's the matter, I say?"

"Will you permit me to offer you an explanation?" remarked Sir Norman.

"None appears to be necessary," interposed Mrs. Shelmerdine. "It is not customary for my daughter-in-law to manifest so much emotion. I have never known her shed a tear before. No doubt she is grieved at your departure, Sir Norman."

"Madam, you are entirely mistaken, I can assure you."

"If she is grieved because Sir Norman is going, I am not," observed Bootle, with a discordant laugh. "I should be glad if he would hasten his departure."

"It will be impossible for me to remain longer after these observations," said the young baronet. "But, at least, let me explain ——"

"Useless—quite useless! I am not to be imposed upon!" cried Bootle. "I am not so blind as you suppose. I have seen what has been going on. This is not the first time that I have surprised you making love to my wife. You forget the scene in the library on the night of the ball. Explain that, if you can."

"It is easily done, Sir, if you will only dismiss your unfounded and, I must say, ridiculous suspicions."

"My unfounded and ridiculous suspicions! ha! When I find my wife closeted with a person whom I know to be in love with her—when I find her profoundly agitated and in tears—I am told that my suspicions are ridiculous and unfounded—ha! ha!"

"You are behaving most unwisely, Sir," said Sir Norman, sternly. "I have always acted as your friend."

"I don't desire your friendship," cried Bootle. "In those confounded French comedies, 'mon meilleur ami' always plays the traitor."

"Then you refuse to listen to me?" said Sir Norman.

"I decline to be made a dupe," rejoined Bootle.

With some difficulty Sir Norman restrained himself. Turning to Mrs. Bootle, he said,—

"Pray make my excuses to Mr. Shelmerdine, coupled with my best thanks for his hospitality. I leave my defence in your hands. Adieu!"

Coldly saluting Mrs. Shelmerdine and Bootle, he then left the boudoir. Proceeding to his own room, he rang the bell, and directing Emile to pack up his trunks, and send them after him to the station, quitted the house.

Leaving him to proceed to Bury, we shall return to the boudoir.

"I shall not endure this any longer, Bootle," cried his wife, as soon as Sir Norman was gone.

"Do as you please," he cried. "If you are for a separation, I sha'n't oppose it."

"A separation! Oh, darling boy! is it come to this?— so soon!"

"I am no longer a darling boy!" he retorted, savagely. "I am an injured husband—that's what I am."

"You have gone crazy, I believe," said his wife.

"I may well be crazy, after what I have seen and heard in this boudoir. Have you any explanation to give?"

"None! I won't make any."

"My son has a right to be satisfied," said Mrs. Shelmerdine.

"I *will* be satisfied, or ——"

"Don't say any more now," interrupted his mother. "Come along!"

And she forced him out of the boudoir.

They had not been gone more than a minute when Léontine, who had been on the watch, made her appearance. She perfectly understood what had happened, and felt that the moment was propitious to the execution of her scheme.

"Ah, Madame!" she exclaimed, in accents of profound commiseration, "what frightful usage you have to submit to!"

"I will submit to it no longer, Léontine," rejoined Mrs. Bootle. "He has threatened me with a separation. Be it so. Dear mamma leaves to-morrow. I shall go with her."

"That would give a complete triumph to Madame Shelmerdine. To send Madame back to her family, beaten, humiliated, is precisely what that dreadful mégère desires. Her task will then be accomplished. In my poor judgment you ought to take no such course, Madame. Either remain here, and defy your vindictive belle-mère, or fly. Were I in your place, Madame, I would unhesitatingly embrace the latter alternative."

"I cannot remain here, that is certain, Léontine. That frightful mégère, as you call her, will kill me. She has regained all her influence over my husband, and has quite set him against me."

"That is perfectly true, Madame. Monsieur is a totally changed man. Emile and myself have both remarked it. It will be impossible for Madame to maintain such an unequal contest. She must yield."

"Never, Léontine! I will fly rather than yield!"

"Then Madame decides!" cried the soubrette, with irrepressible satisfaction.

"Yes—no! I cannot decide now. I am bewildered."

"But the moment is come when the decision must be made, Madame. Pardon me, if I say you can no longer hesitate. The plan proposed by your adorer must either be carried out or abandoned. Will you write to him?"

"No. Let Emile write."

"To what effect, Madame?" asked Léontine, trembling with anxiety.

"To say I will come," replied the other, in a low voice.

"Madame has decided well," cried the soubrette, joyfully. "It shall be done at once."

And she hurried away, fearing lest her mistress should change her mind.

The fatal step was taken. No, not yet taken. Léontine might be recalled. The struggle between good and ill was still going on in the infatuated lady's breast, when her mother entered the boudoir.

"On what errand is Léontine gone?" cried Mrs. Flaxyard. "She looked exulting as she came out, but became greatly confused on beholding me. I fear there is something wrong going on."

"Don't trouble yourself about Léontine, dear mamma, but direct your attention to me. I require your sympathy— your counsel. I am quite prostrated by a terrible scene which I have just had with Bootle and his mother. Their unjust suspicions have well-nigh distracted me. Will you believe it?—Sir Norman has been sent away! Bootle talks of a separation, and I don't know what."

"This is dreadful! But it must be set right without delay. I will speak to Mr. Shelmerdine myself."

"No, mamma, don't. Perhaps the storm may subside, now that the cause of it—Sir Norman—is removed."

"There is something beyond Sir Norman in the quarrel, I fear," remarked Mrs. Flaxyard. "Has Captain Musgrave nothing to do with it? I must own that I thought Léontine was charged with a secret message to him when I met her just now. If a face ever expressed detected guilt, hers did. I shall always feel uneasy while you retain those French servants. But never mind them now. Do let me try and make up this quarrel between you and Bootle. With Mr. Shelmerdine's aid, I am sure I can do so."

"No, dear mamma, you must let me battle it out. I cannot—will not—humble myself to the old lady. Anything rather than that. If she and Bootle persist in annoying me, I will run up to town, and pass a short time with you at the Acacias."

"Not a bad plan, my dear. Go up with us to-morrow."

"No, thank you, mamma. I would rather wait a few days. Bootle may improve when we are left to ourselves. But in order to spare dear Mr. Shelmerdine's feelings—for I don't want him, or papa, or even Hornby, to know of this quarrel—you can ask me to come to you. This will serve as an excuse, in case I should find it necessary to take the step."

"I will do as you desire, my dear, though I had far rather have you under my own charge. That dreadful Musgrave haunts me for ever. Don't deceive me. He is not privy to this plan, I trust? He has not suggested it? Mind, I won't allow him to visit at the Acacias."

"He won't even know that I am there, mamma. It is by no means certain that I shall come."

"You have no arrière-pensée in what you have just proposed?"

"Not the slightest, dear mamma. How frightfully suspicious you are!"

"I cannot help it," groaned her mother. "I am full of uneasiness. Do nothing imprudent, my dear child."

"Mamma!"

"Well, I will say no more!" cried Mrs. Flaxyard. And with a look at her daughter full of maternal anxiety and affection, she left the boudoir.

Léontine was not recalled, and did not reappear till later on in the day. She then informed her mistress that a letter to Captain Musgrave had been sent off by Emile.

So the fatal step was taken.

CHAPTER XIX.

THOUGH Mrs. Flaxyard had by no means shaken off her misgivings, and did not feel sure that she was doing right, she complied with her daughter's suggestion, and urged her very strongly to run up and spend a few days at the Acacias. If Bootle did not choose to accompany his wife, he could come and fetch her back. Bootle, who fancied he understood why the proposition was made, offered no objection, but said his wife might please herself; and so the plan was settled. Mrs. Bootle promised to write to dear mamma as soon as she could fix a day for the visit. Hornby, who, as we know, had an attraction in the neighbourhood, said he should soon run down again, and Mr. Shelmerdine told him to come when he liked—he would always have a room at Belfield. So the Flaxyards took their departure; the old gentleman and his son enchanted with their visit, but Mrs. Flaxyard full of anxiety about her daughter.

As she drove back alone from the station, whither she had accompanied them, Mrs. Bootle felt more wretched than she had ever done in her life. She had parted with her family for ever, for she could not, and did not, expect they would ever see her again, after the fatal step was taken. Her mother's anxious looks and whispered words of counsel filled her with remorse. How fond her mother was of her! —how proud her father was of her! how was she requiting their affection? And then Mr. Shelmerdine, who was almost as fond of her as her own father—who had always sided with her—who had steadily refused to believe any ill of her—what would he think of his little pet when he found out how wickedly she had deceived him? He would never allow her name to be breathed in his hearing again. She did not care what Mrs. Shelmerdine might think of her. That implacable woman could not judge her more harshly than she did now. But poor Bootle! he certainly loved her, and how infamously she was acting towards him! If he would only thrown himself on his knees, and own he was wrong, she would stay with him. She could not find a single excuse for her conduct. On the contrary, it assumed the darkest dye. She was deceiving and abandoning all who loved her—a father and mother who idolised her—a husband who, foolish as he was, loved her—a splendid home— numberless friends—and for whom? She did not dare to ask herself that question. Yet she had not power to resist the temptation held out to her.

All these feelings of compunction, we regret to say, were dissipated when she found herself once more closeted with Léontine, and subjected to the evil influence of that designing creature. Léontine, who well knew what mischievous arguments to employ, soon laughed her out of her irre- solution, and kept her steady to her purpose. But the weak, misguided lady had now a difficult part to play, and, clever actress as she was, it was almost beyond her powers. If she could have ventured to do so, she would not have left her boudoir; and she almost thought of feigning in- disposition, but Léontine discouraged this course. She did not, however, appear till dinner-time, and as there were three or four guests, as usual, she got through the evening tolerably well.

Was it fancy, or did Mr. Shelmerdine really regard her with anxiety? His kindness almost overcame her.

For the first time John seemed to discover that there was

some misunderstanding between her and Bootle, and strove to set it right. Mrs. Shelmerdine was colder and more repelling than ever. Perhaps in consequence of what his father said to him, Bootle showed a slight disposition to make up the quarrel; but his mother checked him, and it came to nothing.

Next day, Mrs. Bootle had more remorseful qualms, but they soon yielded to the remedies applied by Léontine, and the bitter tonic administered by her mother-in-law.

Poor Bootle was certainly coming round. No doubt about that. Very little encouragement might have brought him round altogether. But he got none. When Mrs. Bootle announced her intention of going up to town on the following day, he seemed half inclined to offer to go with her; but his mother frowned at him, and the words stuck in his throat. Mrs. Bootle begged to be allowed to take Emile with her, as well as her femme-de-chambre; and Bootle, having the most perfect confidence in the valet, readily assented. Subsequently he gave some private instructions to Emile, to which the valet, laughing in his sleeve, promised careful attention.

Again there was a little dinner-party, so that the evening passed off tranquilly. John told his daughter-in-law that he quite understood why she was going to visit her mamma, but he would engage that all should be right when she came back.

The eventful day arrived. Mrs. Bootle showed no wavering. All preparations had been made by Léontine, who had been secretly employed in packing up the trinkets and other matters that her mistress desired to take with her.

When the time for departure came, and Knowles announced that the carriage was ready, Mr. Shelmerdine asked Bootle if he did not intend to take his wife to the station; whereupon the foolish fellow, acting upon his mother's advice, replied,—

"No, Sir, I leave that office to you," and without a word more, marched off to his own room.

The parting between Mrs. Bootle and her mother-in-law was cold enough, and Mrs. Bootle was glad to hurry away to the carriage, for at that moment she could scarcely repress her emotion. Emile and Léontine were there, and all the boxes having been got in, there was nothing to wait for. So Mrs. Bootle, having taken leave of Belfield for ever, as she supposed, took her seat; John followed; and the carriage was driven off to the station.

No sooner was his wife gone, than Bootle repented his conduct, and, ordering out the dog-cart with the utmost despatch, hurried after her to the station. Perhaps he was too late, for neither she, nor the vigilant Emile, nor the sharp-eyed Léontine saw him before the train started. Even if he had been there, it was not likely that Mrs. Bootle would have seen him, for her eyes were full of tears. She clung to her father-in-law as if she could not tear herself from him, and when he had assisted her into the coupé, which was reserved for her and Léontine, and bade her an affectionate adieu, she sank back in the carriage in an hysterical state.

John felt very uneasy, but Léontine assured him that her mistress would be better presently; but, in spite of all the soubrette's assiduities, and the application of a powerful vinaigrette, Mrs. Bootle had not recovered when the train started.

Just at that very last moment a person, who had arrived late, with the assistance of the guard managed to spring into a back carriage.

End of the Sixth Book.

BOOK VII.

SAVED.

CHAPTER I.

LAST SCENE BUT ONE OF THE DRAMA.

AFTER many fruitless attempts to enliven her mistress and engage her in conversation, Léontine gave up the attempt in despair, and amused herself as best she could.

Mrs. Bootle continued silent and abstracted till Stafford was reached, when, raising herself for the first time, she let down the window, and, hearing the name of the place bawled out by the railway porters, expressed her surprise that they had got so far.

While she looked out, her attention was drawn towards a tall, striking-looking personage, habited in deep mourning, whose handsome but wasted features and long grey beard seemed familiar to her. This gentleman was looking eagerly into the different carriages as if in quest of some one. All at once he caught sight of her, and his glance of recognition told her it was Myddleton Pomfret. In another instant, and before she could draw up the glass, he was beside the coupé.

"I have been looking for you," he cried. "Will you permit me a little private conversation with you—strictly private?" he added, glancing at the soubrette. "I have something of the last importance to say to you."

His manner was so earnest, that, though much frightened, Mrs. Bootle did not hesitate, but desired Léontine to get into another carriage. Upon which Pomfret immediately opened the door to let out the femme-de-chambre. But Léontine did not seem inclined to obey, and addressed some very determined remonstrances to her mistress, and it was not until Pomfret ordered her in an authoritative tone to descend that she complied.

Just at this moment Emile ran up with the greatest alarm depicted on his sallow countenance. Instead of interfering with the strange gentleman, as Léontine expected, he hurried her off to his own second-class carriage, and left Pomfret to get into the coupé without hindrance. In another moment the door was shut by the guard, and shortly afterwards the train quitted Stafford.

"I ought to offer you a thousand apologies, Madam, for this extraordinary proceeding," he began; "but the motive that has induced me to take it will, I hope, plead my excuse."

"I am quite sure you would not act in this manner without adequate reason, Mr. Pomfret," she rejoined. "No apology, therefore, is necessary. But do, pray, tell me by what magical process you knew that I was travelling by this train."

"From whatever source I obtained the information, Madam, it would appear to be correct, since I have found you," he rejoined. "You must not forget that your journey to town has long been planned."

"Ah! you learnt it from Sir Norman?" she cried.

"You have guessed rightly," he rejoined. "But I must pray you to listen to me." His voice became sterner as he proceeded:—

"You were in Paris when Captain Musgrave was there

with his unfortunate bride. You believed he had married a widow, did you not?"

" I was told he had married the widow of Julian Curzon."

" Not the widow. Julian was alive at the time of the marriage—alive, I repeat—but she supposed him dead, and, having mourned him long, deemed herself free to take another husband. She gave her hand to Musgrave, who . had practised the blackest treachery to win her. He knew that Julian lived. He knew that Julian was returning from India—but that knowledge only made him hurry on his devilish scheme. Julian arrived too late. The marriage had taken place. He followed them to Paris. He saw the unfortunate victim. Horrified at the unintentional wrong she had committed, she fled from the wretch who had betrayed her."

" Oh! did he do this?" cried the listener.

" You know with what levity he treated the affair, feeling sure that the terrible secret would be kept by both those whom he had so deeply wronged. But you do *not* know how he subsequently persecuted his victim, driving her almost to madness by forcing himself into her presence. His last visit to her was to obtain money for a purpose which you will easily conjecture, and the violence which he used upon that occasion hastened her death."

" Oh, horror! Can I have loved such a man? I comprehend your object in giving me these dreadful details. You have opened my eyes to the abyss that was yawning before me. Heaven be thanked, it is not too late to retreat! You have come to my rescue. Do not desert me. I may need your support. I will not meet him."

" Can you give me the assurance that you have torn the villain from your breast—that you sincerely repent the step you have taken—and that henceforward you will devote yourself to your husband? Can you answer these questions from your heart, and without mental reserve?"

" I can," she replied, with an earnestness that carried conviction of her sincerity. " I am fully sensible of my folly—my wickedness—but I will err no more. I know not how I could be infatuated by him, but I despise myself for yielding to his arts. You shall find how I will treat him anon."

24—2

"You will not see him," said Pomfret, almost solemnly.

"You think he will not keep his appointment?"

"He cannot keep it," he rejoined, in the same solemn tone. After a pause, he added, "You cannot doubt who I am."

"You are Julian Curzon—are you not?"

"Yes. I am the unhappy man whose wife was torn from him by that villain—whose existence has been blighted by him. You will wonder why I did not avenge the injury I received; but, while Sophy lived, I could not avenge it. I was forced to bear my wrong in patience. Fate has been kinder to me at the last than it had been before. I had been detained by serious illness in Egypt, and hurried back, incited by a presentiment of ill. I arrived in time to pronounce the forgiveness which she sought—to receive her latest sigh. She expired in my arms. Oh! the agony of that moment! But I will not recal it—or I shall be utterly unable to proceed. My heart seemed crushed; but when I partially recovered from the shock, I felt some consolation in reflecting that her troubles were over. As I gazed upon her inanimate features—so placid!—so beautiful! — so angelic in expression!—I would not have called her back, even if I had possessed the power. I never quitted her till she was laid in her coffin—and I then bade her an eternal adieu. But I distress you by these details."

"Heed me not! go on! go on, I entreat you!" she cried. "These tears will do me good."

His voice changed as he proceeded:—

"It was a simple funeral, yet most touching to all who witnessed it. She was buried in a pretty country churchyard, in a spot which she herself had chosen. There were few mourners, but they all mourned deeply. Chief among them were an elderly lady, who loved her as a daughter, and an old female servant, who loved her little less. Eva and her aunt were there, and at a little distance stood two old men-servants weeping—yes, weeping! Her gentleness, her patience under suffering, had won their hearts."

"She was indeed an angelic creature!" exclaimed the listener.

A moment elapsed before Pomfret could control his emotion. He then went on:—

"All was over. The mourners were gone. The assistants at the sad ceremony had departed. One person alone lingered in the churchyard. When the coffin, containing all he loved, was lowered into the ground, he felt that his heart would burst, if he longer repressed his grief, and he hurried away. He now returned to the grave, but with very different emotions. Grief had given place to the fierce desire of vengeance. His eyes were dry. Fire burnt within his breast. As he stood by her grave, he raised his hand to heaven, and vowed never to rest till he had avenged her. With one last look into the grave, he quitted the churchyard."

"And this is your present purpose?" she cried. "He justly merits death at your hands for the foul wrong he has done her and you. But do not let the thirst of vengeance lead you to throw away your own life. He is a skilful duellist. I dread the result of the encounter."

A singular and almost terrible smile played upon Pomfret's pallid features.

"Hear what I have to tell," he said, in a sombre voice. "Having formed the resolution I have mentioned to you, I entered the carriage that was waiting for me, and drove to Hylton Park, with the intention of taking leave of Eva. I found Sir Norman with her. He had just returned from Belfield. Though the fire of vengeance, only to be quenched by blood, was raging fiercely as ever in my breast, I could not but rejoice to learn that she had at last consented to make him happy."

"And they will be happy," cried Mrs. Bootle. "I am sure of it."

"They will," said Pomfret, emphatically. "But to proceed. My purpose must have been written in my looks, for Sir Norman instantly divined it. Eva too suspected it, though she did not seek to deter me from its execution. Presently she quitted the room with her aunt, and left me alone with Sir Norman, who added fresh fuel to my wrath by acquainting me with the villain's infamous designs in regard to yourself. Had I not determined to act, Sir Norman himself would have taken measures to defeat them. But he entirely approved of my plan, and, tearing himself from Eva, hurried off with me to town.

"Immediately on our arrival, he proceeded to the hotel at which Musgrave was staying, and found him there. A meeting was arranged to take place next morning at Calais. As my enemy had the choice of weapons, and was a master of fence, he chose the sword. This was immaterial to me. All I desired was to have him before me. Mine was the righteous cause, and Heaven, I felt sure, would strengthen my arm. Swords were procured. We started by the French mail train, and crossed on a calm starlight night to Calais. Musgrave was accompanied by his friend, Captain Saint-Quintin. During our passage the seconds conferred together, and all was arranged.

"On arriving at Calais, Sir Norman and myself repaired to Quillac's Hotel, as agreed upon. We neither of us retired to rest, but passed the time in conversation, and I gave my friend full instructions as to how he should act in case I fell.

"As soon as it became light, we entered the coach which was waiting for us in the court-yard of the hotel, and drove to the place of rendezvous—a retired spot, outside the walls, on the road to Boulogne. We were accompanied by a surgeon, and alighting at a little distance from the ground, which was screened from observation by low sandhills, proceeded to it on foot. Sir Norman carried the swords, wrapped in a cloak, and the surgeon a case of instruments.

"Shortly afterwards, my adversary and his second appeared on the ground. Both were smoking, but they threw away their cigars as they came up, and formally saluted us. The seconds then stepped aside to consult, and while they were engaged, we, the principals, prepared for the conflict. It was a sharp frosty morning, and the ground was quite hard, but my breast still burnt like fire, and I did not feel the cold.

"As soon as we were ready, Sir Norman offered the swords to Musgrave, who bowed, took one, and, as he did so, glanced significantly at his second. He felt sure of killing me.

"Taking the other sword, I advanced to meet him. We saluted, and in an instant were engaged. Apparently he was determined to make short work of it. After a few rapid passes, he made a feint, and then, with the quickness of lightning, delivered a thrust, which I successfully parried, and before he could recover, my sword passed through his heart."

"He is dead!"

"He is dead," echoed Pomfret. "Sophy is avenged."

A pause succeeded. The lady sobbed audibly. Pomfret waited till she became calmer, and then said, sternly,—

"He does not deserve your pity. He had but one redeeming quality—courage. He would have betrayed you, as he betrayed all others. Had he lived, you would still be in danger. Yet I must admit that he made a slight attempt at reparation. As he sank into the arms of Saint-Quintin, who rushed to his assistance, he made an attempt to speak, but failing to do so, pointed to his coat, which was lying on the ground. Searching it, I found this packet. It contains some letters, which may be of consequence to you."

And he delivered the packet to her.

"Alas! alas!" she cried. "Was I wrong in pitying him?"

"I have no more pity for him than for a wild beast!" cried Pomfret. "But to finish my narration. Seeing he was dead, we left the body to the care of Captain Saint-Quintin and the surgeon, who undertook to make the necessary depositions before the authorities that the man was fairly killed in a duel. We returned by the first packet to Dover. All that then remained for me to do was to acquaint you with the event, and give you the letters. So rapid had been my movements, that I was fortunately in time to accomplish this before any step likely to compromise you could be taken. And as it was important that I should see you before your arrival in town, I came on to Stafford."

"Oh! how can I thank you!" she cried. "You have indeed, saved me!"

"You owe no thanks," he rejoined. "I thought only of avenging Sophy, when I slew him. But since I have been instrumental in saving you, I am entitled to give you a piece of counsel."

"I will obey you implicitly. What is it you enjoin?"

"Immediately on your arrival in town, dismiss those French servants, who have aided Musgrave's base design.

Fear nothing from them. They are harmless now their employer is gone. Sir Norman came with me to Stafford, and is in another part of the train. We shall see him at the Euston station. Leave him to deal with them."

" It had already occurred to me to act as you suggest. But I felt afraid to take so decisive a step, knowing how completely I am in the power of the perfidious wretches."

" Get rid of them. I repeat, you have nothing now to fear. Proceed at once to your father's house, and then write to your husband."

" I will—I will !" she cried. " I will acknowledge all my faults—make my peace with him—and entreat him to come for me."

Pomfret showed no disposition to continue the conversation, and his stern expression as he sat back in his corner almost alarmed his companion. The silence was prolonged till they were nearing London, when she addressed him.

" Forgive me if I venture to ask what you now propose to do ?" she inquired, glancing at him timidly.

" I shall proceed without delay to India," he rejoined, in a sombre tone. " All my arrangements are made. I have no further business here. Nor shall I return. The last tie that bound me to this country is sundered."

" Time will soften your affliction, and then you will think differently," she rejoined. " Fresh feelings will be awakened in your breast. You are yet young enough to love again."

" Love again !" he exclaimed, bitterly. " Never! My only desire is to rejoin her I have lost."

CHAPTER II.

THE LAST SCENE.

HEN they arrived at the Euston station, Pomfret got out first, and assisted his companion to alight, At the same moment Sir Norman and Bootle— yes, Bootle himself, to his wife's amazement !— descended from a back carriage, and hastened towards her. It was evident from their manner that a perfectly good understanding subsisted between them.

"What ! darling boy, is that you ? " she cried. "This is indeed an agreeable surprise. Have you really travelled in the same train with me ? "

"Yes, I have," he rejoined. "I was so miserable when you left me, that I hurried off to the station, and just got there in time to spring into one of the hind carriages. I should have joined you at Stafford, but Sir Norman stopped me, as he wished to give me some explanation. I now know all."

The young baronet gave her a reassuring look, which informed her that the darling boy did not quite know *all.*

"I've been a great fool to quarrel with you," pursued Bootle. "But I'm very sorry, and promise never to be jealous again."

"And I'll never give you cause to be jealous again, dearest boy, be sure of that," she rejoined. " I ought to ask forgiveness. I'm far more in fault than you."

" Well, I won't attempt to justify my conduct. I know it's inexcusable," said Bootle. " But I may say that my absurd jealousy of Sir Norman—for I now know how absurd it was—was entirely caused by some remarks made by that diabolical Musgrave, who, I am glad to learn, has met with his deserts."

" Yes, he'll trouble you no longer," said Sir Norman. " Mr. Pomfret," he added, presenting that gentleman, "has freed you from a designing villain."

" I am greatly obliged to you, I am sure, Mr. Pomfret," said Bootle. " I should have been obliged to take him in hand myself if you had not got the start of me."

" I had deep wrongs to redress," observed Pomfret.

" Of course I don't mean to compare my wrongs with yours," said Bootle. " But the scoundrel behaved infamously in setting me against Sir Norman. Shall I tell you what he said, my dear?" he added to his wife.

" On no account, darling boy. It would be useless to do so now. I am only surprised that you could lend an ear to his base insinuations, since you knew how passionately Sir Norman is attached to Eva."

" I was an idiot, as I have already owned," said Bootle.

" Then since you are perfectly convinced of your error in regard to Sir Norman," remarked Pomfret, "let me have the satisfaction of hearing that all your doubts are dissipated. Of Musgrave you had cause to be jealous—but he is gone."

" And with him every doubt has vanished," said Bootle. " I must own that I felt a little jealous of you, Mr. Pomfret, when I beheld you get into the carriage with my wife. But Sir Norman soon dispelled my fears. And to prove the opinion I entertain of you, I beg to say that there is no person—not even Sir Norman himself—whom I shall be more delighted to welcome at Belfield than you."

" I am starting at once for India," rejoined the other. " Consequently, I cannot have the pleasure of visiting you."

" Well, when you return, then."

"I shall never return."

While this conversation took place, Emile and Léontine had been occupied in getting together the things. Both were exceedingly uneasy, wondering what would happen. They now came forward, and Emile enquired of his master if he should engage a cab.

"For yourself and the drôlesse with you, if you think proper, malheureux, but not for me and Mrs. Bootle," rejoined our young friend, haughtily. He had been cautioned by Sir Norman.

"Comment, Monsieur!" cried Emile. "Perhaps you will be good enough to express yourself more clearly."

"Allez au diable! You are both discharged. Is that clear?"

"Discharged, at a moment's notice! Monsieur cannot mean what he says!"

"But I do mean it, gredin. I have no further occasion for your services. Here's payment for your wages," he added, taking out a pocket-book, and giving him a couple of bank-notes. "Ten for yourself—a fiver for Léontine."

"You will interfere, Madame? You will not permit this injustice to be done?" cried the soubrette, rushing up to Mrs. Bootle,

"I shall not interfere at all," returned the lady, coldly. "I entirely approve of the proceeding. You can both go about your business."

"Not yet, Madame. I have some revelations to make to Monsieur. I shall show him how he has been duped."

"No, you won't," said Bootle. "Monsieur refuses to listen to any of your revelations. He is quite aware of all your tricks."

"Shall I take any message from Madame to Captain Musgrave?" inquired Emile, spitefully.

"Yes, if you can find him," rejoined Bootle. "But you'll have to seek him below. He was killed in a duel yesterday."

"Milles diables! tué!" ejaculated Emile, recoiling. "Allons donc, Léontine!"

And he hurried away with the soubrette.

While the scene just described took place, Myddleton Pomfret stood apart; but at its termination, and when the French servants were gone, he advanced towards Mrs. Bootle, with the evident design of bidding her farewell. But before he could offer his adieux, she flew towards him, and yielding to her impulsive nature, seized his hand, and cried,—

"You must not—shall not—leave us in this manner. Do remain with us for a month—even for a week—and if no change takes place in your feelings during that time, I will no longer try to prevent your departure. But give me an opportunity of proving the gratitude I owe you. We will do all we can to soothe your affliction. Stay with us, I entreat you!"

"I am fully sensible of your kindness," he rejoined, gently, but firmly. "But my resolution is taken."

"I am afraid your efforts to induce my poor friend to change his purpose will be as ineffectual as my own," said Sir Norman, coming towards them with Bootle. "I have employed every argument—but in vain. Though, as you are aware, he is Eva's guardian, and ought to give her away, he will not remain for our nuptials."

"My presence at your marriage would be ominous," said Pomfret. "You are better without me."

"Still, neither Eva's happiness nor mine will be complete unless you are present," urged Sir Norman.

"Stay, and make us all happy!" cried Mrs. Bootle.

"Time was when I could not have resisted such an appeal; but I must resist it now," said Pomfret. "My task is ended. I rejoice to think that I have removed some few thorns from your path, so that henceforward your course will be unobstructed. Heaven keep you in it! Farewell, Madam! farewell for ever!"

Pressing her hand gently, he bowed to her husband, and, taking Sir Norman's arm, quitted the platform with him.

She continued gazing after him till he was lost to sight, and then sighed deeply, feeling sure she should never behold him again.

Shortly afterwards Bootle came to hand her to a cab, in which her luggage had been placed by a railway porter. They then drove to the Acacias, where, though quite unexpected, they were most warmly welcomed by Mrs. Flaxyard, who was truly rejoiced to find that a reconciliation had taken place between them.

The news imparted by her daughter astonished and delighted Mrs. Flaxyard. She had no fears for the future, since the French servants were discharged, and Captain Musgrave effectually removed. On his return from the City with Hornby, old Flaxyard, who knew nothing about the quarrels of the young couple, was immensely delighted to see them, and laughed very heartily when he learnt that Bootle would not be left behind, but had come up with his wife, though in a separate carriage. He, too, was glad that Emile and Léontine were gone. Hornby was of the same opinion, and both father and son thought it a good job that Musgrave had been disposed of.

There is generally a tolerable dinner at the Acacias, go when you will, and invariably good wine. Bootle felt so comfortable after emptying a bumper of his father-in-law's unexceptionable claret, that he wondered how he could ever have been such a fool as to quarrel with his pretty little wife, who smiled at him so bewitchingly from the opposite side of the table.

But we have been getting on too fast, and must go back for a moment to Pomfret and Sir Norman. On quitting the station they proceeded to the Euston Hotel, and on the way thither Pomfret remarked :—

"All is arranged in regard to Eva's property. I have given full instructions in writing to my solicitor, Mr. Wilson, of Lincoln's Inn Fields, and have appointed Mr. Flaxyard and Mr. Shelmerdine trustees under the marriage settlement, with Mr. Wilson. I hope this meets with your approval.

"Entirely so," said Sir Norman.

"One word more, and I have done," pursued Pomfret. "My will is lodged with Mr. Wilson. You and Eva have an interest in it. Therefore, if anything happens to me, apply to him. It may not be long before the application will be necessary."

"I wish I could remove this melancholy impression from your mind," observed Sir Norman.

"Impossible," rejoined the other. "My release cannot be far off. When you hear of it, rejoice."

At the door of the Euston Hotel a carriage was drawn

up, in which sat Eva and her aunt. Expecting to find his ward there, Pomfret was fully prepared, as he thought, for a short parting interview with her. But all his firmness now deserted him.

As he approached the carriage with Sir Norman, Eva would have alighted, but he motioned her to sit still. Straining her hand, he gazed at her for a moment with inexpressible tenderness, and the look was never effaced from her memory.

Quite overcome by emotion, he then murmured in broken accents :—

"All my wishes are known to Sir Norman. He will explain them to you. Heaven bless you, and grant you years of uninterrupted happiness! Farewell for ever!"

He then plunged into the hotel. Sir Norman did not attempt to follow him, and neither he nor Eva saw the unhappy man again.

EPILOGUE.

A few words will suffice to complete our Tale.

The ill-fated Julian Curzon (for we will now restore to him his rightful name, though he himself never resumed it) died on his voyage to India, and is buried at Madras.

On reference to the will, which was deposited with Mr. Wilson, and, indeed, had been prepared by that gentleman, it appeared that Julian had bequeathed a lac of rupees to Eva, and a like sum to Sir Norman. The residue of his property, which amounted to nearly six thousand pounds, was left to Celia Leycester.

Before the sad tidings came of the death of their friend, the nuptials of Sir Norman and Eva had been solemnised. They are now residing at Hylton Castle, which has been completely restored, and is now what it used to be in the days of Sir Norman's progenitors—one of the finest places in Surrey.

Another wedding, which took place about the same time as that just mentioned, has to be recorded. Hornby Flaxyard was united to Milicent Huncoat, and the marriage promises well. Hornby may be considered a lucky fellow, for he got a very good fortune with his wife. They have fixed their residence in Westbourne Terrace, and live in capital style.

Bootle is darling Bootle still, and idolises his pretty little wife, who has left off flirting, and has become very fond of him. They are now at Belfield.

Mrs. Bootle gets on better than she did with her austere mother-in-law—though they have an occasional wrangle—but the little lady still retains as firm a hold as ever upon the affections of worthy Mr. Shelmerdine.

THE END.

PRINTED BY W. H. SMITH AND SON, 186 STRAND, LONDON, W.C.

21—2—78

www.ingramcontent.com/pod-product-compliance
Lightning Source LLC
Chambersburg PA
CBHW030901270326
41929CB00008B/526